Into the Ocean

VIKINGS, IRISH, AND ENVIRONMENTAL CHANGE IN ICELAND AND THE NORTH

Into the Oceans

VIKINGS, IRISH, AND ENVIRONMENTAL CHANGE IN ICELAND AND THE NORTH

Kristján Ahronson

UNIVERSITY OF TORONTO PRESS
Toronto Buffalo London

Toronto Buffalo London
www.utppublishing.com

ISBN 978-1-4426-4617-9

Library and Archives Canada Cataloguing in Publication

Ahronson, Kristján, 1975– , author
Into the ocean : Vikings, Irish, and environmental change in Iceland and the north / Kristján Ahronson.

(Toronto Old Norse and Icelandic series ; 8)
Includes bibliographical references and index.
ISBN 978-1-4426-4617-9 (bound)

1. Iceland – Antiquities. 2. Iceland – Antiquities, Celtic. 3. Viking antiquities – Iceland. 4. Caves – Iceland. 5. Paleoecology – Iceland. 6. Environmental archaeology – Iceland. I. Title. II. Series: Toronto Old Norse and Icelandic studies ; 8

DL321.A47 2015 949.12 C2014-904290-6

University of Toronto Press gratefully acknowledges the financial assistance of the Centre for Medieval Studies, University of Toronto, in the publication of this book.

University of Toronto Press acknowledges the financial assistance to its publishing program of the Canada Council for the Arts and the Ontario Arts Council, an agency of the Government of Ontario.

University of Toronto Press acknowledges the financial support of the Government of Canada through the Canada Book Fund for its publishing activities.

À ma famille
À mon fils Dafydd Mathieu
a fy nghariad i Lowri Angharad

Contents

Acknowledgments

General

I gratefully acknowledge the support of the Social Sciences and Humanities Research Council of Canada and also of the Centre for Medieval Studies (Toronto). This book emerged from conversations with Professor William Gillies (Edinburgh), Professor Andy Dugmore (Edinburgh), Dr Fraser Hunter (National Museum of Scotland), Professor Thomas Charles-Edwards (Oxford), Professor Ann Dooley (Toronto), and Alex Woolf (St Andrews), and I thank them for their advice, vision, and criticisms. I also wish to give particular thanks to Professor Sir Barry Cunliffe (Oxford) and Professor Ian Ralston (Edinburgh) for their insight, as well as to Professor Jonathan Wooding (Sydney) for his helpful and perceptive comments on a draft of the book. Additionally, I am grateful to Ian MacKenzie (Edinburgh) and Craig Angus (National Museum of Scotland) for their kind assistance with illustrations. The tireless editing and support of Dr Lowri Ahronson sustained this book. I am also grateful to Professor Andy Orchard (Oxford), Suzanne Rancourt, Barbara Porter, Angela Wingfield, and the University of Toronto Press for all of their assistance. I wish to thank the anonymous reviewers for their helpful comments, which improved the work.

Non-specialist Proofreading

Ken Ahronson, Phil McLean, Deryck Aubrey, Dr Andy Newsham (Sussex), Dr Tõnno Jonuks (Tartu), and Sam Thompson very kindly commented on draft chapters and helped me to work towards my goal of accessible scholarship.

Introduction

Dr Jonathan Henderson (Edinburgh) generously contributed his specialist knowledge of bird migrations to the ideas of this chapter.

Chapter 1

I was fortunate to meet with Professor Hermann Pálsson (Edinburgh) early in my research for the first chapter, and I profited from that conversation. Importantly, Professor Richard Sharpe (Oxford) pointed me towards the oft-forgotten work of Eugène Beauvois, and Peter Allmond of the Bodleian Library kindly obtained Beauvois's articles that had recently disappeared from the stacks – including his crucial 1875 paper. Professor Andrew Wawn (Leeds) and Professor Donald Meek (Edinburgh) independently then sparked my efforts to contextualize the Chevalier scholar among his contemporaries. Professor Carole Hillenbrand (Edinburgh) introduced me to Norman Sicily, while Professor Jeremy Johns (Oxford) supplied specialist knowledge on the medieval Arabic world, and Dr Ben White (Birmingham) assisted with translations.

Chapter 2

Chapter 2 was written in response to a challenge from Professor Ian Simpson (Stirling), and I am indebted to him for this. Dr Attila Tanyi (Liverpool) helpfully commented on my philosophy.

Chapter 3

I am grateful to Dr Simon Taylor (Glasgow) for introducing me to Scotland's place names and for generously sharing his discovery of the *Papies Holm* name. Dr Peder Gammeltoft (Copenhagen) provided much specialist advice and kindly commented on a draft of chapter 3. Exceptionally, he has turned his own pen to the subject and kept me abreast of this work. I am also pleased to thank, for his advice and assistance, Dr Arne Kruse (Edinburgh). Additionally, I am grateful to Professor Ian Simpson (Stirling) and Dr Barbara Crawford (St Andrews) for inviting me to take part in their Scottish Papar Project.

Chapters 4 to 7, Seljaland Section

Professor Rory McTurk (Leeds) and Professor Gísli Pálsson (Iceland) were crucial in fostering my interdisciplinary interest in the Icelandic past. Mjöll Snæsdóttir, Guðrún Sveinbjarnardóttir, and the Þjóðminjasafn Íslands (National Museum of Iceland) welcomed me into Iceland's archaeological community. Crucially, my fieldwork at Seljaland profited from the steadfast encouragements of Hálfdan Ómar Hálfdanarson and Kristján Ólafsson of Seljaland. Additionally, Þórður Tómasson (í Skógum) provided helpful advice.

Preliminary 2001 fieldwork was assisted by Professor Andy Dugmore, Professor Tom McGovern (CUNY), and Dr Sophia Perdikaris (CUNY) as well as their students from the City University of New York. This preliminary assessment was carried out in parallel with magnetic susceptibility research by Dr Martin Kirkbride and Donald Ashburn, both of the University of Dundee.

2001 FIELD TEAM: Guðmundur H. Jónsson (co-director), Florian Huber (excavation and survey), Dr Alan Macniven (assistance), and Raymond Meaney (assistance).

Post-excavation: Dr Kate T. Smith (tephrochronological analysis).

Institutional support: Þjóðminjasafn Íslands (equipment) and Department of Geography at the University of Edinburgh (logistics).

2002 FIELD TEAM: Dr Jessica Bäcklund (co-director), Dr Kate T. Smith (tephrochronology), Dr Tõnno Jonuks (tephra contours), and Dr Kerry-Anne Mairs (field illustrations).

Post-excavation: Dr Jessica Bäcklund (sample column processing), Ian G. Scott (publication illustrations), Gardiner Molloy (advice on stone working), and Chris Doherty of the Research Laboratory for Archaeology and the History of Art at Oxford (geological analysis).

Institutional support: Páll Marvin Jónsson of Háskóli Íslands á Vestmannaeyjum (equipment, accommodation, and facilities), National Museums of Scotland (equipment), Department of Geography at the University of Edinburgh (equipment and logistics), Þjóðminjasafn Íslands (equipment), the people of Seljaland (accommodation), and Fornleifastofnun Íslands (logistics).

I am grateful to the sympathetic work of those responsible for two documentary films made in 2002: the Dutch team of Paul Klotz and Merel Brandon (*Crossing Caves*, premiered 1 May 2003), and Elín Hirst of Icelandic National Television (broadcast 1 September 2002).

Chapter 5

Crucially, I wish to thank Dr Kate T. Smith (Exeter) for her help, as well as Guðrún Larsen (Iceland) for her comments and analysis. Additional thanks must go to Dr Peter Hill (Edinburgh) and Dr Anthony Newton (Edinburgh).

Chapter 6

I am particularly grateful to John Higdon, formerly of the Canadian Museum of Civilization, for his generous assistance in preparing the geographic information system (GIS)–mapped images for publication.

Chapter 7

For the sculpture collection, presentation, and analyses here I am indebted to Ian G. Scott (methodological guidance and publication illustrations), Pauline Scott, and my 2001 and 2002 field teams – particularly to Dr Kerry-Anne Mairs (field illustrations), Dr Jessica Bäcklund (co-director 2002), and Dr Tõnno Jonuks (assistance with photographic lighting). Kristján Ólafsson loaned the electrical equipment necessary for our work, and the Department of Geography at the University of Edinburgh provided the logistical framework. Ian MacKenzie very helpfully assisted in scanning and editing digital images.

Professor Ann Dooley inspired the work in this chapter. Furthermore, conversations with Professor Thomas Charles-Edwards on the subject of cross sculpture provided important insight, while the support and guidance of Ian Fisher (Glasgow) has been essential to the analyses presented here. Kristinn Schramm (Edinburgh and Iceland) kindly proofread my translations.

I apologise to those I have overlooked in these acknowledgments.

Illustrations, Tables, and Abbreviations

Illustrations

Tables

Abbreviations

KV Kverkarhellir
NMS National Museum of Scotland
OI Old Irish
ON Old Norse
RCAHMS Royal Commission on the Ancient and Historical Monuments of Scotland
RLAHA Research Lab for Archaeology and the History of Art, University of Oxford
SLJ Seljaland

Into the Ocean

Introduction

The following story, which was told me in Thorshavn [the main town of the Faroe Islands] by an old man, explained the Westman strain in the people of Suderoe [southernmost of the islands] to its narrator's complete satisfaction …

"A long time ago a small foreign vessel anchored off Suderoe. On board there was a woman, the captain's wife. Now the Faroemen were very rude in those days, and the chief man on the island, who lacked a wife at the time, went out to the ship with many boats full of his followers, seized the woman, and took her ashore. The crew of the ship was small, the islanders were many; and the captain was forced to leave his wife to her fate and to set sail with all speed. As he departed, his cry was heard on shore: '*Ma femme! Ma femme!*' To this day there is a village on Suderoe called after her, Famöyen, for she was forthwith married to her captor, and the people thought that her name was Fam. And this proves that the people of Suderoe are Irish, for I have heard that *femme* is the Irish for wife!"

Nelson Annandale, *The Faroes and Iceland*[1]

The alleged method of the professional scientist is: start from observations, observe, and go on observing. The alleged method of the professional historian is: start from documents, read documents, and go on reading documents.

These alleged methods are exactly analogous, and both are precepts which cannot be carried out: they are logically impossible. You cannot start from observation: you have to know first *what to observe*. That is, you have to start from a problem. Moreover, there is no such thing as an uninterpreted observation. All observations are interpreted in the light of theories. Exactly the same holds for documents. Is my train ticket to London a historical document? Yes and no. If I am accused of murder, the ticket may possibly serve to support an alibi, and so become an important historical document … Nevertheless, I should not advise a historian to start his work by collecting used railway tickets.

A historical document, like a scientific observation, is a document only relating to a historical problem. And like an observation, it has to be *interpreted*. This is one of the reasons why people may be blind to the significance of a document, and destroy it.

Karl R. Popper, *The Myth of the Framework*[2]

Carved and rock-cut sculpture identifies a poorly understood facet of early Christianity, whether on Skellig Michael, rising as it does out of the north Atlantic Ocean twelve kilometres off the coast of southwest Ireland, or perched on the Heimaklettur cliff face in Iceland's Westman Islands. The special or sacred places marked by simple sculpture at Inishbofin off the Connemara coast, at St Ninian's Cave in Galloway, at Iona in the Inner Hebrides, at Aird a'Mhòrain on the Outer Hebridean island of North Uist, at the Isle of Noss in Shetland, and at hundreds of other Atlantic places span a zone stretching from the Irish and Scottish coasts to Iceland. Established "certainties" and fundamental ambiguities characterize this northern region. For example, Scotland's western islands are known as a core area for early medieval monastic communities, which are thought to have produced simple cross sculpture as the result of devotional impulse, and yet the nature and extent of early Christian settlements beyond the Gaelic-speaking world is unclear. Similarly, Old Norse speakers are seen to dominate this north Atlantic zone by the late Viking Age, but the timing and the way in which this region was transformed are difficult to perceive.

By looking to Iceland, we may be able to resolve some of these ambiguities. Along with New Zealand, Iceland was among the last significant land masses to be settled by human populations. In comparison to the rest of Europe, then, Iceland was settled very late. Scandinavian groups are generally believed to have entered an "empty" landscape under their own pioneering initiative in the late ninth century; however, a role in this process has also been posited for Ireland's and Scotland's early medieval monastic communities. As can be seen in both above-ground archaeological features and Iceland's sediments, the earliest settlement established patterns of social organization, land use, and resource exploitation. The island was transformed: native mammal, bird, and fish populations were exploited, domesticates appeared, woodland was reduced, and the native vegetation cover altered. These human impacts set in motion or accentuated processes that have resulted in modern-day Iceland's unstable soils and eroded landscape.

For all these reasons, this book aims to cast new light on our understanding of the relationships between the peoples of this north Atlantic zone in the early medieval period. A wide range of scholarship has been involved in exploring this topic, which is often only fully understood once we begin to unravel the sometimes disparate historiographies. The scholarship includes archaeological, medieval literature, place-name, and palaeoenvironmental studies; yet, applying the results of such diverse research also foregrounds a fundamental challenge: how may one work between disciplines?

Problem and Context

The north Atlantic islands have proven importance as an arena for investigating cultural diffusion, the movements of people, and the interactions between humans and their environments, with the chronology of Iceland's settlement being critical to these larger questions (on account of that island's enviable sequence of dated volcanic airfall or tephra). Specifically, scholarship has recently been excited afresh by the uncertainties surrounding the Viking Age's Scandinavian and early Christian communities (called *papar* in later Norse literature),[3] and we may be drawn to this field of research by its complex interplay of established "certainties" and fundamental ambiguities. Throughout the book our focus shall be to engage with these inherent complexities. For example, a fluorescence of Gaelic monasticism is well established for the early medieval period, with individuals and monastic foundations of the "Irish school" penetrating large areas of Europe (figure 1) and contemporary authors such as Dicuil[4] (Tierney 1967) and Adomnán (Anderson and Anderson 1991; Sharpe 1995) describing north Atlantic travels and settlements. Therefore, we may perceive that journeys north from the Gaelic world are plausible, and, given the clearly documented impulse to seek a *desertum* (or wilderness) in the Ocean (Charles-Edwards 1976; Wooding 2000, 2011), exploration of the northern seas may have seized upon a variety of catalysts, perhaps including observation of migratory bird routes[5] (Cunliffe 2002: 119). However, in spite of Dicuil's and Adomnán's accounts and the early (but problematic) proposals by scholars such as Eugène Beauvois (Beauvois 1875), the extent and character of these northern settlements is very poorly grasped – as is their relationship to the Viking Age Scandinavians who came to dominate this region by the ninth or early tenth centuries.

As mentioned earlier, given the range of fields deployed in exploring our topic, it is crucial to try to unravel the various histories of scholarship dealing with these questions, and to consequently improve our own analysis. We shall therefore begin with a consideration of the historical dimension to this problem, and specifically of nineteenth-century legacies. Chapter 1 explores the ancestry of research on north Atlantic migrations by looking to medieval

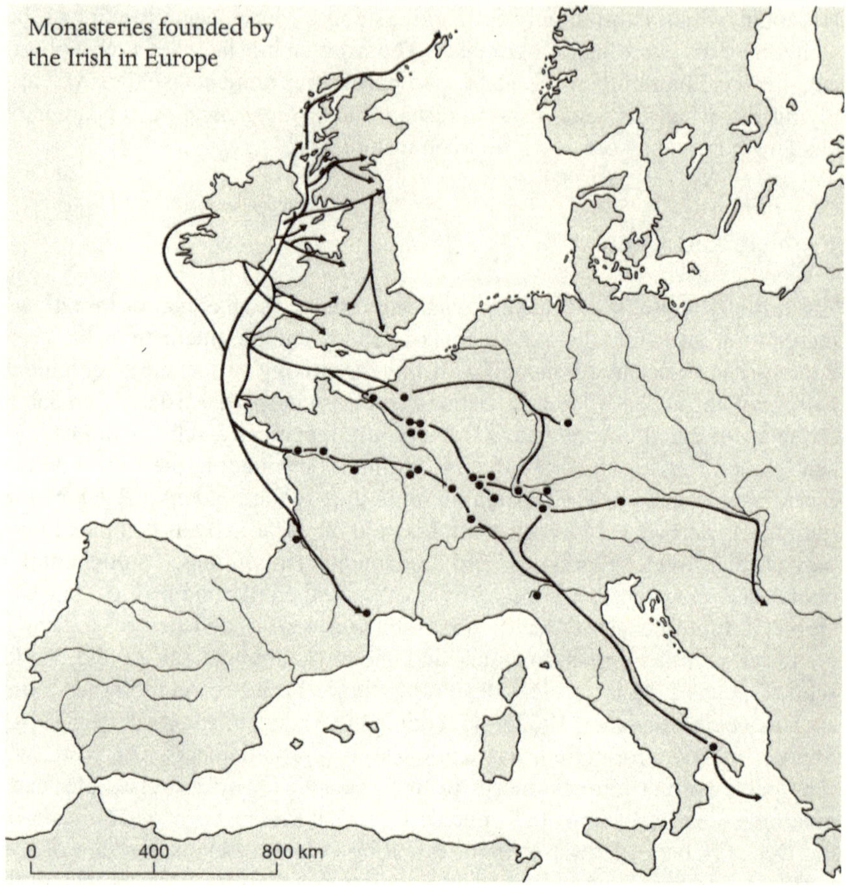

Fig. I.1 The travels of the Irish *peregrini* in the fifth to eighth centuries, and the settlements and monasteries that they founded. Taken from Cunliffe (2001: 472 , fig. 10.25), by permission of Oxford University Press (www.oup.com).

literature and assessing the contributions of antiquarian scholars, such as the otherwise forgotten Eugène Beauvois. Consideration of this earlier work is empowering, and we are fortunate that recent developments – in several fields – enable a more sophisticated analysis of early medieval populations and human-environmental interactions in the north Atlantic islands. Thus we may profit from linguistic and place-name research on Scandinavian-Gaelic contact (Gammeltoft 2004b), catalogues of Iceland's artificial caves (Hjartarson et al. 1991) and Scotland's west-coast cross sculpture (Fisher 2001), and studies considering the role of early Christian communities in the agricultural development of Scotland's northern and western isles (Simpson and Guttman 2002; Simpson et al. 2005) and of the earliest cereal cultivation in the Faroe Islands (Edwards et al. 2005). In order to draw together the strands of work on archaeological, Celtic, Norse, and palaeoenvironmental materials, however, we must deal with the problems inherent in integrating them. From the outset, chapter 2 responds to these concerns by formulating a theoretically grounded method for fruitful conversation between disciplines. Applying this method, we may reposition scholarship in difficult (and interrelated) areas that have frustrated researchers. Thus chapter 3 explores the toponymy of *Pap-* names (which have been associated with settlements of the aforementioned papar), with a focus on Hebridean *Pab(b)ay* islands and *Paible* places. In turn, chapters 4 to 7 tackle the artificial caves of southern Iceland. An earlier generation of scholars tentatively related these sites to the first settlement of Iceland by monastic communities of Gaels, and, though remaining enigmatic, these caves are the best-preserved and most numerous medieval structures in Iceland. Therefore, this "Seljaland section" establishes a chronology of cave construction, occupation, and human-environmental interactions at the Seljaland site in southern Iceland. The results are concrete and gain strength from innovative exploitation of volcanic airfall (tephra) for studies of past environments. Let us start, therefore, by assessing the nineteenth-century contribution to this compelling field of study.

1 Nineteenth-Century Legacies: Literature, Language, and the Imagining of the St Lawrence Irish

By the 1880s growing social and economic problems in Western Europe were encouraging a new emphasis on conservatism and the rigidity of human nature, and hence on ethnicity … The problems of the Industrial Revolution were becoming increasingly evident, especially in Britain where it had been going on the longest, in the form of slums, economic crises, and growing foreign competition. At the same time, the political supremacy of the middle classes was being challenged by the first labour movements. As a result of these developments, the younger generation of intellectuals turned against the idea of progress …

The efforts that were made to externalise conflicts encouraged a growing emphasis on racial doctrines. It was argued that French, Germans, and English were biologically different from one another and that their behaviour was determined not by economic and political factors, but by essentially immutable racial differences …

Disillusionment with progress, together with the belief that human behaviour was biologically determined, promoted growing scepticism about human creativity. Writers and social analysts maintained that people were not inherently inventive and that change was contrary to human nature and potentially harmful to people. It was argued that a static condition was most congenial to human beings, who were naturally predisposed to resist alterations in their styles of life. This led to declining credence in independent development, a belief that particular inventions were unlikely to be made more than once in human history, and hence a growing reliance on diffusion and migration to explain cultural change. It also encouraged an increasing interest in the idiosyncratic features associated with particular ethnic groups rather than with the general characteristics of successive stages of cultural development …

Increasing reliance on diffusion and migration, as well as the concept of cultures as ways of life related to specific ethnic groups, were soon evident in the work of German ethnologists such as Friedrich Ratzel (1844–1901) and Franz Boas (1858–1942). Ratzel, a geographer and ethnologist, … argued that, because the world was small, ethnologists must beware of thinking that even the simplest inventions were likely to have been made more than once, let alone repeatedly. Both invention and diffusion were described as capricious processes; hence it became impossible to predict whether a particular group will borrow even a useful invention from its neighbours. Ratzel argued that because of this it was necessary to rule out the possibility of diffusion in order to prove that the same type of artifact had been invented more than once.

Bruce Trigger, *A History of Archaeological Thought*[1]

Dans un précedent mémoire, j'ai exposé et cherché à expliquer ce que les Islandais nous apprennent de la Grande Irlande ... Ces circonstances nous empêchent de la chercher autre part que dans la péninsule comprise entre la baie de Fundy et le golfe et l'estuaire du Saint-Laurent; elle correspondait donc au Nouveau-Brunswick et à la Gaspésie.

Eugène Beauvois (1835 – after 1912), "Les relations précolombiennes des Gaëls avec le Mexique"[2]

Le récollet Christian Le Clerq, qui avait habité douze ans la Gaspésie, sur la rive droite du Saint-Laurent, y retrouvait au XVIIe siècle, de nombreux restes du christianisme, notamment le culte de la croix et des reminiscences du *pater*; et le jésuite, Joseph-François Lafitau, assure que le christianisme était, chez les sauvages du Canada, une réminiscence plutôt qu'une nouvelle croyance, et qu'ils regardaient la croix comme le symbole de la religion autrefois enseignée à leurs ancêtres. A ces traces de la propogation du christianisme dans le basin du fleuve et du golfe Saint-Laurent, avant les voyages de Jacques Cartier et de Champlain, il faut ajouter les ruines d'édifices qui ne peuvent avoir été élevés par des sauvages. Les Anglais ont trouvé dans l'île de Terre-Neuve des restes de murs en pierre.

Eugène Beauvois, "La découverte du Nouveau Monde par les Irlandais et les premières traces du Christianisme en Amérique avant l'an 1000"[3]

Looking back to earlier generations of scholars and paying particular attention to the legacy of the nineteenth century, we see that in this period the fast-paced discoveries of medieval literature held special appeal for interdisciplinary efforts. Thus medieval accounts such as those of Vínland sparked a search that eventually led to Helge and Anne-Stine Ingstad's spectacular discovery of the L'Anse-aux-Meadows site in Newfoundland – and to the vindication of what were initially speculative ideas. For a number of nineteenth-century scholars, engaging with medieval literature and interdisciplinary problems led to the proposal of bold ideas, at times very ambitious and short lived. In this first chapter I shall argue that these scholars explored medieval texts with a particular and theory-impregnated combination of imagination and insight. Therefore, the question I foreground is this: how may we benefit from the work of these earlier (and often wild) scholars and the medieval literature they deployed?

There is some antiquity to modern suggestions of Gaelic settlement in Iceland by early Christian communities, and some of archaeology's pivotal figures were interested in the topic, such as the University of Toronto's Sir Daniel Wilson (for example, Wilson 1851: 483–6). In the introduction we touched upon the claims of Dicuil as well as Ari fróði and the other writers of the medieval *Íslendingabók* and *Landnámabók*, and upon the way in which Adomnán's writings (alongside Irish voyage literature) provide an early medieval and monastic context for northern journeys into the Ocean (*Íslendingabók*: ch. 1; *Landnámabók*: ch. 1; Benediktsson 1968: 4–5, 31–2; Pálsson and Edwards 1972: 14; Tierney 1967: 72–7; Anderson and Anderson 1991; Sharpe 1995). We may thus perceive that the idea of early Christian settlement across the north Atlantic islands was sparked long ago by study of medieval texts and was fuelled by complementary material from other fields, such as the occurence of *pap*-element place names across the region.

Norse and Celtic scholarship have approached this topic differently. A Celtic literature perspective identifies early Christian writers such as Dicuil to be operating within a coherent tradition. For instance, Jonathan Wooding provides a survey of the "historical context of voyaging by monastic *peregrini* in the Atlantic between c. 560 and 800 AD" (Wooding 2000: 227), while Thomas O'Loughlin investigates what the stories of such journeys may have symbolized for their intended audiences (O'Loughlin 1999). Importantly, what Dicuil describes as contemporary journeys into the Ocean are consistent with Thomas Charles-Edwards's investigation of the attested historical phenomenon of the *peregrinatio* drive within Irish society, in some cases to find a desert place in the Ocean (Charles-Edwards 1976). The situation is different for late medieval Norse literature, however, where descriptions of *papar*/*papæ* (an Old Norse word) might be characterized as odd and poorly understood. From a Norse perspective, the *papar* passages are exotic and lack the three-dimensionality of the Celtic literature on this topic.[4]

Investigations of the relationship between Atlantic Gaels and the island Norse at the end of the first millennium AD gained momentum in the nineteenth century, when scholars such as Daniel Wilson and Eugène Beauvois deployed medieval literature (some only recently discovered, such as the *Historia Norvegiæ*), place names, folklore, and archaeological material to investigate this topic. Enigmatic medieval descriptions of a Greater Ireland (Írland et mikla), somewhere in the Atlantic Ocean, proved fertile ground for the imaginations of early researchers such as Beauvois. This generation of scholarship may today seem outdated; however, I suggest that contextualizing the work of these writers within the academic and social milieu in which they operated enables a more sensitive realization of their continuing contribution to scholarship. In addition, such a realization holds out the possibility for modern-day investigators, with an effort, to work towards an awareness of the mortality of our own ideas. Bruce Trigger makes a similar claim at the outset of his *History of Archaeological Thought* (and touches upon a counter-position):

> In recent years a growing number of archaeologists have come to agree with the philosopher and archaeologist R.G. Collingwood that "no historical problem should be studied without studying … the history of historical thought about it" (Dunnell 1984: 490; Collingwood 1939: 132). Historical investigations of archaeological interpretation have multiplied, and more sophisticated methodologies have been adopted (Trigger 1985). This approach is not, however, without its critics. Michael Schiffer has asserted that graduate courses should cease to be "histories of thought" and instead should systematically expound and articulate current theories (Schiffer 1976: 193). His position embodies the view that the truth or falseness of theoretical formulations is independent of social influences and hence of history but can be determined by applying scientifically valid procedures of evaluation to adequate bodies of data. Taken to an extreme, this view implies that the history and philosophy of archaeology are totally unrelated to each other. (Trigger 1989: 1–2)

Counter to Schiffer, I wish to underscore the idea that formulating an effective *new* solution to a problem demands familiarity with the *historical dimension* of that problem. This is consistent with the view outlined in the next chapter, that science is the social process of proposing (and refuting) testable solutions to a problem. Correspondingly, familiarity with earlier formulations of a problem (and corresponding solutions) increases the robustness of a study by enabling a researcher to enter that debate confidently and intelligently because he or she understands the history of that debate.

Thus we shall explore the history of Írland et mikla scholarship, a survey of which demonstrates continuity of argument between present-day scholarship and the antiquarian past. There are three reasons that we focus upon studies of Írland et mikla descriptions in medieval Icelandic literature (as an area within the larger field of Norse-Gaelic research): first, scholars investigating Írland et mikla often deployed multidisciplinary materials, some of which we shall revisit in later chapters; second, Írland et mikla research is in need of a dedicated treatment; and third, substantial exploration of this scholarship is achievable in a small-scale study.

Problem and Context

In his essay on studying Celtic literature, Matthew Arnold articulates tendencies in late-nineteenth-century scholarship. His comments are of general relevance for the period's scholarship:

> We want to know what all this mass of documents really tells us about the Celts. But the mode of dealing with these documents, and with the whole question of Celtic antiquity, has hitherto been most unsatisfactory. Those who have dealt with them have gone to work, in general, either as warm Celt-lovers or as warm Celt-haters, and not as disinterested students of an important matter of science. One party seems to set out with the determination to find everything in Celtism and its remains; the other, with the determination to find nothing in them. A simple seeker for truth has a hard time between the two. (Arnold [1867] 1962: 307)

Modern-day discussions of medieval texts describing Írland et mikla are part of a continuum of scholarship stretching back to the nineteenth century. In the passage above Arnold points to an important obstacle to realizing the historical dimension of research: many of the earlier writers were operating with explicit aims and theoretical frameworks that we do not share. (For Arnold, these are "warm Celt-lovers" and "warm Celt-haters.") Thus I propose our first problem to investigate: *how to approach scholars such as Beauvois and the medieval literature they deploy.*

All discussions of Greater Ireland spring from descriptions of the place (or what appear to be descriptions of the place) in three Icelandic texts, dated from the late eleventh to thirteenth centuries. Unless otherwise noted, all translations are mine. In *Landnámabók*, Ari fróði describes how his great-grandfather "*varð sæhafi til Hvítramannalands; þat kalla sumir Írland et mikla*" (*Landnámabók*: S122; Benediktsson 1968: 162; drifted to "men of white"-land, that some call Greater Ireland), and that this lies west in the Ocean, near Vínland the good. The *Landnámabók* passage relates Írland et mikla to another name, that of Hvítramannaland. In *Eiríks saga rauða* the author describes a place "*Það ætla menn Hvítramannaland*" (*Eiríks*: ch. 12; Halldórsson 1985: 432; that people believed was "men of white"-land) where "*gengu menn þar í hvítum klæðum ok æpðu hátt ok báru stangir ok fóru með flíkr*" (*Eiríks*: ch. 12; Halldórsson 1985: 432; go men there in white clothing and yell loudly and bear poles and wave pieces of cloth). The third passage, from *Eyrbyggja saga*, does not specifically mention Írland et mikla or Hvítramannaland but does have elements in common with the *Landnámabók* and *Eiríks saga rauða* passages, namely describing a place west of Ireland where "*helzt þótti þeim, sem þeir mælti írsku*"

(*Eyrbyggja*: ch. 64; Sveinsson and Þórðarson 1935: 176–7; they thought that they spoke Irish).

Alongside *Pap-* names, these Írland et mikla accounts have long frustrated analysis – and encouraged nineteenth-century diffusionist-influenced researchers such as Eugène Beauvois to propose wild ideas, such as settlements of early Christian Gaels in Canada (Beauvois 1875). Engaging with this largely forgotten scholarship demands understanding. Some of this earlier work was exceptional but also incorporated what we might today dismiss as wild or racially driven ideas.

Thus our first task shall be to focus upon the Grande-Irlande tradition in the late-nineteenth-century scholarship of Beauvois; what follows is the result of a comprehensive survey of his published work and a detailed study of one key text. When one explores writers such as Beauvois, a crucial question that arises is how to separate out strong scholarship, relevant to modern-day research, from the antiquated elements. Here we shall take a two-pronged approach to contextualizing Beauvois's Írland et mikla research: (1) relate Beauvois's scholarship to the wider historiography of the topic, and (2) set Beauvois's ideas alongside nineteenth-century concepts of diffusionism and racial determinism (racial ideas that in turn became associated with national identities).[5] Importantly, investigating these earlier "outdated" authors reminds us that our own theoretical frameworks will in time become distasteful to future researchers. This realization of the mortality of our ideas cautions us; we should be wary of placing too much confidence in theory-led conclusions inspired by isolated material that is unsupported by coherent bodies of data. We shall return to this caution in the next chapter when we touch upon Karl Popper's idea that "tests can be graded as more or less severe" (Popper 1994: 94), with coherent bodies of data enabling a more severe test than scattered "incoherent" data.

In 1875, Beauvois published "La découverte du Nouveau Monde par les Irlandais et les premières traces du Christianisme en Amérique avant l'an 1000." In this long contribution to the first Congrès international des américanistes, Beauvois argued that a medieval migration of early Christian Gaels across the Scottish and north Atlantic islands led to the founding of a Grande-Irlande along the St Lawrence. Though largely forgotten today, Beauvois was a prolific scholar and involved in some of the great debates of his day, such as Eben Norton Horsford's Norumbega claims (Beauvois 1879a; Wawn 2001: 198–200; 2003: 151; Barnes 2001: 62–70), and a preliminary bibliography of his periodical publications demonstrates this. An initial assessment of his output is tabulated below by decade and by journal.

That he was well received (at least by conference delegates) is suggested by comments introducing his papers, such as "M. Beauvois, après s'être excuse de demander la parole, alors que les conclusions de son mémoire n'on été contestées par aucun des honorables préopinants" (Beauvois 1877a: 59). Or, as Lucien Adam writes in the proceedings of the fifth Congrès international des américanistes: "M. Beauvois vient de nous faire connaître loyalement quel a été son plan de campagne. De session en session, il a successivement occupé, sans rencontrer de contradicteurs, des positions grâce auxquelles il a pu cheminer depuis l'extrémité septentrionale du Canada jusqu'au centre du Mexique" (Beauvois 1883b: 97).

Beauvois was part of a continuum of scholarship investigating Írland et mikla. A survey of selected research demonstrates that Hvítramannaland "*Þat kalla sumir Írland et mikla*" (that some call Greater Ireland)[6] has fired academic imaginations, with scholars attempting to locate the place in either physical or literary space. Though medieval references are limited, the two place names Hvítramannaland and Írland et mikla have been studied since the nineteenth century (Sorenson and Raish 1996). Described as somewhere in the west, near Vínland,[7] Hvítramannaland or Írland et mikla remains problematic after more than a hundred years of scholarship.

The following selected review, concentrating largely upon dedicated discussions of the medieval Icelandic texts, reveals some of the main trends in scholarship. Approaches to the topic follow two main directions (at times explored by the same authors): either one accepts a "realistic" inspiration (which can be located on a conventional map), or one imagines an origin in Irish myth. A number of scholars (including Beauvois) apply the textual descriptions to identify an Atlantic coast or island. A variant of this approach has been to set aside the Írland et mikla descriptions and to concentrate instead on analysis of the two place names, again with the goal of identifying which *real* place was being named (for example, Iceland or the Gaspé). A fundamentally different view equates Hvítramannaland with an other world from Irish myth.

As outlined above, one approach taken throughout the nineteenth and twentieth centuries sought to locate these names on modern-day maps, with varying levels of precision. In 1842, Karl Wilhelmi identified Hvítramannaland and Írland et mikla in today's eastern United States (Wilhelmi [1842] 1967). The suggestion of Hvítramannaland as a place somewhere in this area persisted, for instance in Rudolf Cronau's work (Cronau 1892). Writing later that century, Beauvois disagreed with "les savants, passablement nombreux, qui ont publié, traduit ou commenté les documents relatifs à la Grande Irlande ou *Hvítramannaland*" (Beauvois 1875: 41), arguing instead for his Grande-Irlande on the southern shore of the St Lawrence seaway (Beauvois 1875; figure 1.1).[8] Beauvois's ideas were discussed by Emile Schmidt and later Peter de Roo (Schmidt 1879; de Roo 1900) and then took on a life of their own; a

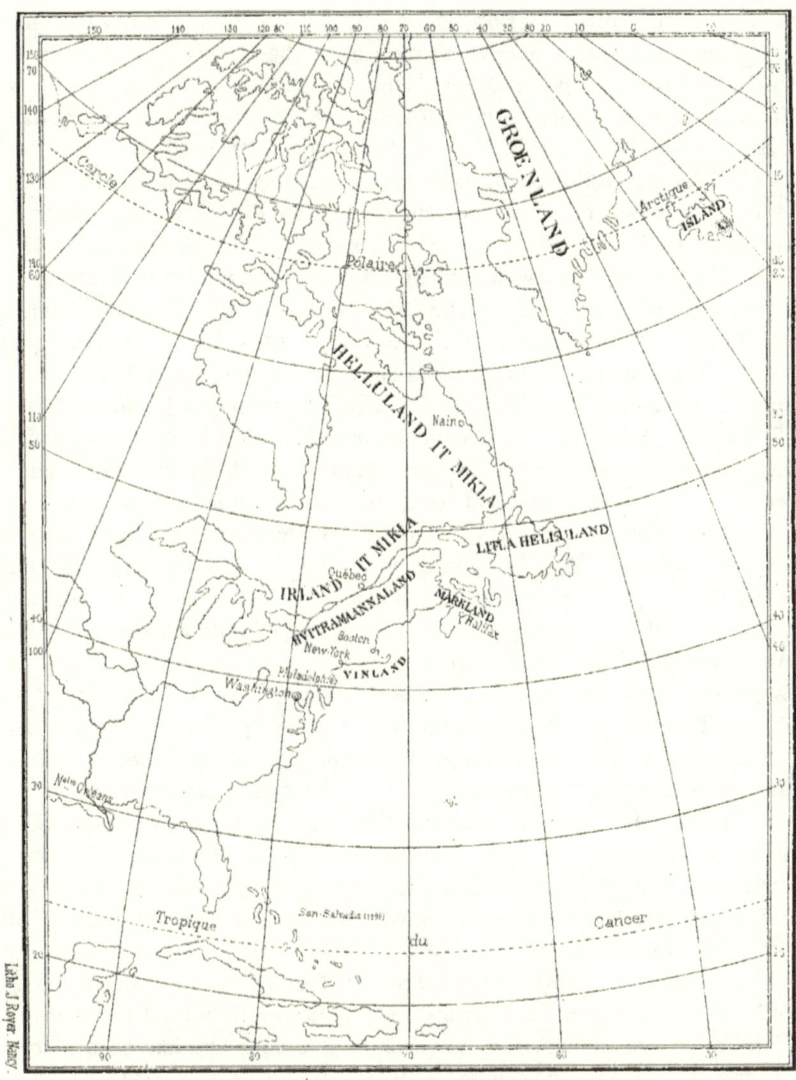

Figure 1.1 “Carte des découvertes Irlandaises et Islandaises selon Mr. E. Beauvois.” Taken from *Congrès international des Américanistes* (Beauvois 1875: 84). Lithography by J. Royer.

generation later, William H. Babcock revisited suggestions of early Irish journeys to North America in Beauvois's old forum, the Congrès international des américanistes series of proceedings (Babcock 1915).

Contemporary with Beauvois, Gustav Storm saw Iceland as a more likely prospect (Storm [1887] 1888: 65, 68 [361]; Nansen 1911: 43n1; Young 1937: 122). L.D. Scisco, followed by Halvdan Koht, made a fresh proposal in the early years of the twentieth century, suggesting that the place names described western Ireland (Scisco 1908: 379, 515; Koht 1909: 133; Nansen 1911: 43n1; Young 1937: 122–3). The twentieth century was to see a number of innovative ideas put forward. Jean Young, in 1937, contemplated a dual physical origin for the medieval traditions, both off the coast *and* on the coast of western Ireland (Young 1937). Four years later, Halldór Hermannsson proposed that the names remember a western Irish baptismal place (Hermannsson [1944] 1966). In 1962, Geoffrey Ashe held that Greenland, possibly Nova Scotia, or the eastern United States was meant by Hvítramannaland (Ashe 1962: 144–56). A generalized view of Írland et mikla and Hvítramannaland gained prominence in this period. The following year, Tryggvi Oleson understood the place names as Greenland or the New World generally *or* possibly the eastern Canadian Arctic (Oleson 1963: 97–9).[9] Most recently, Kirsten Seaver argued that these place names and traditions demonstrate a medieval Icelandic knowledge of lands in eastern Canada (Seaver 1999: 526).

Beginning in the twentieth century a rival perspective has challenged this approach. Taking inspiration from ideas of a Celtic other world, an approach was formulated that instead proposed Hvítramannaland and Írland et mikla as learned constructs rather than real places (for instance, comparable to an Irish Tír na Fer Finn). For example, Edmund Hogan included the following passage in his *Onomasticon Goedelicum Locorum et Tribuum Hiberniae et Scotiae* in which he refers to Wilhelmi's ideas (Wilhelmi [1842] 1967: 75–81): "*Tír na Fer Fionn*; in romantic tales ... this may be 'Hvitra Manna Land' (Land of the White Men), also called 'Irland et Mikla' (Great Ireland), the name given by the Danes to the E. Coast of the United States of America, nr Florida, when Ari, K. of Lein., was wrecked in the year 983" (Hogan 1910: 638). A problem with the Tír na Fer Finn comparison, however, is its unique and late occurrence in the Stonyhurst larger Irish volume dated ca. 1700 (St B. 718) (Hogan 1910).[10] Continuing from Tír na Fer Finn parallels, Fridtjof Nansen's *In Northern Mists* compared Hvítramannaland to the promised land in the Irish *Navigatio Sancti Brendani abbatis* (Nansen 1911: 43–50). However, it would be for later scholars to build upon Hogan's equation of Tír na Fer Finn and Hvítramannaland. A generation (or two) later, Jean Young, Halldór Hermannsson, and Gabriel Turville-Petre all suggested that the Icelandic texts describe a mythical land

(Young 1937: 124–5; Hermannsson [1944] 1966; Turville-Petre 1953: 48). Similar ideas continued in the works of Hermann Pálsson, Tryggvi Oleson, Magnús Magnússon, Paul Edwards, and Ólafur Halldórsson (Pálsson 1960; Oleson 1963: 101–2; Magnússon and Pálsson 1965: 102n1; Pálsson and Edwards 1972: 61n48; Halldórsson 1985: 364–6). In 1996 and 2000, Hermann Pálsson once again expressed variations of this view, as did Helgi Guðmundsson in 1997 (Pálsson 1996: 224–6; 2000: 29; Guðmundsson 1997: 67n47).

A difficulty with the "learned construct" argument is its reliance upon a Celtic other world overseas. Whether or not one accepts a Celtic other world across the seas, James Carney and John Carey challenge its antiquity (Carney 1963: 40–1, 40n9; Carey 1983: 36–43), while David Dumville stresses the fantastic nature of journeys into the supernatural worlds of the *echtrai* and *immrama* tale types (Dumville 1976: 82–3).[11] However, Seamus Mac Mathúna identifies Irish literary motifs from the *Navigatio Brendani* in the Hvítramannaland and Írland et mikla passages (Mac Mathúna 1999: 186–7), but the aforementioned difficulty remains: the other-worldly supernatural elements we would prefer, in order to bolster an interpretation of Hvítramannaland as Irish-inspired literary invention, are absent. Instead, our texts – even if fictional – describe events set in a "real" world familiar to the authors.[12] For instance, Gustav Storm compared the phrase *Írland et mikla*, or Greater Ireland, to places such as Magna Græcia, the Greek colony in Italy, and Svíþjóð it mikla (Greater Sweden), the Scandinavian settlement of Rus' in Russia and Ukraine (Storm [1887] 1888: 65; Nansen 1911: 48). Storm's interpretation of the phrase (as describing an Irish colony or Gaelic place outside Ireland) has been explored by Geoffrey Ashe, Hermann Pálsson, and Helgi Guðmundsson (Ashe 1962: 151; Pálsson 1960: 52; Guðmundsson 1997: 67n47).

Hermann Pálsson presented a view that mediates between the literary and physical worlds. He has been followed or considered by Jakob Benediktsson, Helgi Guðmundsson, and Mac Mathúna (Benediktsson 1968: 162n2; Guðmundsson 1997: 68n47; Mac Mathúna 1999: 187). Pálsson proposed *Hvítramannaland* as a learned secret name for Alba through conflation with the Latin *albus* (white) (Pálsson 1960: 52). Thus, he interpreted *Hvítramannaland* as a learned Icelandic rendering of "land of the men of Alba." Alternatively, Nansen understood the *hvítra-* (white) element in *Hvítramannaland* as related to the Scandinavian concept of the holy (or Christian) (Nansen 1911: 44).

In summary then, a survey of Hvítramannaland and Írland et mikla scholarship points to a field with a number of *ideas*, often neither fully supported nor refuted, and frequently propounded as points of faith (or fashion) in learned footnotes and brief discussions. Longer studies are rare, with Beauvois publishing the most extensively on the topic, whereas late-twentieth-century investigations were dominated by Pálsson and, later, Mac Mathúna. Most important, however, is the discovery that critical dialogue with earlier scholars, such as Beauvois, by twentieth-century writers is minimal. For instance, Pálsson and Mac Mathúna have raised the level of the debate with fresh rigour and a historical awareness, though they both appear unaware of Beauvois's contributions to the field – despite his prolific output illustrated in table 1.1. Mac Mathúna and Pálsson are not alone in this. Beauvois's ideas continued in popular literature, but scholars such as Nansen, Young, Hermannsson, Turville-Petre, and Benediktsson do not engage with his substantial body of work, though they and later writers explore comparable ideas and materials.[13] Correspondingly, if we conceive of scholarship (or science) as a public *community* enterprise, where ideas are proposed and subjected to mutual criticism, then the fostering of rigorous scientific research in this field mandates the study of earlier ideas such as Beauvois's, and their consequent integration into our discussions.

Hypothesis

With a fascinating combination of imagination and insight, late-nineteenth-century scholars such as Beauvois engaged with historical materials that are still prominent today. In particular, Beauvois was exceedingly well read and prolific and had an impressive command of contemporary literature. Thus the problem at hand is how to approach scholars such as Beauvois and the medieval literature they deploy.

In his *History of Archaeological Thought* and *Sociocultural Evolution* Bruce Trigger provides a contextual model with which to explore Beauvois's claims for his Grande-Irlande. In short, Trigger suggests that nineteenth-century scholars operated within a theoretical framework that accepted diffusionist and racial ideas. I propose that, by remembering this theoretical framework, the contribution of Beauvois and other scholars may be realized and fully integrated with modern-day research.

In particular, trends in nineteenth-century folktale theory elaborate Trigger's ideas regarding diffusionism. In his chapter "Theories of the Folktale," Stith Thompson sums up why the field proved particularly fertile for such ideas: "A study of tale collections shows clearly that many tales are widely distributed over the globe. What is the nature of this distribution, how did it occur, and why?" (Thompson 1946: 368). Writing in 1819, the Grimm brothers were the earliest scholars to grapple with these questions.[14] In contrast with later workers, Wilhelm Grimm felt that straightforward diffusion did not explain the wide distributions mentioned above. Grimm did not "deny the possibility, nor in

Table 1.1 Beauvois's publications in periodicals, sorted by decade and periodical

Decade	Number of publications	Periodical and volume/year
1850s	1	*Revue orientale et américaine* **1859**
1860s	0	
1870s	5	*Congrès international des américanistes* **1, 2, 3**
		Annales de philosophie chrétienne **1877**
		Revue orientale et américaine **1879**
1880s	12	*Congrès international des américanistes* **4, 5**
		Le Muséon: Revue internationale. Études de linguistiques, d'histoire et de philosophie **2, 3, 5, 6, 7, 8**
		Revue de l'histoire des religions **6, 7, 10, 18**
		Revue des questions historiques **1885**
1890s	6	*Le Muséon* **10, 12, 15, 17**
		Congrès international des américanistes **1892**
		Revue des questions scientifiques **2**
1900s	4	*Revue des questions scientifiques* **3**
		Journal de la société des américanistes de Paris **1**
		Le Muséon **1904, 1907**

particular instances the probability, of a story's passing over from one people to another, and then firmly rooting itself on the foreign soil" (Grimm 1856: 427ff; 1884: 575ff; Thompson 1946: 369), but he felt this was exceptional. Instead, he appealed to Indo-European theory to explain similarities between tales (Thompson 1946: 370). In the mid-nineteenth-century a diffusionist school of thought emerged – first tentatively by Loiseleur Deslongchamps and then as dogma in Theodor Benfey's work (Deslongchamps 1838; Benfey 1859; Thompson 1946: 376). Benfey championed the mechanism of diffusion to explain similarities between tales across the world. Benfey imagined an ultimate Indian origin for most folktales and charted the routes of their diffusion to Europe, though later scholars influenced by Benfey, such as Reinhold Köhler and Emmanuel Cosquin, suggested non-Indian origins for some folktales (Thompson 1946: 376–9). Andrew Lang, however, challenged outright these Indianist and Indo-European mythological theories, instead proposing a mild form of polygenesis. Polygenesis theory understands that "resemblances in stories are due to an independent invention in many places, since they are made up of beliefs, customs, etc. which are common to peoples of the same stages of culture" (Thompson 1946: 380; Lang 1893).

By the second half of the nineteenth century Trigger perceives that "most Western historians and social scientists" held diffusionist ideas (Trigger 1998: 96). He defines and points to the prevalence of diffusionism (and the related concept of migrationism) in this period:

> They [most Western historians and social scientists] rejected the claim that change came about as a result of the same innovation being made independently in different places as they were needed. Instead they relied on migration and diffusion to explain the changes observed in the historical and archaeological record. Migrationary explanations tended to be more pessimistic about human creativity than were diffusionist ones. Diffusionists assumed that humans were better able to copy other people's ideas than to innovate. Migrationists believed that people were unable or unwilling to change their ways and therefore all cultural change had to come about as the result of immigrants with their distinctive cultures replacing or blending with established groups. (Trigger 1998: 96)

As John Francis Campbell's *Popular Tales of the West Highlands* (first edition 1858–60) demonstrates, however, Trigger may be overstating and overpolarizing the case. For instance, Campbell writes in his second edition that "there are, of course, two ways of accounting for … [resemblances between medieval romances]. Those who believe in creations of the human brain will look on the traditions as fragments of a ruined romance. Those who think that *creations* of the brain are very rare will look on traditions as the quarry whence materials have been taken by a succession of romancers, who said nothing about their mine of wealth" (Campbell 1893: 246). Furthermore, Campbell himself does not (in the end) follow diffusionist thinking. He sees similarities in tales between different peoples as arguing *not* for diffusion but instead for a common origin (that is, the diffusion of *people*, with a continuity of ideas): "The only possible deduction from these facts seems to be that these are traces of a mythology once common to Celts, Scandinavians, Italians, Germans, and mayhap ancient Greeks, Romans, Egyptians, and Aryans" (Campbell 1893: 262). To support his point, he gives the example of stories of "mysterious western lands": "In a note, I find that Cardigan Bay was once the site of a submerged country; the same, no doubt, which can be traced in Breton, in Irish, in Manks, and Gaelic; in Norse, and in Italian, a country submerged for wickedness, and whose houses can be seen under water, and occasionally rise to the surface; a tradition common to many nations which bears upon that of the mysterious western land hidden in the mist, which once was the Isle of Man, and is now to the westward of Man" (Campbell 1893: 273). Campbell was a part of the world in which Beauvois operated. Nonetheless, these scholars agree that, in the period Beauvois was writing, diffusionist (and the related migrationist) ideas were theoretically credible.

Similarly, racial ideas emerged out of the first half of the nineteenth century to gain prominence in the 1850s. The French scholar Joseph-Arthur, Comte de Gobineau, was a key figure in the articulation and dissemination of racial ideas; by 1855 he had published his four-volume *Essai sur l'inégalité des races humaines* (Gobineau 1853–5). Trigger contextualizes Gobineau:

> A member of an aristocratic and royalist French family, Gobineau exalted the Frankish nobility as the true creators of Western civilization (Bowler 1989: 109). He believed that the fate of civilizations was determined by their racial composition and that the more a successful civilization's racial character became diluted through intermarriage with other groups, the more likely it was to sink into stagnation and decay. Gobineau's writings were to influence European racists from the nineteenth-century composer Richard Wagner to Adolf Hitler. Yet he was not alone ... In both Europe and America novelists, popular writers, and reputable scholars were invoking racial factors as well as environmental ones to explain variations in the degree to which different groups had evolved in the course of human history. (Trigger 1998: 49–50)

The currency of the concept of race in the late nineteenth century had special relevance for archaeological and historical investigations. In this period, "race replaced language as the main criterion that was used to trace the history of ethnic groups" (Trigger 1998: 50).

Separately, it was claimed that only migrations of people (and thus invasion and conquest) could bring "superior culture" to an area (Trigger 1998: 50). A key consequence of these ideas for study of archaeological and historical problems was that "as cultures came to be viewed as biologically inherent in different populations, change was devalued and old customs were treated as more authentic reflections of a people and their culture than were recent innovations or borrowings. The development of racism provided an explanation for cultural variation that had great appeal to romantics because it identified the culturally specific and the exotic as the most essential reflections of human nature and offered reassurance that these aspects of human behaviour and identity were relatively resistant to change" (Trigger 1998: 50). Following this theoretical conception, the "culturally specific," the odd, and the exotic were given special importance in research. In other words, the isolated unusual artefacts or practices of a society were seen as the most essential diagnostic criteria for that society. Furthermore, the application of diffusionism to these exotic and culturally specific traits fostered the proposal of wild ideas; an example to be considered later is how "exotica," such as contact-period stories of the cult of the cross among the aboriginal peoples of southern Québec, led Beauvois to propose an early Christian Irish settlement there. Of course, that is not to say that all scholarship from this period was bound up with these ideas. For instance, in 1858 Thomas Stephens objected to suggestions of a thirty-thousand-strong medieval Welsh migration to North America. Of these claims, Stephens wrote: "Let us put the legend in its proper place in the list of our 'Mabinogion.' Let us show that we are not incapable either of self-analysis or of historical criticism" (Williams 1987: 200–1). Stephens, however, was exceptional; Gwyn A. Williams described him as "one of the sharpest intelligences Wales has produced" (Williams 1987: 200). In contrast, the epigraphs to this chapter articulate Trigger's ideas regarding the racial determinism and diffusionism so pervasive in nineteenth-century scholarship and juxtaposes these ideas with a passage from Beauvois. Trigger sees diffusionism and migration as well as racial ideas prominent precisely in Beauvois's period. The corresponding hypothesis for us to test, then, may be expressed as follows:

Nineteenth-century scholars such as Eugène Beauvois operated within a theoretical framework that accepted diffusionist and racial ideas. By allowing for this theoretical framework, the historical dimension that Beauvois and others contribute to scholarship may be realized and fully integrated with modern-day research.

Method

Beauvois imagined early Christian Irish settlement in the north Atlantic islands and, later, eastern Canada. Correspondingly, let us turn to a consideration of research into Canadian prehistory in the "medieval" period, as well as presentation of the principal textual materials describing Írland et mikla and Hvítramannaland.

Much of Beauvois's prolific output expands the ideas he first articulated in his 1875 paper, "La découverte du Nouveau Monde par les Irlandais et les premières traces du Christianisme en Amérique avant l'an 1000." In testing our hypothesis, we shall therefore concentrate on this 1875 paper and test the proposal that Beauvois held diffusionist and racial ideas. To be precise, his paper invites examination in order to identify examples of diffusionist or racist thinking.

In light of the results of this test, the character of Beauvois's scholarship may be assessed through his treatment of Greater Ireland literature. Thus, Beauvois's ideas shall be characterized by their integration with new research in the field. In this way, we explore the historical dimension that Beauvois contributes to scholarship.

Results and Discussion

In his arguments Beauvois explores medieval Atlantic journeys and migrations "into the Ocean," and in later chapters we shall contextualize these ideas with robust archaeological, environmental, and toponymic discussions. In order to empower an intelligent critique of Beauvois's wilder ideas, let us also turn to the northwest Atlantic area in the medieval period.

On the eve of European contact the aboriginal cultures of eastern Canada were characterized by expansion and abandonment of frontiers of settlement, complex interrelationships (including extensive trade networks), and major population migrations or cultural expansions. The fluidity of frontiers may be illustrated by the Palaeo-Inuit Late Dorset culture: southwest Greenland was settled and abandoned by Late Dorset from the eastern Canadian Arctic in the period from 700 to 900 (Damas 1996: 329; McAleese 2004: 358–9). These are the centuries immediately preceding the appearance of what Peter Pope describes as Norse "kin groups, moving for a year or two at a time, as part of normal resource foraging, which sometimes resulted in migration" (Pope 2004: 350). At this time the wider region of Greenland and eastern Canada was inhabited by a number of peoples in complex interrelationships: "The Dorset people of the eastern Canadian Arctic and northern Greenland, the ancestors of the Labrador Innu, the Newfoundland Beothuk, and the Maliseet and Micmac [Mi'kmaq] of the southern Gulf of Saint Lawrence and Nova Scotia … had divided this territory into a multicultural region of discrete homelands" (Odess et al. 2000: 193). That extensive trade networks existed is clear; deposits of meteoric iron from northwest Greenland were traded throughout the eastern Canadian Arctic (Sutherland 2000: 242; Schledermann 2000: 248–50, 254). Major migrations or cultural expansion also occurred: the Thule culture (which we relate to the modern Inuit) expanded eastwards from the western Arctic roughly a thousand years ago, completely replacing the Late Dorset culture over the following centuries (McAleese 2004: 359–61; Odess et al. 2000: 198–200; Sutherland 2000).

Further south, in the general region that Beauvois imagined as Grande-Irlande, archaeological investigation and ethnographic analogy enable a sketch of first millennium AD populations inhabiting some of the inland areas in proximity to the St Lawrence seaway. In the Ottawa river valley, for instance, people subsisted by hunting and fishing, alongside the gathering of fruits, nuts, and other foods. Hunters favoured white-tailed deer, but other species were pursued, including moose and bear as well as small-game species such as beaver and muskrat. The meat of these animals was consumed, and the hides used for clothing, containers, and other purposes. Bones could be crushed for their marrow or worked to fashion tools such as fish hooks, harpoons, and needles. Fish were important, and spring spawning runs and summer populations were particularly exploited. Several hundred individuals congregated in macro-bands for the spring and summer, along the shores of lakes and rivers near fishing sites. At this time of the year, varied and easily accessible resources were plentiful and encouraged socializing and feasting within and between macro-bands. For most of the autumn, efforts were made to build up a winter food supply. Fishing and communal white-tailed-deer hunting dominated, while wild rice, nuts, and other plant resources were gathered. By the end of the autumn, camp was abandoned and the macro-band splintered; individual micro-bands moved to interior wintering grounds. Winter sustenance depended upon food supplies accumulated during the autumn, supplemented by the occasional hunted white-tailed deer and small game. These Middle Woodland populations occupied a given territory and buried dead in mounds near the macro-band camps. There they interred individuals who died during the warm season, as well as the disarticulated skeletons, incomplete and often burned, of those who had died in the winter camps. The winter dead were probably buried or kept until the following spring (or perhaps even several years later), when a burial festival was held and the dead interred near the macro-camp (Laliberté 1999: 74–6; McAleese 2004: 356–7; Wright 1999).

This brief outline of eastern Canadian later prehistory empowers informed assessment of Beauvois's ideas and the literature he deploys. Beauvois begins his 1875 study with the mandate that "nous avons d'abord à traduire aussi littéralement que possible trois documents islandais, où il est parlé de la Grande-Irlande" (Beauvois 1875: 42). Dating from the late-eleventh to thirteenth centuries, three principal textual materials are associated with Írland et mikla and Hvítramannaland. These Icelandic texts include *Landnámabók*, *Eiríks saga rauða*, and *Eyrbyggja saga*.

The earliest version of *Landnámabók* is thought to originate in the late-eleventh and early twelfth centuries, but the text is not fixed until ca. 1300 (Pálsson and Edwards 1972: 3–8; Corráin 1998: 440).[15] The lost earliest version, thought to have been compiled by Ari fróði, was used by the thirteenth-century redactors of *Landnámabók*. *Landnámabók* begins by appealing to foreign authority in order to locate Iceland, and then charts the tentative process of the Norse land claim to the island (Taylor 2003: 4–5). A driving force behind the first prose texts, such as *Landnámabók*, may be perceived as the desire to establish the legitimacy and respectability of the new society that emerged in early Iceland, and it was through the telling of stories and genealogical accounting that this goal was pursued (Taylor 2003: 8; Hastrup 1998: 116; Clunies Ross 1997: 11). In the following passage we have an account of Ari's great-grandfather:

> Þeira son var Ari. Hann varð sæhafi til Hvítramannalands; þat kalla sumir Írland et mikla; þat liggr vestr í haf nær Vínlandi enu góða; þat kallat sex dœgra sigling vestr frá Írlandi. Þaðan náði Ari eigi á brutt at fara ok var þar skírðr. Þessa sǫgu sagði fyrst Hrafn Hlymreksfari, er lengi hafði verit í Hlymreki á Írlandi. Svá kvað Þorkell Gellisson segja íslenzka menn, þá er heyrt hǫfðu frá segja Þorfinn [jarl] í Orkneyjum, at Ari hefði kenndr verit á Hvítramannalandi ok náði eigi brutt at fara, en var þar vel virðr. (*Landnámabók*: S122; Benediktsson 1968: 162)[16]

> (Their son was Ari who drifted to White Men's Land ["men of white"-land], which some people call Greater Ireland. It lies in the ocean to westward, near Vinland the Good, said to be a six day sail west from Ireland. Ari couldn't get away, and was baptized there. This story was first told by Hrafn Limerick-Farer who spent a long time at Limerick in Ireland. Thorkel Gellisson quoted some Icelanders who had heard Earl Thorfinn of Orkney say that Ari had been recognized in White Men's Land, and couldn't get away from there, but was thought very highly of.) (Pálsson and Edwards 1972: 61)

Eiríks saga rauða is dated to the mid-thirteenth century (Magnússon and Pálsson 1965: 34). In common with *Graenlendinga saga*, *Eiríks saga rauða* testifies to Norse prominence in sailing and navigation in the Atlantic seas around Greenland, from the eleventh century into the period in which these texts were written (Perkins 2004: 38). Specifically, one might propose that *Eiríks saga rauða* was written to celebrate Guðríðr Þorbjarnardóttir, perhaps in order to support ambitions to sanctify in some way one of her twelfth-century descendents in the Hólar diocese of northern Iceland (Perkins 2004: 35). The *Eiríks saga rauða* passage below may derive elements from the earlier *Landnámabók* account:

> Hǫfðu þeir sunnanveðr ok hittu Markland ok fundu Skrælinga fimm; var einn skeggjaðr ok tvær konur, bǫrn tvau. Tóku þeir Karlsefni til sveinanna, en hitt komsk undan ok sukku í jǫrð niðr. En sveinana hǫfðu þeir með sér ok kenndu

> þeim mál ok váru skírðir. Þeir nefndu móður sína Vethildi ok [fǫður] Óvægi. Þeir sǫgðu at konungar stjórnuðu Skrælingalandi; hét annarr Avaldamon, en annarr hét Valdidida. Þeir kváðu þar engi hús, ok lágu menn í hellum eða holum. Þeir sǫgðu land þar ǫðru megin gagnvart sínu landi, ok gengu menn þar í hvítum klæðum ok œpðu hátt ok báru stangir ok fóru með flíkr. Þat ætla menn Hvítramannaland. (*Eiríks*: ch. 12; Halldórsson 1985: 432)[17]
>
> (They had southerly winds and reached Markland, where they met five natives. One was bearded, two were women and two of them children. Karlsefni and his men caught the boys but the others escaped and disappeared into the earth. They took the boys with them and taught them their language and had them baptised. They called their mother Vethild and their father Ovaegi. They said that kings ruled the land of the natives; one of them was called Avaldamon and the other Valdidida. No houses were there, they said, but people slept in caves or holes. They spoke of another land, across from their own. There people dressed in white clothing, shouted loudly and bore poles and waved banners. This people assumed to be the land of the white men ["men of white"-land].) (Hreinsson 1997: 17)

Eyrbyggja saga also appears to originate in the mid-thirteenth century (Pálsson and Edwards 1973: 12). The saga has a complicated structure, with many strands that follow the interweaving relationships between families (and individuals) from the late-ninth century to the early-eleventh century. In relation to *Landnámabók*, we mentioned the literary impulse to establish legitimacy and respectability for Iceland's new society. As with other early Icelandic prose works, *Eyrbyggja saga* has been seen to chart "a community progressing from lawlessness to collective responsibility" (Pálsson and Edwards 1989: 2). Though not actually naming Írland et mikla or Hvítramannaland, the following text is drawn from "the dying cadences of the narrative" (Pálsson and Edwards 1989: 10) and is associated with the *Landnámabók* and *Eiríks saga rauða* passages (the relevant section is long; the first part of *Eyrbyggja*'s chapter 64 is given below):

> Þat var ofarliga á dǫgum Ólafs ins helga, at Guðleifr hafði kaupverð vestr til Dyflinnar; en er hann sigldi vestan, ætlaði hann til Íslands; hann sigldi fyrir vestan Írland ok fekk austanveðr ok landnyrðinga, ok rak þá langt vestr í haf ok í útsuðr, svá at þeir vissu ekki til landa; en þá var mjǫk á liðit sumar, ok hétu þeir mǫrgu, at þá bæri ór hafinu. Ok þá kom þar, at þeir urðu við land varir; þat var mikit land, en eigi vissu þeir, hvert land þat var. Þat ráð tóku þeir Guðleifr, at þeir sigldu at landinu, því at þeim þótti illt at eiga lengr við hafsmegnit. Þeir fengu þar hǫfn góða; ok er þeir hǫfðu þar litla stund við land verit, þá koma menn til fundar við

> þá; þeir kenndu þar engan mann, en helzt þótti þeim, sem þeir mælti írsku; brátt kom til þeira svá mikit fjǫlmenni, at þat skipti mǫrgum hundruðum. Þessir menn veittu þeim atgǫngu ok tóku þá hǫndum alla ok bundu ok ráku þá síðan á land upp. (*Eyrbyggja*: ch. 64; Sveinsson and Þórðarson 1935: 176–7)[18]
>
> (Towards the end of St Olaf's reign Gudleif set out west to Dublin on a trading voyage, intending to sail on from there to Iceland, but west of Ireland he ran into easterly and then north-easterly gales, and the ship was driven out to sea first west and then south-west, well out of sight of land. This was late in the summer, and they kept making vows to do all sorts of things if they could get back to land. At last, land came into view. It seemed very large, but they'd no idea what country it could be. Gudleif and his crew decided to put in, not wanting to struggle against the sea any longer. They found a safe harbour, and after a little while some people came down to meet them. They didn't know who the inhabitants were, but they seemed to be talking Irish. Soon a great crowd gathered there, hundreds of them. They attacked the crew, took them all prisoner, shackled them, and marched them some distance inland, where they were taken to a court to be tried and sentenced.) (Pálsson and Edwards 1973: 193–4)

The three late medieval Icelandic passages describe a realistic (fictional it may be, but *not* fantastic),[19] significant place located *somewhere* in the north Atlantic (in some proximity to Earl Þórfinn's Orkney, according to *Landnámabók*), connected with Gaels or Gaelic Christianity and sometimes *skrælings*, set in the past, and at times named Írland et mikla or Hvítramannaland. It is worth remembering that these texts were composed when the Greenland settlements were thriving and the Norse adventures in eastern Canada were a recent memory. Surviving literature and archaeological material point to interaction between the Norse and the aboriginal peoples of the northwest Atlantic, collectively named *skrælings* by them (Sutherland 2000). Thus, certain elements of these passages could derive from contemporary stories of westward journeys and settlements.

In his 1875 article Beauvois used the medieval Icelandic texts presented above. Initially his argument concentrated on the eastern north Atlantic. He identified a number of enigmatic medieval descriptions of early Christian monastic migration to Iceland by Gaels and integrated these with *pap*-element place names found in the Scottish islands, Faroe Islands, and Iceland. Beauvois looked to the early-ninth-century geography that included an account of the most northerly islands of the world, written in Frankia by the Gaelic cleric Dicuil. Beauvois understood Dicuil's descriptions to identify a Faroese monastic community harried by "*Normannorum*" (Northmen), as well as an Icelandic settlement. These interpretations of Dicuil's account are geographically plausible. Furthermore, Beauvois contextualized Dicuil's accounts within the early Christian tradition of seeking desert places in the Ocean, a tradition clearly described in early monastic literature from Iona. Beauvois married this robust monastic literature to enigmatic late-medieval writings from the Scandinavian world that described Gaelic communities of "white-clothed"[20] *papae* or *papar* in the Scottish islands and Iceland previous to the Viking Age's Scandinavian domination of this region. In short, Beauvois's 1875 paper begins by arguing for settlement in Iceland by early Christian Gaels.

In making this argument, Beauvois demonstrated an impressive awareness of the most current (and often difficult to access) materials of his day. Furthermore, he applied a critical approach to dismiss both Wilhelmi's ideas (which located Hvítramannaland in Florida) and the suggestions of a medieval Welsh migration to North America[21] (Beauvois 1875: 71n2, 78, 85–6). His work is an early articulation of literature- and toponym-based arguments still current today. As an optimistic construction (and this is what he initially claimed to be making), his ideas regarding Iceland were critical and emerged from a familiarity with medieval insular and Scandinavian literature, though twentieth-century archaeologists rightly criticized the lack of associated archaeological material for this hypothesis. He went too far, however, when he loosed his imagination upon the west after losing traces of early Christian Gaels in Iceland. As he himself admits, "Là, nous perdons leurs traces, mais, une fois lancés sur la piste, nous ne pouvons plus nous arrêter; nous franchissons d'un bond la distance qui sépare l'Irlande de l'Amérique" (Beauvois 1875: 65). Beauvois imagined early Scandinavian "pirates" forcing Christian communities from the Northern Isles of Scotland and the Faroe Islands to flee north to Iceland and west from there: "enfin, ils allèrent les relancer jusqu'en Islande et … [les contraignirent] à émigrer de nouveau … se rejêter vers l'ouest" (Beauvois 1875: 77). Ultimately, Beauvois based his westwards speculations upon the three medieval Icelandic texts given above, and to these he introduced the twelfth-century (that is, roughly contemporary) Arabic *Book of Roger* by Idrisi. Beauvois believed that these texts described a Grande-Irlande in the Atlantic. His underlying assumption was that Grande-Irlande had a reality beyond the potentially related Icelandic texts. From this material, Beauvois imagined a settlement of Gaels (still Christian but no longer a monastic community) in the Gaspé and southern Québec. Two seventeenth- and eighteenth-century authors pointed Beauvois to Québec: Christian Le Clerq and Joseph-François Lafitau. Specifically, Beauvois cited Le Clerq's Récollet accounts from the Gaspé of "nombreux restes du Christianisme, notamment le culte de la croix et des réminiscences du *pater*" (Beauvois 1875: 86; Le Clerq 1691), and the Jesuit

Lafitau's[22] belief that the cross was an old religious symbol for eastern Canada's aboriginal peoples (Beauvois 1875: 83–6; Lafitau 1723).

In proposing early Irish communities in Québec, Beauvois demonstrated the peculiar consequences of integrating diffusionist and racial ideas in late-nineteenth-century scholarship. Earlier in the chapter, we visited Trigger's suggestion that the combination of racism and diffusionism appealed to romantics "because it identified the culturally specific and the exotic as the most essential reflections of human nature and offered reassurance that these aspects of human behaviour and identity were relatively resistant to change" (Trigger 1998: 50). Beauvois acted in just this way when he wrote that "ces faits remarquables sont aujourd'hui bien connus, même en dehors des pays scandinaves; mais les savants, passablement nombreux, qui ont publié, traduit ou commenté les documents relatifs à la Grande Irlande ou *Hvítramannaland* (Pays des hommes blancs), ont négligée de mettre en relief et en regard, pour les comparer entre eux, une foule de petits détails qui s'éclairent mutuellement et confirment la véracité des sagas scandinaves" (Beauvois 1875: 41). Here Beauvois stresses the "foule de petits détails," in other words the odd and the exotic, as holding the key to his field of research. Beauvois accepted diffusionist ideas; he worked from Le Clerq's and Lafitau's descriptions of crosses to imagine mechanisms for the cross symbol to spread from the Old World to the New. Correspondingly, he embraced racial doctrines and the rigidity of human nature, not only for Gaels but also for the aboriginal peoples. Beauvois understood Gaels as going bravely into the unknown Ocean because that is what Gaels do; it is in their nature. For instance, Beauvois claimed that "les traditions de leur race les portaient à sonder l'inconnu … d'arracher à la mer le secret de son immensité" (Beauvois 1875: 77). He also followed biological determinist thinking when he saw aboriginal peoples as racially incapable of constructing the stone structures that he had heard of along the St Lawrence and in Newfoundland.[23] He wrote that "les ruines d'édifices … ne peuvent avoir été élevés par des sauvages" (Beauvois 1875: 86).

Thus, Beauvois's arguments were coloured by the theories he accepted (though, of course, a mass of historical research has been needed to give us the vantage points we now enjoy). In addition, Beauvois (like many of his contemporaries) placed too much confidence in the straightforward accuracy of medieval literature, not paying sufficient attention to the social role of these texts for the communities that created and preserved them. For instance, recent commentators (in contrast to earlier scholars) explore how the *Landnámabók* text was written as a work that "focuses on a nation's appropriation of space" (Taylor 2003). Nevertheless, Beauvois's treatment of the Grande-Irlande passages reveals thoroughness in his methods and an impressive command of contemporary scholarly literature. Furthermore, he added fresh data to the debate that has not been appreciated by subsequent scholarship. First, in exploring the idea of early Christian settlement of the Faroe Islands, he presented a folk tradition collected by the pastor J.H. Schrœter on the island of Suðuroy:

> Quelque temps avant que les Norvégiens s'emparassent des Færeys, il s'y était établi des hommes que le narrateur considérait comme des saints, attendu qu'ils avaient la puissance de faire des signes et des miracles, de guérir les blessures et les maladies, aussi bien des hommes que des animaux; ils savaient prédire si l'année, la pêche ou l'état sanitaire, seraient favorables. Ils ne vivaient pas comme les autres hommes; car leur nourriture se composait de lait, d'œufs, de racines et d'algues: ils avaient des chèvres domestiques qu'ils trayaient; mais ils ne tuaient aucune créature et ne versaient pas le sang. Les seuls objets qu'ils acceptassent comme presents ou en rénumération de leurs services, étaient le pain azyme, le poisson sèché, et le *vadmel* (bure) pour se vêtir. On montre plusieurs localités où ces gens auraient habité; par exemple, un endroit situé en dehors de Kvalboy, où l'on peut voir que le sol a été nivelé pour être converti en pâturage; de même, près du village, nommé *í Hovi*, etc., ainsi que dans quelques-unes des autres îles. A l'arrivée des Norvégiens, qui étaient très-violents, quelques-uns de ces gens s'éloignèrent par mer; d'autres se réfugièrent dans des cavernes. Les derniers que l'on dit s'être conservés, demeuraient dans une caverne de l'île de Nálsoy; on doit y avoir vu des cendres, loin à l'intérieur, vers la fin du siècle précedent. (Beauvois 1875: 68n1; Schrœter 1849–51: 146–7)

As with all folk traditions, the passage above is a complex material. First, because of questions of transmission and the teller's concerns regarding style, the story should not be taken as a straightforward and honest account of a distant past; however, it is of interest that later scholars seem unaware of the tradition. Second, and of special relevance as an additional example of the Grande-Irlande name, he introduced a medieval Arabic description of a place "*Irlandah-al-Kabirah*/Irlande-la-Grande" (Beauvois 1875: 81; *Idrîsî*: VII, 2; Jaubert 1836; Bresc and Nef 1999: 461). The name appears in the Chevalier P. Amédée Jaubert's early-nineteenth-century translation of Idrisi's *Book of Roger.*[24] Writing in Norman Sicily, al-Idrīsī completed his *Book of Roger* circa 1154, and the work is important for our purposes because of its detailed geography of western Europe (Bresc and Nef 1999; Oman 1971; Perkins 1993; Dunlop 1957; Wittek 1955). As mentioned in note 20 to this chapter, Sicily in the Norman period experienced close connections to northwest Europe. This included Scandinavian Britain, as implied by "the presence in southern Italy and Sicily of more than a handful of Normans who still bore Norse personal names"

(Johns 2002: 4). In addition, medieval Icelandic reports of Norwegian crusaders spending a long and comfortable period in Sicily at Roger's court indicate direct connections between Scandinavia and Sicily (Doxey 1996: 149). In researching his book, Idrisi and his informants took advantage of these connections, collecting detailed information on the regions; for instance, even the inland settlement of Oxford may be identified in his geography (Beeston 1950: 275; Wittek 1951: 1045).

For Beauvois to propose that Idrisi's geography should include a description of what the Icelandic texts name Írland et mikla was plausible, given Jaubert's translation below:

> Entre l'extrémité de l'Écosse, île déserte, et l'extrémité de la Hirlanda (de l'Irlande), on compte 2 journées de navigation, en se dirigeant vers l'occident.
>
> L'Irlande est une île très-considérable. Entre son extrémité supérieure et la Bretagne on compte 3 journées et demie de navigation.
>
> De l'extrémité de l'Angleterre à l'île de Danes, 1 journée.
>
> De l'extrémité septentrionale de l'Écosse à l'île de Reslanda (l'Islande), 3 journées.
>
> De l'extrémité de l'Islande à celle de l'Irlande la Grande, 1 journée.
>
> De l'extrémité de l'Islande, en se dirigeant vers l'orient, à l'île de Norbagha (Norwège), 12 milles.
>
> L'Islande s'étend sur un espace de 400 milles de long sur 150 milles de large. (*Idrîsî*: VII, 2; Jaubert 1836)[25]

Beauvois connects the "Irlande la Grande" in this passage with the roughly contemporary Icelandic Írland et mikla descriptions and suggests that Idrisi received his information "peut-être dans un de ses voyages sur les côtes de l'Angleterre, ou plutôt encore à la cour de Roger II, roi de Sicile, pour lequel il composa son ouvrage" (Beauvois 1875: 81). He supports this proposal by elaborating that Roger was grandson of "Tancrède de Hauteville, dans le Cotentin, et par consequent originaire de la Normandie où certaines familles avaient conservé des relations avec la Norvège, patrie de leurs ancêtres" (Beauvois 1875: 81–2). Beauvois's suggestion of Scandinavian information being integrated into the *Book of Roger* is plausible because of the key role that Palermo (and Sicily generally) seems to have played in the diffusion of scholarship between the Arabic and Latin worlds (Jehel and Racinet 2000: 195). As mentioned earlier, there was much contact between Sicily and northwest Europe in the twelfth century: court members were Anglo-Norman, distinguished Scandinavians visited the court, and Scandinavian mercenaries operated on the island (Doxey 1996; Haskins 1911). Nevertheless, the information in the *Book of Roger* on Scandinavia is poor, while details on Anglo-Norman Britain appear to have been transmitted to Idrisi from French to Greek and then to Arabic (Johns 2001; Haskins 1911). Thus it may be that the informant, or informants, for these areas was a French-speaking Anglo-Norman rather than Scandinavian.

Furthermore, deeper investigation of this Idrisi passage favours an alternate reading. Working from an Arabic edition of this section, published by A.F.L. Beeston in 1950 (Beeston 1950: 270, 280), the following is a literal translation of the sentence in question: "And between the extremity of the island of (Ruslanda) and the extremity of [the] island of (Burlanda) the large [is] a day of navigation" (Jeremy Johns, personal communication; Ben White, personal communication). The "island of Ruslanda" has been variously interpreted as part of Scotland, the Faroe Islands, or Iceland (Dunlop 1947: 117; Stevenson 1948; Beeston 1950: 277–8), while the Iceland identification is supported by the most recent editors (*Idrîsî*: III, 2; Bresc and Nef 1999: 461). Turning to "Burlanda," Beeston studied five of the six extant *Book of Roger* manuscripts and noted that they mostly agree in giving the form *b.rlanda* (one manuscript reads *ġ.rlānda*). Beeston suggested that *b.rlanda* represents a scribal miscopying of an original *l.rlanda*, from the French *l'Irlande*. This compares with the form *lanqualtara* (l'Angleterre) given by Idrisi elsewhere in the *Book of Roger* and would be consistent with the idea of a French-speaking Anglo-Norman informant (Beeston 1950: 273). Paul Wittek, however, has argued that *b.rlanda* may equally be a miscopying of *irlanda*, while the *ġ.rlānda* variant may be explained as incorporating an initial glottal stop in order to make *irlanda* more emphatic (Wittek 1951).[26]

Importantly, Beeston's rendering of the phrase as "the extremity of [the] island of Ireland the large" questions Jaubert's (and Nef's) translation of *Irlande la Grande*. We are dealing with the genitive case here, which means that the definite article drops out (thus the translation's bracketed *the*), while the feminine singular adjective *kabīrah* (the large) could relate to either of the feminine nouns "island" or "Ireland" – though relating *kabīrah* to "island" would be more normal (Johns, personal communication; White, personal communication). Thus Beeston translates the phrase as "the extremity of the large island of Ireland" (Beeston 1950: 280). This grammatical approach to the Idrisi passage poses serious problems for Beauvois's suggestion that what Icelandic texts called Írland et mikla was also included in the *Book of Roger*. Beeston, however, did not consult all six manuscripts, and Jaubert and Nef's translation remains a possibility; it may be that we are dealing with variation between manuscripts here. Owing to this question regarding Jaubert's translation and the way in which Idrisi's passage may be read to locate a place called Irlande la Grande in the north Atlantic, Beauvois's suggestion that Idrisi's Irlanda al-kabīrah is the same as his Grande-Irlande needs further investigation before it can be decisively refuted. Specifically, it would be useful to understand the reasons for Jaubert and Nef translating as they did.

In fairness to Beauvois, Idrisi (if this is what he intended) may not be alone in giving a north Atlantic location for Irlande (la Grande). For instance, the name Iraland(e) appears to describe a northern place in an Old English passage attributed to Ohthere, a chieftain from the north of Norway. The Old English *Orosius* was compiled at King Alfred's court sometime between 871 and 900 and incorporates travel information provided by Ohthere (Page 1995: 45–8). The Ohthere passage follows:

> Ohthere sæde þæt sio scir hatte Halgoland þe he on bude. He cwæð þæt nan man ne bude be norðan him. Þonne is an port on suðeweardum þæm lande þone man hæt sciringesheal. Þyðer he cwæð þæt man ne mihte geseglian on anum monðe, gyf man on niht wicode & ælce dæge hæfde ambyrne windæ & ealle ða hwile sceal seglian be landeæ & on þæt steorbord him bið ærest Iraland, & þonne ða igland þe synd betux Iralande & þissum lande; þonne is þis land oð he cymð to sciringesheal, & ealne weg on Þæt bæcbord Norðweg. (*Orosius*: I.i; Lund et al. 1984: 21–2; Bately 1980: 16, 17)
>
> (Ohthere said that the district where he lived is called *Halgoland*. He said no-one lived to the north of him. In the south part of Norway there is a trading-town which is called *Sciringes heal*. He said that a man could scarcely sail there in a month, assuming he made camp at night, and each day had a favourable wind. He would sail by the coast the whole way. To starboard is first of all *Iraland* and then those islands which are between *Iraland* and this land, and then this land until he comes to *Sciringes heal*, and Norway is on the port side the whole way.) (Lund et al. 1984: 21–2)

The text given above appears to locate Iraland(e) in the north Atlantic. This is one of the very earliest uses of the place name *Iraland*, an Old Norse name that seems to originate with Ohthere, as *Hybernia* is used for Ireland in the rest of the *Orosius* text. The locating of Ohthere's Iraland has been a matter of debate for some time. In 1855, J. Bosworth discarded the argument that modern-day Scotland inspired Ohthere's Iraland (Bately 1980: 193–4; Bosworth 1855: 46n54). In the early twentieth century D.F. Emerson (and later K. Malone) posited that the passage preserved medieval views on the position of Ireland, while W.A. Craigie followed J. Ingram and Bosworth in emending the text to **Isaland* and identified the place as Iceland (Bately 1980: 193–4; Emerson

1916: 458; Malone 1930: 143; Malone 1933: 78; Craigie 1917: 200–1; Bosworth 1855: 46n54; Ingram 1807: 63, 79–80q, 110n33). In 1957, W.C. Stokoe proposed that Ohthere was referring to the first sea route to Ireland (from northern Norway) (Bately 1980: 193–4; Stokoe 1957: 304). More recently, Niels Lund proposed that one of Alfred's scholars may have introduced the references to Ireland, the Orkney Islands, Hebrides, and Britain in order to aid the English reader in understanding the text (Lund et al. 1984: 11–12). Lund also explored the counter-position that geography suggests emending Ireland to Iceland; this is a point that Christine Fell supported (Lund et al. 1984: 12; Fell 1984: 63). In advocating that *Ísland* was misunderstood in the text as *Iraland*, Fell (like many before her) accepted that the island referred to by the name Iraland was in fact the island known today as Iceland (Fell 1984: 63). Two important difficulties for efforts to emend *Iraland(e)* to *Ísland* are that (a) the word *Iraland(e)* is unambiguous in the Ohthere passage (figure 1.2), and (b) it is unclear that the northern island of Iceland was known by the name Ísland during the late-ninth-century period of Norse settlement there. For instance, later Icelandic tradition gives Snæland / Snjóland as the name for Iceland used by the earliest Norse land claimers (*Landnámabók*: H2, S5, H5; Benediktsson 1968: 33, 37). Furthermore, the use of *Iraland(e)* in the Ohthere passage may be the earliest surviving occurrence of this name. Thus perhaps we should hesitate in emending the *Orosius* text to the potentially problematic *Ísland*, and (bearing the difficulties outlined above) also consider that the Iraland name need not necessarily refer to modern-day Ireland. To elaborate another of Fell's points, it is certainly possible to imagine that Ohthere gave the wrong directions and that Ohthere and / or the Old English *Orosius* writer may have been mistaken (Fell 1984: 63). Strictly speaking, however, the text of the late-ninth-century Ohthere passage appears to locate its Iraland(e) in the north Atlantic. If Iḍrisi's twelfth-century Irlanda al-kabīrah is also to be located in the north Atlantic (as argued above, this has yet to be established), then it is formally possible that these two descriptions could be related to each other or, along with the Írland et mikla passages, draw upon a common medieval tradition of an Irlande (la Grande) in the north Atlantic.

Although Beauvois seems to have been unaware of Ohthere's Iraland(e), the multiple occurrences of Greater Ireland in Icelandic and Arabic texts drove his diffusionist- and racial-determinist-coloured arguments. Nevertheless, in order to decisively refute his idea that these texts may be related to each other, it would be necessary to first refute Jaubert's (and Nef's) translation of *Irlanda al-kabīrah* as "Irlande la Grande." Next, we might set the Old English Iraland(e) of *Orosius* alongside the Icelandic Írland et mikla passages in order to achieve a better understanding of the problems they pose. Furthermore, the way in

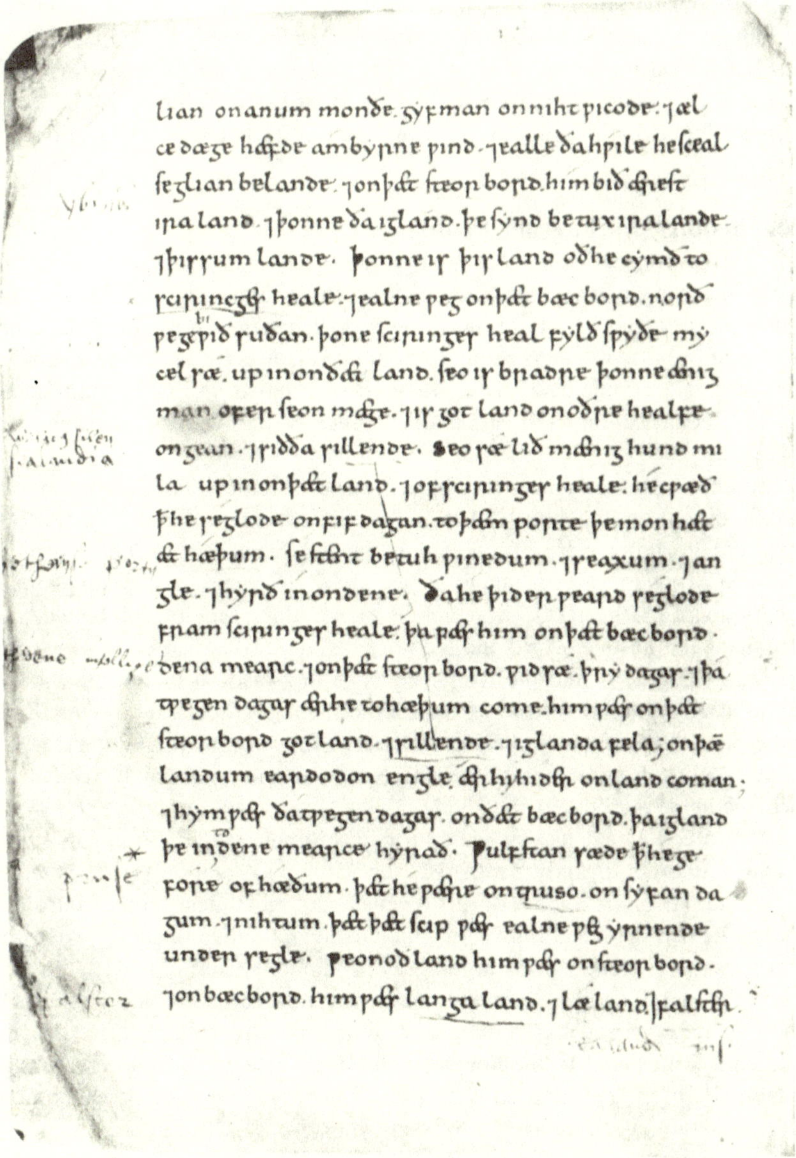
lian on anum monðe. gyf man on niht wicode. 7 æl
ce dæge hæfde ambyrne wind. 7 ealle ða hwile he sceal
seglian be lande. 7 on þæt steorbord him bið ærest
iraland. 7 þonne ða igland. þe synd betux iralande
7 þissum lande. þonne is þis land oð he cymð to
sciringes heale. 7 ealne weg on þæt bæcbord. norð
weg. wið suðan. þone sciringes heal fylð swyðe my
cel sæ. up in on ðæt land. seo is bradre þonne ænig
man ofer seon mæge. 7 is gotland on oðre healfe
ongean. 7 siððan sillende. seo sæ lið mænig hund mi
la up in on þæt land. 7 of sciringes heale. he cwæð
þæt he seglode on fif dagan. to þæm porte þe mon hæt
æt hæþum. se stent betuh winedum. 7 seaxum. 7 an
gle. 7 hyrð in on dene. ða he þiderweard seglode
fram sciringes heale. þa wæs him on þæt bæcbord.
dena mearc. 7 on þæt steorbord widsæ. þry dagas. 7 þa
twegen dagas ær he to hæþum come. him wæs on þæt
steorbord gotland. 7 sillende. 7 iglanda fela; on þæm
landum eardodon engle. ær hi hider on land coman.
7 hym wæs ða twegen dagas. on ðæt bæcbord. þa igland
þe in to dene mearce hyrað. Wulfstan sæde þæt he ge
fore of hæðum. þæt he wære on truso. on syfan da
gum. 7 nihtum. þæt þæt scip wæs ealne weg yrnende
under segle. weonoðland him wæs on steorbord.
7 on bæcbord him wæs langa land. 7 læland 7 falster.

British Library, MS. Cotton Tiberius B. i, f. 13v (f. 11v *old foliation*)

Figure 1.2 Folio from Cotton Tiberius B manuscript of the Old English *Orosius*. © British Library Board, Cotton Tiberius B. i, f. 13v.

which the Írland et mikla descriptions incorporate ideas of an early Christian settlement of Gaels on an Atlantic island may be profitably investigated alongside insular early Christian literature – and alongside the work outlined elsewhere in this book, which posits a horizon of early medieval settlement in southern Iceland with sculpture indicating affinities in the insular worlds.

Conclusions and Further Problems

Many of the areas of research we explore today first took form in the nineteenth century, and investigation of the *historical dimension* of scholarship is important because it fosters critical rigour and an awareness of the mortality of our ideas. The problem we have grappled with has been that of approaching late-nineteenth-century scholars and, specifically, the medieval literature they deployed.

The solution presented here has been drawn from study of Eugène Beauvois's prolific output on the subject of Írland et mikla (Greater Ireland). Beauvois's ideas on the topic were articulated in his 1875 paper, "La découverte du Nouveau Monde par les Irlandais et les premières traces du Christianisme en Amérique avant l'an 1000," in which he explored the relationship between the early medieval insular world and the north Atlantic islands. Beauvois was fascinated by journeys into the Atlantic Ocean and made a literature- and toponym-based argument for early Christian settlement of Iceland by Gaels. Thus, this aspect of his work is relevant in light of the way in which later chapters suggest connections between Atlantic Scotland and southern Iceland in the early medieval period.

Therefore, we have assessed the historical dimension that Beauvois's work provides. In order to study Beauvois's scholarship in detail, we first related his work to the theoretical ideas of diffusionism and racial determinism current in his day. Armed with materials with which to contextualize Beauvois, we examined the critical rigour of his arguments (as demonstrated in his 1875 paper). Thus assessed, his ideas were integrated with new research on the topic. Our study in these pages has reintegrated otherwise "forgotten" materials that Beauvois contributed to the debate; Schrœter's example of Faroese folklore and Idrisi's Irlanda al-kabīrah were part of his arguments, but these complex yet enigmatic materials have since been overlooked.

More important, however, the revisiting of Beauvois's 1875 study demonstrates that appreciation of the historical dimension may be a spur to future research. At the heart of his arguments Beauvois found that a handful of medieval Icelandic and Arabic references suggested to him the existence of an

Atlantic place called Grande-Irlande, peopled by early Christian Gaels. Understanding the diffusionist and racial determinist thinking with which he operated empowers us to be both sceptical of his suggestions of an early medieval Irish settlement in Québec and appreciative of the problem with which he engaged. For instance, it is true that medieval Icelandic, potentially Old English, and (less probably) Arabic literature describes a (Greater) Ireland in the north Atlantic, which in the Icelandic tradition is associated with Gaels and early Christianity (among other things). In addition, revisiting Beauvois's scholarship has demonstrated that one should be wary of placing too much confidence in theory-led conclusions inspired by isolated material and unsupported by coherent bodies of data.

2 A Fruitful Conversation between Disciplines

Although I am an admirer of tradition, and conscious of its importance, I am, at the same time, an almost orthodox adherent of unorthodoxy: *I hold that orthodoxy is the death of knowledge, since the growth of knowledge depends entirely on the existence of disagreement.* Admittedly, disagreement *may* lead to strife, and even to violence. And this, I think, is very bad indeed, for I abhor violence. Yet disagreement may also lead to discussion, to argument, and to mutual criticism. And these, I think, are of paramount importance …[1]

But is a fruitful discussion between different frameworks really possible? Let us take an extreme case. Herodotus, the father of historiography, tells an interesting though somewhat gruesome story of the Persian King, Darius the First, who wanted to teach a lesson to the Greeks living in his empire. It was the custom of the Greeks to burn their dead. Darius "summoned," we read in Herodotus, "the Greeks living in his land, and asked them for what payment they would consent to eat up their fathers when they died. They answered that nothing on earth would induce them to do so. Then Darius summoned the … Callatians, who do eat their fathers, and he asked them in the presence of the Greeks, who had the help of an interpreter, for what payment they would consent to burn the bodies of their fathers when they died. And they cried aloud and implored him not to mention such an abomination."

Darius, I suspect, wanted to demonstrate the truth of something like the myth of the framework. Indeed, we are given to understand that a discussion between the two parties would have been impossible even with the help of that interpreter. It was an extreme case of a "*confrontation*" – to use a term much in vogue with believers in the myth of the framework, and a term which they like to use when they wish to draw our attention to the fact that a "confrontation" rarely results in a fruitful discussion.

Let us assume that this confrontation staged by King Darius actually did take place as Herodotus narrates it. Was it really fruitless? I deny that it was. Admittedly, it does not seem that mutual understanding was achieved. And the story shows that we *may* be faced, in some rare cases, by an unbridgeable gulf. But even in this case, there can be little doubt that both parties were deeply shaken by the experience, and that they learned something new. I myself find the idea of cannibalism just as revolting as did the Greeks at the court of King Darius. And I suppose my readers will feel the same. But these feelings should make us all the more perceptive and the more appreciative of the admirable lesson which Herodotus wishes us to draw from the story. Alluding to Pindar's distinction between nature and convention, Herodotus suggests that we should look with tolerance and even respect upon customs or conventional laws that differ from our own. If this particular confrontation ever took place, some of the participants may well have reacted to it in the enlightened way in which Herodotus wishes us to react to his story.

This shows that there is, even without a discussion, a possibility of a fruitful confrontation among people deeply committed to different frameworks. *But we must not expect too much*: we must *not* expect that a confrontation, or even a prolonged discussion will end with the participants reaching *agreement*.

Karl R. Popper (floruit 1930–94)[2]

Thinkers have been trying to establish theories and methods for science for well over two thousand years. Among the many eminent philosophers of science, only a relatively small number have tried to integrate abstract scientific method (for example, logic, mathematics) with the "messy" data of the world. In exploring recent theories, Karl Popper's ideas hold special appeal for the kind of interdisciplinary thinking advocated in the previous chapter, where the works of literature scholars, linguists, folklorists, archaeologists, and historians were interwoven to empower a more sophisticated understanding of nineteenth-century scholars and their continuing contribution to scholarship. In particular, interdisciplinary workers may be particularly drawn to the conceptualization of scientific method advocated by Karl Popper (and his adherents). For these reasons, let us consider how Popper's conceptualization may be brought to bear upon the limited and diverse scatter of materials available to our study of the north Atlantic's early medieval past. As an exploration of problems related to the diffusion of culture, movements of people, development of societies, and environmental change, this book depends upon the possibility of fruitful interplay between disciplines. Equally, we may find inspiration in Popper's inclusive concept of science as a critical process with a unity of method. In elaborating this conceptualization, Popperian theory seeks to account for the progress of science as well as its fragile and uncertain existence, and commends the intelligent practice of "self-aware" science, outlining how scholars should integrate research from many fields (because, in the absence of such a method, they already do this). In short, articulation of Popperian "best practice" offers a framework in which our interdisciplinary approach can receive an apt theoretical grounding. In studying the early settlement of the north Atlantic, the following chapters revisit difficult areas of Viking Age scholarship, each of which has frustrated researchers: first, the toponymy of Hebridean *Pap-* islands and, second, the chronology of cave construction, occupation, and human-environmental interactions in southern Iceland. The merits of our method will be demonstrated through the success of its application to these problem areas and through its power to integrate them into an interdisciplinary discussion.

As we have seen in chapter 1, a wide range of scholarship has been involved in exploring the relationships between early medieval Atlantic Scotland, Iceland, and the Faroe Islands, and this continues to be the case today with a range of archaeological, medieval literature, place-name, and palaeoenvironmental scholars interested in the topic. Clearly, a multidisciplinary approach is needed for fruitful integration of these diverse studies. It is, however, necessary first to propose an answer to the methodological questions that multidisciplinary materials present, and we should choose a framework within which to confront these materials that is both particular and coherent. As mentioned above, Popper advocates a common method for his conception of science: the critical discussion of testable ideas. Although he has critics, Popper provides an elegant and influential system. By applying his proposals, this chapter presents a working solution to the problem of interdisciplinary dialogue. Although this goes beyond our remit in this book, it would be fruitful in further work to explore certain basic aspects of Popper's method and to consider how the application of Popperian thinking contained in these pages may, on the one hand, be integrated with discipline-specific theoretical approaches and, on the other hand, be used to develop Popper's own ideas.[3]

Problem and Context

Disciplines do not exist in isolation; indeed, some scholars argue "that most of the disciplinary boundaries that characterise the Western social sciences are arbitrary" (Trigger 1989: 373; Wolf 1982: 7–9), or that "a so-called scientific subject is merely a conglomeration of problems and tentative solutions demarcated in an artificial way. What really exists are problems, and scientific traditions" (Popper 1992: 69). Correspondingly, there is an urgency to enabling scholars legitimately to "import" results from one discipline to another – because it will be done regardless. April and Robert McMahon articulate this urgency with reference to the importation of ideas regarding language relationships, from linguistics to archaeology and genetics: "We must face the prospect that if linguists do not attempt to provide quantification in our own terms, archaeologists and geneticists will increasingly be forced to supply their own. If these do not correspond to linguists' intuitions about degrees of relatedness among languages, we are condemned to fighting a perpetual rearguard action against these externally imposed figures; and if we still do not supply linguistically coherent alternatives, we are not likely to be taken seriously by scholars in other disciplines" (McMahon and McMahon 2003: 21). McMahon and McMahon make a strong case for thinking about the interdisciplinary application of results. In addition, their arguments become ever more relevant when leading scholars such as Colin Renfrew write that there is a need "to work towards a unified reconstruction of the history of human populations ... because we certainly do not have such a unified history at the moment" (Renfrew 1999: 1–2; McMahon and McMahon 2003: 19).

Pressures for framing interdisciplinary discussion are most keenly felt in disciplines that operate in areas of convergence for separate theoretical traditions, such as Celtic studies or archaeology. If we turn to archaeological research, Bruce Trigger points to a good tradition of integrating physical science studies and at the same time criticizes how "there is little general awareness of the value of combining the study of archaeological data with that of historical linguistics, oral traditions, historical ethnography, and historical records, although it is clear that many archaeological problems can be resolved in this way" (Trigger 1989: 356). Trigger identifies this reluctance to integrate research from other cultural fields with a "desire to push the interpretative potential of archaeology as far as possible without relying on other disciplines for information about the past ... partly justified by the fear that interdisciplinary approaches can degenerate into an exercise in dilettantism" (Trigger 1989: 356). He argues, however, that this fear does not "nullify the value of interdisciplinary research, provided that it is understood that such studies must exploit the historical potential of each discipline to the greatest extent possible, using its own data and methods before comparisons of findings are attempted" (Trigger 1989: 356). The model for conversation between disciplines proposed in this chapter attempts to put thinking such as Trigger's into practice; the hypothesis section outlines ideas for integrating multidisciplinary specialist studies into an interdisciplinary framework.

The materials of this book relate to the early medieval north Atlantic area. For studies of these materials, the urgency of defining a method for coordinating multidisciplinary approaches has been realized for some time. For instance, in 1961 F.T. Wainwright published a fairly extended discussion of the admittedly simplistic and atheoretical method that guided his scholarship (Wainwright

1962: xi–xiii). He provided a pragmatic outline for coordinating historical, linguistic, and archaeological lines of enquiry. Although it lacked a theoretical foundation, Frank M. Stenton insisted "that the strongest argument in its favour [Wainwright's method] is the large volume of firmly based research which it enabled him to carry through" (Wainwright 1962: ix). Wainwright saw two kinds of coordination. First is the simple specialist study for use in another discipline (a kind of coordination common especially in archaeology), such as a specialist toponymic study of an area under archaeological investigation. Second is the grander synthesis of data from many disciplines, a kind of coordination that Wainwright saw as more difficult (Wainwright 1962: 89–97). It is this latter type of exercise that we shall pursue.

An extension of Wainwright's specialist study from another discipline may be identified in Carole L. Crumley's *historical ecology* method (though she would perhaps claim to be trying to integrate data from many disciplines into a grander synthesis). In formulating historical ecology, Crumley organized a team of anthropologists[4] to consider how "to address the important work of environmental historians, anthropologists, geographers, and others who seek to combine evidence of the human past with evidence about the environment by studying the evolution of landscapes" (Crumley 1994: xiii). Crumley recognizes the need for "a comprehensive, interdisciplinary framework reflecting the contributions of social, physical, and biological scientists and humanists" (Crumley 1994: 2). However, her proposal for responding to this need is to privilege one discipline (anthropology) and to outline a method for incorporating material from other disciplines into this discipline's framework:

> Only a handful of disciplines bridge natural and social sciences, the humanities, and the professions; among the most comprehensive and theoretically sophisticated is anthropology.
>
> The advantages of using an anthropological approach to explore the human role in environmental change are considerable. Anthropology, broadly understood, is integrative and comparative; inclusive of temporal, spatial, and cultural dimensions; and dynamic. The discipline's historic focus on the dynamics of change render an anthropological perspective particularly appropriate in unravelling complex chains of mutual causation in human-environment relations. (Crumley 1994: 2)

She goes further, specifically privileging archaeology, ethnohistory, and ethnography (as subdisciplines of anthropology) in her historical ecology. Outlining her reasoning for favouring an archaeological framework, she writes: "Archaeologists have long sought to understand changes through time in regional populations, their distribution, and their economies. Requisite data include evidence for changing human-environmental relationships in the form of remains of human manufacture and elements of the environment related to human activities. It seems evident that archaeology (*sensu lato*) is in an excellent position to render service to a number of fields by proposing a *rapprochement*" (Crumley 1994: 7).

This formulation of historical ecology has the potential to develop methods for using research from other disciplines to investigate anthropological questions, while at the same time informing these anthropological questions with a historical dimension of ecological analysis (Winterhalder 1994: 40). As Winterhalder correctly observes, "it will be a prime challenge of historical ecology to find or to generate concepts that will promote collaborative work among social and natural scientists" (Winterhalder 1994: 40). One can easily imagine that the most important difficulty in formulating historical ecology will be convincing practitioners of other disciplines that archaeology, ethnohistory, and ethnography should be flagged as having "superior" methods. I find Crumley's arguments in this respect far from convincing, as it is unclear that, for instance, an archaeological methodology is inherently superior to a geological one. Certainly an archaeological methodology has advantages when used to answer archaeological questions, and historical ecology could provide one way to incorporate geological or other-disciplinary data into this process. However, to propose that the disciplinary approaches of archaeology are innately superior to those of geology (to continue the example) necessitates knowledge of some standard against which to assess the relative merits of each discipline and runs counter to the more embracing models of science advocated by thinkers such as Popper.[5] Instead, each discipline's methodology is unique and has been developed to answer the historically important kinds of questions that each discipline's data sets respond to (Wainwright 1962).

Nevertheless, Crumley's historical ecology does have merit as a movement *within* anthropology. Historical ecology holds out the possibility (if suitable methods are developed) to permit sophisticated interdisciplinary work of Wainwright's first kind: the incorporation of specialist studies from other disciplines into an anthropological framework in order to answer anthropological questions.

In discussing interdisciplinary coordination, however, one crucial philosophical question emerges: Is conversation between disciplines, between intellectual frameworks, really possible? Popper provides the following useful formulation of a counter position to interdisciplinary dialogue: "A rational and fruitful discussion is impossible unless the participants share a common framework of basic assumptions or, at least, they have agreed on such a framework for the purpose of the discussion" (Popper 1994: 34–5). In other words (according to this view), intellectual frameworks (such as languages or disciplinary backgrounds) act as barriers to mutual intelligibility between those not sharing the same language or disciplinary background. The reason such frameworks operate as barriers, following this formulation, is that in order for participants to have a rational and fruitful discussion, they need first to agree on definitions of terms. Popper observes that behind this view "there is the tacit assumption that a rational discussion must have the character of a justification, or of a proof, or of a demonstration, or of a logical derivation from admitted premises" (Popper 1994: 60). In other words, this view assumes that each participant in a rational discussion is driven by the question of how we can establish or justify our thesis or our theory (Popper 1994: 60).

The view that the ideal of a rational discussion is pursued by a participant justifying his or her own thesis or theory is a *relativist* perspective, which Popper rejects, calling it the "Myth of the Framework." His challenge to this formulation of a rational discussion appeals to the natural sciences: "… [where] critical discussion … does not seek to prove or to justify or to establish a theory, least of all by deriving it from some higher premises, but … tries to test the theory under discussion by finding out whether its *logical consequences* are all acceptable, or whether it has, perhaps, some undesirable consequences" (Popper 1994: 60). In other words, a critical discussion in the natural sciences considers the following questions: "What are the *consequences* of our thesis or our theory? Are they all acceptable to us?" (Popper 1994: 60).

In the following passage Popper applies this formulation of critical discussion to what he sees as the relativist problem; he advocates:

> … comparing the consequences of different theories (or, if you like, of different frameworks) and trying to find out which of the competing theories or frameworks has consequences that seem preferable to us. [We are] … thus conscious of the fallibility of all our methods, although [we] … try to replace all our theories by better ones. This is, admittedly, a difficult task, but by no means an impossible one.
>
> Of course, a proponent of the myth of the framework might criticise this idea. He might say, for example, that what I have called the correct method of criticism in no way allows us to get out of our framework – for, he might insist, the "consequences that seem preferable to us" will themselves be *part* of the framework: that we have here a model for mere self-justification, rather than the critical transcendence of a framework.
>
> But I think that this criticism is mistaken. While we *may* interpret our views in this way, we do not *have* to do so. We can choose to pursue an aim or goal – such as the aim of understanding better the universe in which we live, and ourselves as part of it – which is autonomous of the particular theories or frameworks that we

> construct to try to meet this aim. And we can choose to set ourselves standards of explanation, and methodological rules, which will help us to achieve our goal and which it is *not* easy for any theory or framework to satisfy. Of course, we may choose not to do this: we may decide to make our ideas self-reinforcing. We may set ourselves no task other than one we know our present ideas can fulfil. We certainly can choose to do this. But if we choose to do this, not only will we be turning our back on the possibility of learning that we are wrong, we will also be turning our backs upon that tradition of critical thought (stemming from the Greeks…) which has made us what we are. (Popper 1994: 60–1)

This last section is important because it allows for the possibility of methodological innovation when a discussion from one framework, or discipline, is contrasted with another. This is a point to which I will return later.

Ultimately, Popper's response to the relativist view (that a rational and fruitful discussion is impossible between intellectual frameworks) brings us back to the quotation that prefaces this chapter, with its elaboration of Herodotus's narrative of the Greek and Callatian encounter at Darius's court. Popper argues that we must realize that a confrontation, encounter, or discussion may have fruitful results without achieving agreement. With reference to Herodotus's narrative, Popper articulates this point: "This shows that there is, even without a discussion, a possibility of a fruitful confrontation among people deeply committed to different frameworks. *But we must not expect too much*: we must *not* expect that a confrontation, or even a prolonged discussion, will end with the participants reaching *agreement*" (Popper 1994: 36–7). Popper then, provides a philosophical foundation upon which a methodology for interdisciplinary coordination may be constructed so long as the potential limitations of such coordination are realized and that we are prepared not to expect too much.

Given that the overarching concern of this book is to tackle difficult key areas for study of the early medieval Atlantic region, encompassing Atlantic Scotland, the Faroe Islands, and Iceland, we may now pose our problem in the form of a question:

> How may we formulate a method for exploring the multidisciplinary materials available to us, and how may we integrate study of these disparate materials?

Hypothesis

This section strives to formulate a model for interdisciplinary dialogue without privileging one discipline over another. The proposal to be elaborated here is this: if individual specialist studies are phrased accurately and accessibly, then they may be integrated with other similarly phrased studies into an interdisciplinary discussion. Behind this proposal is the thinking that if one writes clearly, then one's ideas may be thoroughly understood and thus effectively criticized. By advocating an inclusive concept of science with a unity of method, Popper provides the theoretical basis for this hypothesis and indeed points towards interdisciplinary conversation as a natural goal.

Popper, however, makes an important assumption in his work: namely that the world is real (even though our perception of reality is imperfect). This *realist* assumption grounds Popper's ideas and may be contrasted with *idealism.*[6] In its most straightforward formulation, idealism proposes that "the world (which includes the present reader) is just my dream" (Miller 1983: 221). A number of workers in cultural fields have been influenced by idealism. Recent trends in archaeological research, for instance, have incorporated greater idealism than previously and "express growing doubts that anything approaching an objective understanding of the past is possible" (Trigger 1989: 354). Trigger has linked this growth to the growing despair, felt by those desiring change, with corporate-led capitalist society[7] (Trigger 1989: 354–5). Popper argues that idealism is irrefutable (and correspondingly that the same is true for realism): "Whatever you, the reader, may do to convince me of your reality – talking to me, or writing a letter, or perhaps kicking me – it cannot possibly assume the force of a refutation; for I would continue to say that I am dreaming that you are talking to me, or that I received a letter, or felt a kick" (Miller 1983: 221). Following this logic, idealism may be proposed but not refuted – and thus cannot be the refutation of realism it is sometimes claimed to be. Nonetheless, the challenge of accommodating realist, idealist, and other fundamental philosophical concerns leads one into a big unresolved area of debate. For the purpose of this book, however, I accept the realist assumption, though being explicitly aware that it is an assumption (Miller 1983: 220–5; Popper 1972: ch. 2).

Popper's concept of science is crucial to the conversation between disciplines advocated in this chapter. First of all, Popper challenges Bacon's ideal of observation devoid of theory;[8] he demonstrates that "a mind so purged [of theory] would not only be a pure mind: it would be an empty mind" (Popper 1994: 86). In other words, he argues that a theory-free observation is not possible. All observations are interpretations of data informed by theory of some form (Popper 1994: 86). Correspondingly, Popper denies both *repetitive induction* ("no amount of observation of white swans establishes that all swans are white" [Popper 1994: 104]) and *eliminative induction.* Advocates of eliminative induction believe that by refuting false theories, a "true" theory may be proven. A fundamental problem with establishing a theory as true is that the potential number of competing theories is infinite, whereas "as a rule at any particular moment only a finite number of theories" may be considered (Popper 1994: 105). Similarly, Popper's method is against *positivism* (though he has been falsely criticized as a positivist in the past).[9] In Popperian science no theory may be proven to be true, though testing a theory may show it to be untrue. This idea of falsifiability is crucial to Popper's conception of science.

Popperian science may be expressed by the formulation of PROBLEM → THEORIES → CRITICISM (where criticism incorporates attempts at refuting the theories proposed) (Popper 1994: 101). The following seventeen theses define his method for science:

1. All scientific knowledge is hypothetical or conjectural.
2. The growth of knowledge, and especially of scientific knowledge, consists in learning from our mistakes.
3. What may be called the method of science consists in learning from our mistakes systematically: first, by taking risks, by daring to make mistakes – that is, by boldly proposing new theories; and second, by searching systematically for the mistakes we have made – that is, by the critical discussion and the critical examination of our theories.
4. Among the most important arguments which are used in this critical discussion are arguments from experimental tests.
5. Experiments are constantly guided by theory, by theoretical hunches of which the experimenter is often not conscious, by hypotheses concerning possible sources of experimental errors, and by hopes or conjectures about what will be a fruitful experiment. (By *theoretical* hunches I mean guesses that experiments of a certain kind will be theoretically fruitful.)
6. What is called scientific objectivity consists solely in the critical approach: in the fact that if you are biased in favour of your pet theory, some of your friends and colleagues (or failing these, some workers in the next generation) will be eager to criticise your work – that is to say, to refute your pet theories if they can.
7. This fact should encourage you to try to refute your own theories yourself – that is to say, it may impose some discipline upon you.
8. In spite of this, it would be a mistake to think that scientists are more "objective" than other people. It is not the objectivity or detachment of the individual scientist but of science itself (what may be called "the friendly-hostile cooperation of scientists" – that is, their readiness for mutual criticism) which makes for objectivity.
9. There is even something like a methodological justification for individual scientists to be dogmatic and biased. Since the method of science is that of critical discussion, it is of great importance that the theories criticised should be tena-

ciously defended. For only in this way can we learn their real power. And only if criticism meets resistance can we learn the full force of a critical argument.

10. The fundamental role played in science by theories or hypotheses or conjectures makes it important to distinguish between testable (or falsifiable) and non-testable (or non-falsifiable) theories.

11. Only a theory which asserts or implies that certain conceivable events will not, in fact, happen is testable. The test consists in trying to bring about, with all the means we can muster, precisely these events which the theory tells us cannot occur.

12. Thus, every testable theory may be said to forbid the occurrence of certain events. A theory speaks about empirical reality only in so far as it sets limits to it.

13. Every testable theory can thus be put into the form "such and such cannot happen." For example, the second law of thermodynamics can be formulated as saying that a perpetual motion machine of the second kind cannot exist.

14. No theory can tell us anything about the empirical world unless it is in principle capable of clashing with the empirical world. And this means, precisely, that it must be refutable.

15. Testability has degrees: a theory which asserts more, and thus takes greater risks, is better testable than a theory which asserts very little.

16. Similarly, tests can be graded as being more or less severe. Qualitative tests, for example, are in general less severe than quantitative tests. And tests of more precise quantitative predictions are more severe than tests of less precise predictions.

17. Authoritarianism in science was linked with the idea of establishing, that is to say, of proving or verifying, its theories. The critical approach is linked with the idea of testing, that is to say, of trying to refute, or to falsify, its conjectures. (Popper 1994: 93–4)

Popper, then, outlines a method for science based upon the proposal of bold ideas, followed by systematic critical discussion and refutation of testable hypotheses, resulting in the continual identification of further problems. Following Popper, one cannot prove a theory to be true, but instead one *can* prove a theory to be untrue. This critical discussion of testable hypotheses is the process that Popper defines as science – a conception of science that is open and *independent* of differences in materials (for example, place names versus tephra) but *dependent* upon the critical approach of attempting to boldly propose and refute ideas about these materials.

One important point in this approach to science is that *all* observations are theory impregnated. Popper goes so far as to propose that "our very eyes and ears are the result of evolutionary adaptations – that is, of the method of trial and error corresponding to the method of conjectures and refutations" (Popper 1994: 58). Elaborating the visual example, Popper suggests that we have an absolute sense of up and down built into the "ordinary" visual experience. For instance, a square balanced upon one of its corners (a diamond shape) appears different to us than a square with its base flat (a "normal" square). Nevertheless, these observations (theory impregnated in the sense that we perceive the two squares to be different – diamond or square) may be overcome; these observations may be reinterpreted. Through the method of science (that is, critical discussion) we may learn that the diamond and normal square are not different to each other but are in fact the same square shape, in alternative positions (Popper 1994: 58).

Popperian science is not without its challengers; these include such prominent theorists as Thomas Kuhn or P.K. Feyerabend (Kuhn 1970 [1962]; Feyerabend 1975). In contrast to Popper's continually revolutionary science,[10] Kuhn proposes the concept of "*normal science*" and "*extraordinary science*." As Kuhn sees it, normal science consists of three directions for research: "These three classes of problems – determination of significant fact, matching of facts with theory, and articulation of theory – exhaust, I think, the literature of normal science, both empirical and theoretical" (Kuhn [1962] 1970: 34; see also Bird 1975: 161). These characteristics of "normal research" may be understood as puzzle solving. Indeed, Kuhn is struck by how these little normal research problems "aim to produce novelties, conceptual or phenomenal" (Kuhn [1962] 1970: 35). Kuhn also identifies something he calls extraordinary science (or scientific revolution), and he sees this as emerging out of normal science in times of deep crisis, being precipitated by an awareness of a number of unexpected results encountered during normal research (Kuhn [1962] 1970: 34; Stokes 1998: 33). Furthermore, Kuhn advocates hierarchy and a more authoritarian structure for science than Popper does, in order for extraordinary science, that is scientific revolutions, to take place (Ryan 1985: 100–1). Kuhn has influenced Popper: his identification of normal science is seen by Popper as "a danger to science."[11] Popper's emphasis in his later works upon the fragility of the scientific enterprise may be seen as inspired by Kuhn (Popper 1994: 57, 72).

Kuhn is a very important figure in the theory of science, as is Feyerabend, with his "anarchist" epistemology "against method" (Stokes 1998: 36; Feyerabend 1975). As a consequence, their work deserves fuller discussion. In particular, Kuhn's ideas may be significant to the questions raised by this book; the appearance of data challenging conventional wisdom on the early settlement of Iceland can be seen as exactly the conditions for one of his "revolutions." Nonetheless, the purpose of this chapter is not to contrast Popperian science with the models advocated by Kuhn or Feyerabend. It is sufficient for present purposes to acknowledge the presence of alternative approaches to our problem, and possible directions for future research. We return, then, to the business of making explicit our methodology for conversation between disciplines.

As mentioned at the outset of this chapter, a number of scholars question the legitimacy of disciplinary boundaries (Trigger 1989: 373; Wolf 1982: 7–9; Popper 1992: 69). Popper, for instance, sees scientific subjects as "merely a conglomeration of problems and tentative solutions demarcated in an artificial way"; in other words, he defines a scientific discipline as a grouping of historically important problems and traditional (scientific) solutions to these problems (Popper 1992: 69). For Popper, this view is possible because of his conception of the scientific enterprise as being driven by a unity of method. If one accepts Popper's model of science, then perceived differences between the natural and human sciences fade away (Popper 1992: 64–81; 1994: 130–53, 154–84). This is not to say that there are not differences between, for instance, the natural and social sciences, but rather that the similarities are more significant than the differences (Stokes 1998: 75–6; Bird 1975: 158).

Nevertheless, the belief in a fundamental gulf between the natural and human sciences is widespread.[12] Popper's counter-position is this: those practitioners of the human sciences who insist on such a gulf "have a radically mistaken idea of the natural sciences" (Popper 1994: 139). In essence, scholars of the humanities and social sciences have sometimes understood scientific objectivity as something that is uniquely inherent in the data sets of the natural sciences. However, Popper stresses that what may be called scientific objectivity is not inherent in the kinds of data nor based upon the imagined impartiality of natural scientists, but instead is based on the "public and competitive character of the scientific enterprise and thus on certain social aspects of it" (Popper 1994: 69). Thus, scientific objectivity springs from "*mutual rational criticism*, upon the critical approach, the critical tradition" (Popper 1994: 70). This conception of objectivity is shared by all sciences, human and natural, and is dependent not on the materials but upon the particular rigour of the field's critical tradition and standards of clarity (Popper 1994: 70).

As mentioned earlier, Trigger shares this view, seeing the dichotomy of "science and history … at best unconvincing" (Trigger 1989: 374). The corollary of such fundamental questioning of disciplinary legitimacy, of course, is to encourage interdisciplinary work. Trigger, for instance, suggests that interdisciplinary dialogue improves attempts to prove the falsity of solutions to archaeological problems (and thus improves the discipline's critical rigour): "[It is reasonable] to use non-archaeological sources of data, such as oral traditions, historical linguistics, and comparative ethnography, in order to produce a more rounded picture of prehistoric cultures and to rule out alternative explanations that archaeological data alone might not be able to exclude" (Trigger 1989: 377). If one is to carry through such a mandate as Trigger's for interdisciplinary conversation, then a standard of clarity is paramount. This point is vital and one which Popper has stressed at length, for instance in his essay "Against big words" (Popper 1992: 82–95). The argument in a simple form is this: "One cannot tell truth from falsity, one cannot tell an adequate answer to a problem from an irrelevant one, one cannot tell good ideas from trite ones, and one cannot evaluate ideas critically – unless they are presented with sufficient clarity" (Popper 1994: 70–1). This goal of clarity (and thus accessibility) is a crucial one. As an editor of the works of others, I stressed this ideal in the introduction to a collection of articles: "*Atlantic Peoples* outlines a fresh approach to first publication of research on the North Atlantic coasts and islands, here focusing on the Markarfljót and Eyjafjallasveit region of southern Iceland. The ideal expressed here is of accessibility. New research is framed to highlight the potential of inter-disciplinary study, especially between the natural and cultural sciences" (Ahronson 2003a: 50). Standards of clarity allow for accessible scholarship across specialist fields (and thus dialogue and Popperian science). Implicit in the ideal of clarity is an attack upon the authority of "experts" (and the corresponding imprisonment of experts within their specialization). "Expert authority" should be attacked by a "frank acknowledgement of how little we know, and how much that little is due to people who have worked in many fields at the same time" (Popper 1994: x). The argument for clarity means that if one is able to effectively communicate a problem and a tentative solution from a specialist field to a wider audience, then one has little recourse to expert authority. Standards of clarity in scholarship foster academic modesty and the abandonment of authority, as thorough engagement with one's ideas by others will (hopefully) lead to effective and open criticism by the community. In this way, a scholar's well-communicated problem and solution should (without authority) engage with the audience. It may then be considered convincing or unconvincing, and thus open to criticism from all courts. *This is science*.

In editing the *Atlantic Peoples* collection, I aimed to embody Popperian ideals of clarity and science: "Each article follows the same structure. An accessible abstract prefaces while the introduction and conclusion summarise the relevance of the study to a wider audience. Emphasis is placed upon language that allows conversation between disciplines. Every paper is the first publication of new research and the main text presents specialist data and discussion ... The sampling of North Atlantic research in this collection expresses the ideal of publishing work-in-progress: new data and preliminary interpretations are presented in order to encourage dialogue and inform discussion" (Ahronson 2003a: 51, 52). In this book we pursue the same aims but on a larger scale and with a more explicitly theoretical basis.

Our hypothesis to be tested here is therefore that, if individual specialist studies are phrased accurately and accessibly, then they may be integrated with other similarly phrased studies into a fruitful interdisciplinary discussion. This is coordination of Wainwright's second kind: the synthesis of data from many disciplines (Wainwright 1962: 89–97). Following Popperian science makes interdisciplinary conversation a natural goal and does not favour any discipline over another. In order to achieve this dialogue, standards of clarity are vital. Correspondingly, to communicate a problem and a tentative solution effectively, the problem and the solution must be "packaged for export" so that specialist disciplinary knowledge is made accessible without appealing to expert authority. Wainwright gives a straightforward formulation of similar ideas (Wainwright 1962: 104–23), which may be integrated into a Popperian method as follows:

1. Tentatively accept realism.
2. Each discipline that studies the past approaches the past using its own methodologies and terms (for example, an archaeological term is not the same as a historical term).
3. Similarly, each discipline is focused by its terminology on questions that its data sets can attempt to answer. For instance, a place-name study could consider the linguistic background of those who named a locality but cannot consider questions that the data sets do not (usually) respond to, such as whether those who named a locality were tall.
4. Coordinating material from multiple disciplines may permit the refutation of ideas formulated within a discipline, and thus advance scientific dialogue.
5. By accessibly communicating studies (clearly defining a problem, a solution, implicit assumptions, and limitations), that is, by packaging material for export to other disciplines, we allow for better science.

Furthermore, working towards a conversation between disciplines in this way has the added benefit of fostering methodological innovation. By repeatedly restating problem, solution, implicit assumptions, and limitations, we allow for questioning of method as well as results. For example, the *tephra contouring* technique discussed in chapter 6 asks just these sorts of questions. This point will be returned to shortly.

Method

This book focuses on problem areas for several types of scholars of early medieval Scotland, the Faroe Islands, and Iceland. Three key problems for a number of disciplines were selected. These relate to the diffusion of culture, movements of people, development of societies, and environmental change: How should the historical dimension of scholarship, as seen in the Írland et mikla tradition of medieval (and antiquarian) literature, be approached? What can the toponymy of Hebridean *Pap*- islands and *Pap*- farms tell us? And how can southern Iceland's artificial caves be integrated into the island's settlement sequence, and, correspondingly, how does the area's record of human-environmental interactions relate to this settlement sequence?

Mono-disciplinary solutions to multidisciplinary problems such as these have the potential to falsify each other when integrated, thus fostering a more rigorous practice of science. That is not to say that these toponymic, archaeological, environmental, philosophical, literary, and historiographical problems have been integrated from the outset. We should respect the specific critical tradition of each field when elaborating tentative solutions to its problems, because each field's data sets respond best to certain kinds of questions and these are not immediately comparable in an interdisciplinary way. For instance, the archaeological or palaeoecological scholar is able to consider evidence of domesticated animals in a buried layer of volcanic airfall (tephra) but is mostly unable to determine which languages the farmers of these animals spoke. Throughout this process, a long view is maintained: one problem study has the potential to falsify aspects of solutions to another, as long as care is taken to stress the appropriate limitations. The use of interdisciplinary dialogue to falsify single-disciplinary ideas is discussed by Trigger in a passage quoted earlier, where he argues that archaeologists should use non-archaeological sources of data "in order to produce a more rounded picture of prehistoric cultures and to rule out alternative explanations that archaeological data alone might not be able to exclude" (Trigger 1989: 377). The use of clear and accessible language is crucial in this process, as well as an awareness of the very tentative (that is, falsifiable) nature of any "bold" solutions proposed.

Although his is not the only theory of science that considers interdisciplinary research, Popper's approach validates and even encourages interdisciplinary work, such as that of Wainwright. In the same vein, Trigger explains how interdisciplinary dialogue has more power than single-disciplinary work to refute archaeological hypotheses. Consider the following simplified example. A preliminary archaeological survey may interpret a small number of visible structures on a hill as seventeenth-century farm buildings (because today the area is surrounded by extensive open grassland suitable for cultivation). However, place-name study may suggest nineteenth-century environmental change, noting the open grassland as a previously submerged landscape, with the hill carrying an island name and the grassland a lake name. On that evidence, the reasoning that identified these structures as farm buildings is refuted. This example also highlights another important element of Popperian science, namely modesty; we know that our ideas are imperfect but do not yet understand exactly how.

In order to reinforce the use of accessible language, a common structure frames each of the book's chapters. A long quote (or quotes) points to the general problem area, followed by a short introduction that articulates the problem and the solution. An elaboration of problem and context then explores the field, including previous attempts to solve related problems. Next, a hypothesis (or multiple hypotheses) is presented. A tentative solution to the problem is developed, and assumptions inherent in the solution are made explicit. A description of method then applies the hypothesis or hypotheses to the problem, defining the test to be made. Results and discussion follow, considering the outcome of the test and asking how the results of other studies may be incorporated (including results of other chapters). Important in this process is a constant awareness of inherent assumptions and limitations; interdisciplinary dialogue has the potential to falsify aspects of certain solutions but we must not expect too much. Lastly, the entire process is summarized in the conclusions and further problems section, where the wider relevance of the study is discussed. Crucially, the conclusions restate inherent assumptions and limitations in simple language that is accessible to the scholar who is not a specialist in the discipline in question. This final section, most of all, is phrased to enable intelligent interdisciplinary dialogue. Invariably, further problems are raised in the course of the problem-solving process. The conclusion ends with a brief section in which such fertile areas are flagged up for future research.

Results and Discussion

While the concluding chapter is the most appropriate home for a consideration of several results, a point raised earlier deserves further attention at this point: namely, the possibility for methodological innovation *within* a field as a result of interdisciplinary dialogue.

This chapter stresses how a conversation between disciplines is most effective when each study clearly communicates problem, solution (including methodology), assumptions, and limitations. The process has twofold advantages: the critical rigour of a study is increased, and methodological innovation may occur when a technique is adapted from one field to another. The tephra contouring technique pioneered in chapter 6 is just such a case.

Simply put, the tephra contouring technique is an application of an archaeological method to solve environmental questions of landscape change. In archaeological fieldwork an excavator often contours the surface of a deposit and may become very skilled at exposing such surfaces. Volcanic airfall deposits in the Seljaland area of southern Iceland at times form visually distinctive centimetre-scale layers that an excavator may expose across a large area in order to study changes in surface vegetation over time. In essence, the tephra contouring method provides a photographic negative of surface vegetation at the moment the tephra was deposited. For instance, clearly defined circular "holes" in the tephra cover may mark the site of tree trunks and record the trunk diameter at ground level. In other words, tephra contours put into practice ideas such as those entertained by the palaeoecological and archaeological researcher Paul Buckland when he wrote, "The tephra horizons mean that extensive areas are sealed and it would theoretically be possible to excavate and reconstruct entire plant communities" (Buckland 1981: 383). Furthermore, exposing a large contiguous tephra surface allows density of tree cover to be quantified.

Efforts at defining the representativeness of the tephra contours have asked fundamental questions of the commonly used technique of recording an exposed vertical profile, or section (Jones et al. 1999: 27–33). These points are elaborated in chapter 6. For immediate purposes, it is the concept of methodological innovation that is important. The archaeological technique of the tephra contours provides a new method to answer questions of landscape change, and, as a "borrowed" technique, it is itself the result of interdisciplinary dialogue. Furthermore, applying the technique allows assessment of another technique, that of *vertical profile logging*, reminding us of the limitations inherent in that method.

Conclusions and Further Problems

As with the previous section, the effectiveness of my method is best considered at the end of the book. Nevertheless, a review of the contents of this chapter is worthwhile, leading to the presentation of some methodological questions that immediately emerge.

This chapter has explored Karl Popper's conceptualization of science as a critical process with a unity of method. Such a formulation is not limited to the "traditional" (that is, natural) sciences but instead defines science as the process of proposing conjectures and refutations. Thus science is an enterprise that proceeds by first formulating bold solutions to a problem and then attempting to show these solutions to be false.

An explicitly defined interdisciplinary method is needed when exploring problems that arise from fields operating in areas of convergence for separate theoretical traditions, such as Celtic studies and archaeology. Specifically, an interdisciplinary method is crucial in studies such as our exploration of the early medieval north Atlantic, where we deploy archaeological material, medieval literature, place names, and palaeoenvironmental data. F.T. Wainwright elaborated a pragmatic method for such coordination over forty years ago. He identified two kinds of interdisciplinary study: the specialist study from one discipline to another (for example, a study of local geology incorporated into an archaeological site report), and a grander synthesis of research from a number of fields.

High standards of clarity and accessibility are crucial to a Popperian practice of science; well-communicated scholarship fosters dialogue, increases the possibility of refuting one's ideas, and encourages methodological innovation. This last point is important and highlighted by the tephra contouring technique's application of an archaeological method to solve environmental problems of landscape change. The format of this book reflects the theories and methods discussed here.

We have explored a fundamental theory of knowledge. A challenge for future work will be to integrate the thinking outlined in this chapter with fuller treatment of discipline-specific theoretical models. In addition, two methodological questions immediately emerge. In the statement of Popper's seventeen key theses given in the hypothesis section, he proposes that "qualitative tests, for example, are in general less severe than quantitative tests" (Popper 1994: 94). One potential problem is whether a distinction between quantitative and qualitative tests is necessary or valid when one is doing science as described above. To be more precise, if each test (or study) clearly and accessibly communicates its inherent assumptions and limitations, then such a rule-of-thumb distinction between quantitative and qualitative tests becomes obsolete (and a potential source for error). This problem may be worth pursuing further.

A second problem emerges out of Wainwright's two kinds of interdisciplinary coordination. Wainwright distinguished between the integration of specialist study and a larger synthesis of research from many fields. Implicit in our advocated Popperian method is an inclusive concept of science as a process, thus giving minimal relevance to disciplinary boundaries. Indeed, Popper stresses that "what really exists are problems, and scientific traditions" (Popper

1992: 69). Correspondingly no disciplinary approach is privileged over another. Instead, the relative limitations of each study are articulated. One unresolved question, then, is whether there is any distinction in Popperian science between Wainwright's two kinds of coordination; in other words, further investigation may articulate a common method for the specialist study and larger synthesis.

In conclusion, Popper proposes an inclusive concept of science with a unity of method that stresses communication with other researchers in other fields. In other words, Popperian science is a *community* enterprise. Writing from a literary perspective in the 2003 preface to his book *Orientalism*, Edward W. Said provides a useful parallel:

> My idea in *Orientalism* is to use humanistic critique to open up the fields of struggle, to introduce a longer sequence of thought and analysis to replace the short bursts of polemic, thought-stopping fury that so imprison us in labels and antagonistic debate whose goal is a belligerent collective identity rather than understanding and intellectual exchange … By humanism I mean … to use one's mind historically and rationally for the purposes of reflective understanding and genuine disclosure. Moreover, humanism is sustained by a sense of community with other interpreters and other societies and periods: strictly speaking, therefore, there is no such thing as an isolated humanist. (Said [1978] 2003: xvii)

Within his humanism, Said embraces key Popperian ideas when he stresses willingness and ability to communicate effectively across frameworks, for Popper argues that we may work between frameworks, be they intellectual perspectives or disciplinary traditions. This chapter provides a justification and outlines a method for putting our theory of interdisciplinary conversation into practice. In order to understand better the diffusion of culture, movements of people, development of societies, and environmental change across the early medieval north Atlantic, this book applies our method to integrate studies in key problem areas, from a number of disciplinary perspectives.

3 Pabbays and Paibles: *Pap-* Names and Gaelic and Old Norse Speakers in Scotland's Hebridean Islands

The Landnáma states that wherever the Norwegian settlers found monks, or remains of their establishments, they called the places by some name beginning with *Pap*, from *pfaff*, *Papa*, πάππας, a priest – as *Papey*, the Priest's Island; *Papuli*, the Priest's district. In Orkney there are two *Papeys*; the larger Papa Westray, the smaller Papa Stronsay. In the mainland also there is Paplay (*Papuli*); another Paplay in South Ronaldshay; in Shetland two *Papeys*, Papa Stour and Papa Little; and a Papill (*Papilia*) in Unst. In the Hebrides also there are two *Pabbys* (Papey) and a *Pappadil* in Rum.

Sir Daniel Wilson, *Archæology and Prehistoric Annals of Scotland*[1]

A place name denotes a location and, for the namer, articulates meaning given to that place. *Pap-* names, such as those derived from Old Norse (ON) **Papa(r) ey*, are found across a northern region incorporating the Scottish islands, Faroe Islands, and Iceland. Since at least the middle of the nineteenth century these Old Norse names and medieval *papar/papae* descriptions have been used to suggest early Christian migration(s) across the north Atlantic islands. Detailed review, however, highlights unexplored avenues for toponymic study of these names and suggests more complex and nuanced interpretations of the material.

Pap- names are most common in Atlantic Scotland, where *pap-* scholarship is dominated by studies centred on the Northern Isles. The Hebrides are equally endowed with these names and represent a striking gap in scholarship; the *Pap-* names of those western islands are little studied and are only beginning to be integrated with Northern Isles–driven work. Yet, if *Pap-* names are indeed to be related to early Christian Gaels, one would expect this to be most clearly seen in the Hebrides, where sculpture, surviving structures, artefactual material, and contemporary literature are associated with early Christian communities. Let us rigorously assess the proposal that *Pap-* names may be identified with early Christian communities. This chapter therefore highlights the little-studied Hebridean *Pap-* islands and *Pap-* farms and serves to illuminate our specific problem – the postulated relationship between *Pap-* names, communities of early Christian Gaels, and Norse colonists. Previously the argument has appeared straightforward: *Pap-* names describe settlements of early Christian Gaels, called *papar* by the Norse. In this chapter we shall suggest that the argument is simplistic and begs a critical reappraisal. In our reappraisal, we shall revisit and underscore some key points and arguments regarding these names, which I have dealt with at length elsewhere (Ahronson 2007).[2]

Problem and Context

Reflecting upon the distribution of these names (see table 3.1), we may make three observations. First, *Pap-* names are found in a number of places across the north Atlantic region, and they are most common in Atlantic Scotland. Second, the geographical range of *Pap-* names is notable; they appear to be largely restricted to the littoral zones and archipelagos of Scotland and to the northern archipelagos of the Faroe Islands and Iceland. Third, the Hebrides are a core area for these names, albeit being the least studied.

We may also note the new discovery of Papies Holm (Duffus parish, Moray) (Simon Taylor, personal communication). Papies Holm is intriguing, as its occurrence pushes the area of these names southwards into the Moray Firth, which is a region with an early Christian inheritance and where the Viking Age is poorly understood.[3]

To date, *Pap-* names have yet to be found in Ireland or Scandinavia, though certain Scottish and Norwegian names, of another type, betray surface similarities to our group. This other type includes names such as the Paps of Jura (Jura, western Scotland) or Papper / på Papøy (Østfold, southeastern Norway) and may be set apart as they appear to be different from ON *papa(r)* names, though Marteinn Sigurðsson has recently been exploring the relationships between north Atlantic *Pap-* names, topography, and a "breast, teat" etymology (Sigurðsson 2005; 2008). Thus, the Østfold Papper / på Papøy is usually understood in terms of the Norwegian word *pappe* "breast, teat"; and the island's topography supports this interpretation (Gammeltoft 2004a: 38n1). Gammeltoft is critical of the possibility that the north Atlantic *Pap-* names share a common etymology with the Østfold name, and he writes that deriving all these names from ON **pap* "breast, teat" is difficult to support: "Formally, there is no reason why this possibility should not lie behind some *Pap-* place-names in the North Atlantic either. I must, however, immediately concede that I have not

Table 3.1 *Pap*- names from Iceland, the Faroe Islands, Scotland, northwest England, and the Isle of Man. Potentially recent names are represented by +, while ? notes an unclear derivation. This list draws substantially upon the work of Peder Gammeltoft and Aidan MacDonald (Gammeltoft 2004a: 36–7; MacDonald 2002: 26–9).

Country/Region	*Pap*- name(s)
Iceland	Papey (island, S-Múlasýsla) Papafjörður (firth, A-Skaftafellssýsla) Papós/*Papafjarðarós (confluence, A-Skaftafellssýsla) Papýli (lost settlement) Papi (pool in the river Laxá) Papafell (mountain, Strandasýsla) +Papakross (cliff-face carving, Hetta, Vestmannaeyjar) +Papahellir (cave, A-Rangárvallasýsla)
Faroe Islands	Paparókur (cliff ledges, Vestmanna) ?Papurshálsur (cliff ledge, Saksun)[1]
Scotland 1: Shetland	Papa Geo (creek, Aithsting) Papa Little (island, Aithsting) Papa Stour (island, Sandness) Papa (island, Burra) Papil Geo (creek, Noss) Papil Water (loch, Fetlar) Papil (settlement, Burra) Papil (settlement, North Yell) Papil (settlement, Unst)
Scotland 2: Orkney	Papa Stronsay (island, Stronsay) Papa Westray (island, Westray) Papdale (settlement, Kirkwall and St Ola) Papley (district and settlement, South Ronaldsay) +Papleyhouse (settlement, Eday) Ward of Papley (mound, Holm) ?Steeven o'Papy (sea rock, North Ronaldsay)
Scotland 3: Caithness	Papel (tidal rock, Canisbay) Papigoe (creek and district, Wick)
Scotland 4: Moray	Papies Holm (settlement, Duffus parish)
Scotland 5: Hebrides	Bayble/Paibal (settlement, Stornoway, Lewis) Pabanish (rocky hill, Uig, Lewis) Pabay (island, Strath, Skye) Pabay Beag (island, Uig, Lewis) Pabay Mór (island, Uig, Lewis) Pabbay (island, Barra) Pabbay (island, Harris) Pabbay (two islands, South Uist) Paible (chapel and settlement, North Uist) Paible (chapel and settlement, Taransay) Papadil (islets, Rhum) Kilphobull (Kilninian and Kilmore parish, Mull)[2]

Table 3.1 (*continued*)

Country/Region	*Pap*- name(s)
Isle of Man	?Glenfaba (Peel)
Scotland/England: Dumfries and Galloway/Cumberland	?Papy Ha' (Minnigaff, Kirkcudbright) ?Papcastle (settlement, Cumberland)

1 Christian Matras argued that the name *Papurshálsur* is derived from an original **Papýlishálsur* – and thus related to a now lost *Papýli*- name in the Saksun area. He proposes first a loss of *-i-* from **Papýlis-*, resulting in **Papýls-*. Next, the dipthong *-ý-* "uj" becomes *-u-* "u". The final change is that of *-uls-* to *-urs-*, thus **Papuls-* > *Papurs-*, producing the recorded *Papurshálsur* (Matras 1934: 187).

2 Gammeltoft derives this name from Gaelic *cill* 'cell, church' + ON **Papabýli* (Gammeltoft 2001: 301). Alternatively, this name could relate to Old Irish (OI) *popul* (itself derived from Latin *populus*) meaning "people, tribe" or in modern Gaelic "congregation, especially Catholic" (cf. *Cairnpapple* in Lanarkshire).

been able to find any suitable breast-shaped formations on or near any of the localities, apart from possibly *Papa Little* in Shetland which has a tendency to a double-peaked profile.[4] So, although ON **pap*- 'breast, teat' might be a formal possibility, the topography seems to speak against this in most cases" (Gammeltoft 2004a: 38n1). Topography, then, offers one way to distinguish ON **Papa(r)ey* and **Papa(r)býli* names from names containing the Old Norse (or Northern Old English) word for "breast, teat."

It is crucial to emphasize that *Pap*- names were coined by Old Norse speakers. Consequently, our exploration of the Hebridean names calls for a review of current thinking on Scandinavian language use in Atlantic Scotland. In the Viking Age the areas of Scandinavian influence in Scotland saw two power centres emerge: one in the Northern Isles and the other in the Hebrides and Isle of Man.[5] From the Viking Age until the end of the twelfth century, Shetland, Orkney, Caithness, Sutherland, the Hebrides, and the Isle of Man formed a common language area where Old Norse was spoken. In the Western Isles of Scotland a form of Old Norse thus appears to have preceded the late medieval dominance of Gaelic. Old Norse may have flourished in the western part of this area until the mid-thirteenth century, when the Scottish king secured authority in the Hebrides and Isle of Man (though Orkney and Shetland remained "Scandinavian" until 1468–9). An unresolved question is the length of time before Gaelic completely replaced the Old Norse spoken in these western islands, the suggestion being that Hebridean Old Norse disappeared rapidly under Scottish influence. We may be critical of the idea of rapid language loss because Scandinavian speech survived changes in authority in Orkney and Shetland, where the Norn language (derived from Old Norse) was used until the seventeenth and eighteenth centuries. The length of time that Hebridean Old Norse survived and the nature of its decline are therefore unclear (Gammeltoft 2004b: 53–4; 2001: 23–30).

Recent work does, however, provide insights into the transformation in the Western Isles from Old Norse to Gaelic speech. By studying Gaelic and Scandinavian phonetics, grammar, lexical loans, and place names, Gammeltoft is able to perceive aspects of this late medieval language shift in the Hebrides. The distribution of a number of Gaelic phonetic features may result from this shift. The devoicing in Manx and Scottish Gaelic of *b, d, g* to [b_o, d_o, g_o] (in contrast to Irish Gaelic); the initial stress on native words in Scottish Gaelic and in the Irish Gaelic dialects of Ulster and western Connaught; and the supradentalization and retroflection of certain consonant clusters in the Hebrides may have been brought about by Scandinavian interference on Gaelic (Gammeltoft 2004b: 55–9). Similarly, a large-scale shift from Old Norse to Gaelic language may be reflected by the 900–1200 grammatical simplification in Gaelic, which appears to have been greatest in Manx and Scottish Gaelic (Gammeltoft 2004b: 60). Alongside the notable phonetic and grammatical interference, lexical loans into Gaelic are surprisingly slight (c. 200 words), though the combination of significant phonetic and grammatical interference with a small number of lexical loans fits well with models of language shift–induced interference (Gammeltoft 2004b: 61–7). The many Old Norse place names still to be found in the Hebrides are also consistent with the suggestion of a large-scale language shift there:

> That so many place-names of Scandinavian origin remain in existence and have not been replaced by new Gaelic place-names shows that the user-group of these place-names must have continued to live in the area. Had the Scandinavians been driven out in connection with the language change, the survival of anything but perhaps the most central names is hardly conceivable. Only continuity in the user-group could have facilitated the survival of place-names of Scandinavian origin in this number. At the same time, however, the high number of place-names also bear witness to longstanding contacts between Gaelic and Scandinavian speaking people in the area. Had Gaelic-speaking people not already accepted a great number of the place-names, the rate of survival would probably not have been as high as it is. (Gammeltoft 2004b: 71–2)

Thus the existence of such a number of Old Norse place names suggests a continuity of the user group and long-standing contacts between Old Norse and Gaelic speakers. Additional support for this scenario is found in the limited interference of Gaelic upon the Scandinavian languages. The limited lexical loans *from* Gaelic (as the only type of Gaelic interference on the Scandinavian languages) suggest that interference in this direction was not intense and resulted from language contact through bilingualism. Furthermore, that about

8 per cent of these loan words serve a religious function may reflect the Christian influence of Gaelic speakers on Old Norse–speaking communities of the Atlantic area (Gammeltoft 2004b: 64, 67).

Cast against this background (or one like it), research into the *Pap-* names has fallen into three camps. Earlier scholarship has argued that these names testify to "Irish" Christian settlements across Scotland, the Faroe Islands, and Iceland that *predate* the Viking Age (Beauvois 1875: 69–72). In contrast, recent years have explored the idea of late Viking Age "antiquarianism" among the Scandinavian communities of the north Atlantic, proposing that the late Norse coining of *Pap-* names asserts (or invents) continuity with a Christian past (MacDonald 2002; Lowe 2002: 94–5). Another idea admits that *Pap-* names are potentially related to early Christian communities of the seventh and eighth centuries, but nonetheless posits that these names were given by *Norse speakers* in the early Viking Age and thus describe papar within an early Norse context in the Scottish islands, Faroe Islands, and Iceland (Gammeltoft 2004a: 36–41; Lamb 1995: 17–18). Correspondingly, our problem may be phrased in the following way: what do the *Pap-* names of the European north Atlantic (and especially of the Hebrides) reveal about early Christian communities and the Norse?

Hypotheses

Given the wide-ranging interpretations outlined above, understanding the *pap-* element is crucial to the problem of these names. As noted in the introduction and again in chapter 1, the earliest literature to mention the *pap-* element describes *papar* or *papae* as early Christian "Irish" in Iceland, or African Jews in Orkney; in both cases these populations are portrayed to precede Norse settlement there and as having minimal contact with the colonists (*Íslendingabók*: ch. 1; *Landnámabók*: ch. 1; Benediktsson 1968: 4–5, 31–2; Pálsson and Edwards 1972: 14; *Historia*: ch. 6; Ekrem and Mortensen 2003: 64–7). These twelfth- and thirteenth-century texts were written with purpose, and, as we saw in chapter 1, this purpose is especially evident in the case of *Historia Norvegiae*'s Africans "*judaismo adhærentes*/adhering to Judaism" (*Historia*: ch. 6; Storm 1880: 90; Anderson 1922: 331). With regard to the medieval traditions of early Christian settlements encountered by Scandinavians (in contrast to the lone claim of the *Historia Norvegiae*), we may note that these persisted into the modern period. The following folktale from the Faroe Islands is one such example, published in the mid-nineteenth century: "Quelque temps avant que les Norvégiens s'emparassent des Færeys, il s'y était établi des hommes que le narrateur considérait comme des saints, attendu qu'ils avaient la puissance de faire des signes et des miracles, de guérir les blessures et les maladies … A l'arrivée des Norvégiens, qui étaient très-violents, quelques-uns de ces gens s'éloignèrent par mer; d'autres se réfugièrent dans des caverns" (Beauvois 1875: 68n1; Schrœter 1849–51: 146–7).[6] A belief in early Christian (Irish)[7] settlements across the early medieval north is thus of significant antiquity and longevity (see figure 3.1). Similarly, implicit in much earlier scholarship was the argument that *Pap-* names describe settlements of early Christian Gaels, called *papar* by the Norse.[8] Highlighted in this chapter's epigraph, Daniel Wilson relayed *Landnámabók*'s assertion that "wherever the Norwegian settlers found monks, or remains of their settlements, they called the places with some name beginning with *Pap*" (Wilson 1851: 486). Eugène Beauvois was also an early advocate of this idea. Writing in 1875, Beauvois suggested that *Pap-* names remembered early Christian Gaels in Scotland's Northern Isles and Iceland. Of the Northern Isles he writes: "Il n'y a, en effet, plus de restes de l'ancienne population celtique dans les Orcades; mais, bien que les Papas n'y aient pas laissé de descendants, leur nom n'a pas moins été conservé dans ceux des îles de *Papa westra* et *Papa stronsa*, et des localités de *Paplay*. Fordun, qui composa vers 1380 sa chronique d'Écosse parle d'une *Papeay tertia* dont on ne connaît pas la position. De même dans les Shetlands, il y a trois îles qui rappellent les Papas: *Papa stour* (Papey stóra), *Papa little* (Papey lítla) et *Papa*, ainsi qu'un domaine de *Papil*" (Beauvois 1875: 69–70).

The following hypothesis is drawn from Beauvois but applied to the Hebridean case: the distribution of *Pap-* names reflects the settlement of early Christian Gaels before the Viking Age.[9]

Another area of debate is the dating of *Pap-* names. In 2002, MacDonald and Lowe questioned the earlier assumption that the names were coined upon the arrival of Old Norse–speaking colonists. MacDonald instead argued that the likely period for "the creation of all or most of these names is, broadly, the second half of the ninth century and the tenth, but with the overall chronological limits probably varying locally" (MacDonald 2002: 22). He posited that *Pap-* names were inspired by oral and written traditions of contact-period Christian (Irish) communities and thus coined and then applied to places in the landscape retrospectively (MacDonald 2002: 21, 24n6). Lowe, on the other hand, suggested that *Pap-* naming flourished as the twelfth-century fledgling Church "sought to attach itself to something that was much older" (Lowe 2002: 95). Thus, MacDonald posited that the name was coined retrospectively in the late ninth to tenth centuries, while Lowe suggested the twelfth. Their arguments propose the hypothesis that the distribution of *Pap-* names reflects retrospective names given by Old Norse speakers in *either* the late ninth and tenth century *or* the twelfth century.

Figure 3.1 Detail of Kinnaird's 1783 estate plan, with inset of Moray and coastal northeast Scotland; the arrow locates Papies Holm.

Gammeltoft challenges these proposals, and my final hypothesis emerges both from the realization that *Pap-* names are Norse constructions and from linguistic and toponymic arguments for an early dating of the name forms. Gammeltoft argues that *Pap-* island and *Pap-* farm names were coined well before the twelfth century and, as island and generic settlement names, would typically be among the earliest Norse names in the north Atlantic area (Gammeltoft 2004a: 42–3). Our third hypothesis therefore proposes that the distribution of *Pap-* names reflects the character of earliest Norse settlement.

Method

We may thus perceive that *Pap-* names present a difficult area for scholars of both the early Christian Gaelic and the Viking Age Norse worlds. Correspondingly, when the problem posed by their distribution across the European north Atlantic is explored, the Hebrides form a natural focus. These islands were home to a number of early Christian communities and, as we have seen, strong Norse settlement. Therefore, if *Pap-* names are indeed related to early Christian Gaels, then this should be most clearly seen in those western islands where art-historical and archaeological material as well as literature identify early Christian communities.

As highlighted at the outset of the hypothesis section, understanding the *pap-* element is key to the problem of these names. Therefore, let us delve into a linguistic analysis of the place-name element, which may in turn inform our subsequent characterization of the regional distribution of *Pab(b)ay* and *Paible* names in Scotland's Western Isles. Thus empowered, the three proposed hypotheses shall be tested: *Pap-* names (a) reflect the settlement of early Christian Gaels before the Viking Age, (b) are retrospective names given by Old Norse speakers, or (c) reflect the character of earliest Norse settlement.

Results and Discussion

Pap- names, understood to contain the Old Norse masculine noun *papi*, have been proposed to be related to descriptions of early Christian (Irish) papar. In order to further understand these names, let us turn first to a grammatical and etymological analysis. Table 3.2 conjugates ON *papi*, while table 3.3 outlines proposed original forms, meaning, and potential derivations for *Pap-* island and *Pap-* farm names.

Table 3.2 Conjugation of Old Norse masculine noun *papi*

Case	Singular form	Plural form
Nominative	*papi*	*papar*
Accusative	*papa*	*papa*
Dative	*papa*	*pöpum*
Genitive	*papa*	*papa*

Table 3.3 *Pap-* name forms. The ?> notation symbolizes a problematic, though possible derivation. The forms **Paparey* and **Paparbýli* are theoretically possible, but only theoretically so; they have never been recorded in old sources. Furthermore, it is unclear to which extent indications of singular or plural are relevant, especially if these toponymic forms came to be used as a fixed phrase (i.e., outside the grammar of word composition).

Proposed original forms	Meaning	Potential derivations
**Papaey*	'island of *papi* (s.)'	*Papey / Papa / Pab(b)ay*
**Paparey*	'island of *papar* (pl.)'	*Papey / Papa / Pab(b)ay* OR **Paprey* > **Pabra*[1]? > *Pab(b)ay*
**Papaey*	'island of *papar* (pl.)'	*Papey / Papa / Pab(b)ay*
**Papabýli*	'farm of *papi* (s.)'	*Papýli* > *Papil / Papley / Paible*
**Paparbýli*	'farm of *papar* (pl.)'	**Paprýli* > *Papýli* > *Papil / Papley / Paible*
**Papabýli*	'farm of *papar* (pl.)'	*Papýli* > *Papil / Papley / Paible*

1 Though the *Pabra* name form is recorded in Forbes's *Place-Names of Skye and Adjacent Islands*, this name is puzzling: it could derive from **Paparey*, but the possibility is problematic as this source is so late that to postulate the survival of a variant Old Norse form of *Pabra* would be dangerous (Forbes 1923: 272).

These proposed original forms and derivations need elaboration. The case of **Papaey* > *Papey / Papa / Pab(b)ay* is simple: the medial vowel (*Papaey*) is lost owing to Old Norwegian syncope,[10] resulting in the *Papey / Papa / Pab(b)ay* forms. The alternate derivation of **Paparey* > **Pabra* > *Pab(b)ay* is problematic because, after syncope, the uncommon sound combination [-pr-] remains nonetheless possible in Old Norse; thus the loss of [-r-] in **Pabra* > *Pab(b)ay* cannot be understood as a straightforward sound change. The **Paparey* > **Paprey* > **Pabra* > *Pab(b)ay* derivation must therefore be considered unlikely, whereas the proposed **Papaey* > *Papey / Papa / Pab(b)ay* is plausible.

The case of **Papa(r)býli > *Paprýli/Papýli > Papil/Papley/Paible*, however, is less clear. Again, the medial vowel (*Papa(r)býli*) is lost owing to Old Norwegian syncope. The initial [b-] in *býli* is also lost, here because of phonotaxis; a pronunciation of the [-pb-] in **Papbýli* is not permitted according to the set of allowed sequences of speech sounds in Old Norse. Similarly, the [-prb-] in **Paprbýli* is very problematic, so in this instance the [-rb-] would also be dropped. For the *-býli* name then, either proposed original form of **Papabýli* or **Paparbýli* is possible, though **Papabýli* is preferable by analogy with **Papaey* (Gammeltoft, personal communication).

Thus **Papaey* and **Papabýli* are the preferred original forms, though **Paparbýli* is also possible. As may be seen in table 3.2, both singular *papi* and plural *papa* are identical in this conjugation; therefore, the **Papaey* and **Papabýli* names may denote either "*papi* island" and "*papi* farm" or "*papar* island" and "*papar* farm" – or some combination of these.

In his 2002 study of *papar* names, Aidan MacDonald noted that ON *papi* is usually understood to be a borrowing from Old Irish (which itself draws upon a Latin original); he cites F.T. Wainwright, Hermann Pálsson, Paul Edwards and A.O. Anderson as supporting this Irish origin (MacDonald 2002: 15; Wainwright 1962: 100; Pálsson and Edwards 1972: 15n3; Pálsson 1955: 120–2; Anderson 1922: 341n2). However, MacDonald also suggests the possibility of a Germanic source (also derived from Latin *papa*) for ON *papi* (MacDonald 2002: 17). Accepting a Latin source, Gammeltoft has assessed potential Germanic and Old Irish origins for the Old Norse use of *papi* in the sense of "cleric or Christian." Gammeltoft proposes that a Germanic origin for the specifically north Atlantic meaning "cleric or Christian" is highly problematic since Old English *pāpa*, Old High German *pabes*, and East Frisian *pape*, *pâp* were used solely for "pope," and that "pope" is the meaning of Old Danish *papa* or *pave* and Old Norwegian *pafi* or *papi*. It may be countered that Middle Low German *pape* did develop the meaning "cleric," but this is late,[11] and the first mainland Scandinavian use of the word to describe a cleric is the fifteenth-century Swedish *pape* (Gammeltoft 2004a: 39–40).

Alternatively, the north Atlantic meaning of "cleric or Christian" may be compared with the Old High German *phafo* "priest, especially lower clergy," which C.-E. Thors derives from an ultimately Greek rather than Latin origin. Thors proposes that Old High German *phafo* is a loan from Gothic, where *papan* occurs in the Gothic calendar fragment[12] and is itself ultimately drawn from Greek παπᾶς, which in the fourth century held the meaning "clericus minor" and was easily distinguished from πάπας "pope." Thors suggests that both the Greek παπᾶς and πάπας "*egentigen tillhört barnspråket*" (Thors 1957: 37–8; belonged to the sphere of children's language); he also derives Old

Slavic *popu* from Greek *παπᾶς*. Thus it may be that Old High German *phafo* (attested in Middle High German *phaffe*, Middle Low German *pape*, Old Frisian *papa*, and Middle Dutch *pape*, all in the sense of "priest, spiritual") has a Greek rather than Latin origin. However, the word is largely absent from the Nordic languages, occurring only once in the Old Swedish poem *Tio Guds bud*,[13] though this poem includes many "*norvagismer*" (Norwagisms) and "*germanismer*" (Germanisms); Thors suspects the poem's *papa* is just one of these. According to Thors, then, Old High German *phafo* cannot be demonstrated to have entered the Scandinavian languages (Thors 1957: 37–8).

In contrast to the difficulties with a Germanic derivation, an Old Irish source is straightforward: OI *popa/pobba/bobba* held the meaning "father" and was used as a respectful address (following the form *poba* + personal name), whereas the rare OI *papa* or *pupu* described monastic or anchoritic individuals (MacDonald 2002: 15–17; Gammeltoft 2004a: 40–1). A transcription of the early-ninth-century *Martyrology of Oengus the Culdee* (MS Rawlinson B505) describes Enda of Aran as just such a papa: "*Nem macc hui Birn do Dail Birn i n-Osraige 7 comarba Enna Arné ocus is hé sin in papa atberar do bith i n-Arainn*/Nem moccu Birn of the Dál Birn of Ossory and successor of Enda of Aran; and he is that papa who is said to be in Aran" (MacDonald 2002: 15; Gammeltoft 2004a: 41; see also MacDonald 1977: 26). Thus, rather than supporting an Old Germanic derivation, linguistic arguments suggest an Old Irish origin for the north Atlantic use of ON *papi* as "cleric or Christian" (Gammeltoft 2004a: 41). A third possibility, still largely unexplored, is a Pictish source for ON *papi*. Such an origin is conceivable, considering that most *Pap-* names are located in what may have been Pictish-speaking areas at the outset of the Viking Age (Kruse 2005). Further research along these lines is called for.

Looking to the places that *Pap-* names denote, and the way the element is used in name constructions, proves a further avenue for understanding the toponyms. Combining the *pap-* element with "island" or "settlement" is comparable in practice to the naming of an island using a personal name specific, as in the Shetland examples of Hildisay (< ON **Hildirsey* "Hildir's island") and Trondra (< ON **Þrondarey* "Þrondr's island"). Thus, for the namer, the *pap-*, *Hild-* and *Þrond-* elements reflects the idea that papi/papar, Hildir, or Þrondr owned or were the first to settle there. In other words, "a place-name with the element *papi*, m., 'a priest, Christian' with *ey*, f., 'island' or *býli*, m., 'settlement,' signals the association of a locality with the *Papar*, be it their presence at, or ownership of, the locality" (Gammeltoft 2004a: 43).

Following this context of ownership or settlement makes intriguing the Orkney-led claim that *Pap-* sites "are always the most fertile spots of a parish" (Fisher 2002: 45; Smith 1842: 226; Lamb 1995: 15–17). If these names are sited on the best land in a parish, does this signal a favourable role for papar in the local hierarchy? Or, alternatively, could these soils have been improved by papar through agricultural innovation? Work is ongoing to explore and refine these claims for fertile soils; initial efforts targeted the Northern Isles (Simpson and Guttman 2002), while more recent fieldwork looks to the Western Isles (Ian Simpson, personal communication; Simpson et al. 2005). From this exploratory work Simpson et al. were able to perceive that the bulk of these names "are associated with areas of very good to medium quality agricultural land which, with the agricultural land management of the period, would allow good yields" (Simpson et al. 2005: 13). The research of Simpson and colleagues thus promises to make an important contribution to our understanding of the places marked by *Pap-* names.

Study of the *Pap-* name distribution across the Western Isles also suggests important conclusions. The *Pab(b)ay* and *Paible* names are Norse, and a form of Old Norse was spoken in those islands until, at least, the thirteenth century. Norse speakers must have given these names sometime during this period. As Norse names, *Pab(b)ays* and *Paibles* occur in a regular distribution across the Western Isles, respecting modern regional divisions: the Barra islands, South Uist, Harris/North Uist, the Uig area of Lewis, and the Skye area each have one *Pab(b)ay.*[14] Furthermore, when the *Paibles* and other *Pap-* names are included, the population centres in the Stornoway area, Taransay and neighbouring Harris, southwest-facing Uist, and Rum are each found to have a *Pap-* name. Most populated areas of the "Long Island," Skye, and Rum have a *Pab(b)ay* name – and if not, then probably a *Paible* or other *Pap-* name. This distribution of the name element suggests a consistent role for these *Pap-* places within the Norse-speaking regional structure or administration and may be brought to bear upon our hypotheses.

Pap-*names reflect the settlement of early Christian Gaels before the Viking Age*

Fisher has recently pointed to the coincidence of *Pap-* names with early Christian sculpture sites (Fisher 2002), and a number of names demonstrate the early Christian associations of these areas in the Hebrides (cf. the "surrounding" and "selected" names catalogued in my *Viking-Age Communities*). However, the hypothesis outlined above requires one to deny the apparently firm datum that *Pap-* names are Norse, and instead to suppose that those names are either Gaelic or Pictish. It is important to stress that *Pap-* names, though probably a loan from Gaelic, are nevertheless a Norse word form. Furthermore, my inventory of minor names from the Hebridean *Pap-* islands demonstrates that the vast majority of smaller scale names were given by Norse speakers or by more recent Gaelic, Scots, and English speakers (Ahronson 2007: 67–9; 2002b; Taylor 2002). In other words, these Norse-period (or younger) names cannot be older than the Viking Age and thus cannot reasonably be used in locating *earlier* settlements of Christian communities. One attempt to surmount this difficulty proposes that early Scandinavian colonists applied *Pap-* names to recently abandoned sites formerly occupied by early Christian Gaels (Fellows-Jensen 1996: 116). The rebuttal of this idea has been set out as follows, with reference to Scotland's Northern Isles: "Why should it be more relevant to name abandoned *papar* sites than abandoned *pettar* [Pictish or indigenous] sites, the latter often being more distinctive with their broch structures?" (Gammeltoft 2003: 94). In other words, if sites related to the indigenous population of the presumably Pictish-speaking Northern Isles are almost completely lacking *Pettar-* names, then it is difficult to support the proposal that numerous *Pap-* names identify abandoned (and perhaps unremarkable) sites related to potentially marginal communities of early Christian Gaels. Furthermore, Gammeltoft suggests that the evidence from the Northern Isles (presumably also applicable to the Western Isles)[15] encourages the following idea:

> *Papar* lived alongside Scandinavians … for a prolonged period. This fits well with the fact that a large number of *papar* sites are associated with post-Viking Age chapels or graveyards, which presupposes a prolonged period of Christian worship at these sites. Whether this means a continuous clerical presence from pre-Viking Age times or not is uncertain. However, if this is the case, then the presence of the Christian *papar* might well represent attempts at converting the heathen Scandinavians. Judging from the many Christian Scandinavians from Scotland, who, according to *Landnámabók*, settled in Iceland only a couple of generations after settlement of the Northern and Western Isles of Scotland, they seem to have been fairly successful. (Gammeltoft 2003: 94)

In support of Gammeltoft's theory of prolonged coexistence, one may draw on the onomastic truism that place names are often coined by neighbouring groups. England's many *Denby* names are a clear example; these names for isolated "Dane's farms" seem to have been given not by the farms' Scandinavian residents but by their English-speaking neighbours (Gammeltoft 2004a: 44). Another example would be northwest England's *Ireby* names, which have been understood to mark out areas of "Irish" or Gaelic-Norse settlement within the region's larger Scandinavian settlement (Higham 1995). However, even if this were the circumstance in which *Pap-* names arose, the hypothesis under consideration would remain implausible. Certainly, it is possible that settlements of early Christian Gaels did continue into the Viking Age on *Pab(b)ay* islands and *Paible* farms. However, it is also possible that these names are related to an unconnected Viking Age religious movement or are even a product of the contact situation itself – perhaps on an earlier Christian site, or perhaps not. In short, these names are indubitably Norse and were applied by Norse speakers in areas of Scandinavian colonization. To propose that they reflect settlement of early Christian Gaels *before* the Viking Age would be to argue beyond the limits of the place-name material. The minor name patterns on these islands illustrate these limitations: the vast majority of names date to the Norse period or more recent centuries. Simply put, ON *Pap-* names need not be related to pre–Viking Age communities of early Christian Gaels.

Either Pap- *names are retrospective names given by Old Norse speakers in the late ninth or tenth century or the twelfth century*

Or Pap- *names reflect the character of the earliest Norse settlement*

Earlier in this discussion it was suggested that **Papaey* and **Papabýli* names had lost their medial vowel (in this case the middle *a*) through the Old Norwegian syncope, producing *Papey* and triggering the phonotaxis that produced *Papýli*. These changes must have occurred in a Norse-speaking environment and preceded later transformations of these names into Scots and Gaelic, which resulted in the modern *Pab(b)ays*, *Papa(s)*, *Paibles*, and *Papils* (Gammeltoft 2004a: 41). Gammeltoft provides a succinct description of the Old Norwegian syncope: "Syncope is popularly speaking a means of shortening multi-syllabic words and names by a syllable and it probably takes place owing to frequent use of the linguistic element in question … it is important to note that syncope does not take place in the coining process of a name but it is solely the result of frequent use of the coinage" (Gammeltoft 2004a: 42). If Gammeltoft is right about this, the loss of the medial *a* in *Pap-* names was the product of frequent use of these names. Precise dating of the Old Norwegian syncope is difficult, though it may be demonstrated to have already taken place by the time of the earliest Old Norse manuscripts, that is before 1150. In other words, these *Pap-* names must, on linguisitic grounds, have been coined well before 1150 *at the latest* and have been "well-established and often-used place-names prior to the time when the Old Norwegian syncope came into force" (Gammeltoft 2004a: 42).

From his work on Papa Stronsay, Lowe put forward the idea that the founding of twelfth-century ecclesiastical structures led to "retrospective" naming of *Pap-* places (Lowe 2002: 95). However, the linguistic evidence outlined above argues against the suggestion that *Pap-* names are twelfth-century "retrospective" coinages. In addition, the absence of any Norse ecclesiastical names from the catalogued islands (aside from the *Pab(b)ay* name itself) is at odds with the "retrospective naming" idea. Furthermore, if this ecclesiastical name form were late, then one might expect *Pap-* names to be concentrated in areas important for the Church in that later period, as Lowe proposed for Orkney. In the Icelandic case this should suggest that *Pap-* names would occur in the surroundings of the bishop's seats of Skálholt (in the south) or Hólar (in the north). However, the Icelandic examples of these names occur elsewhere on the island, clustered in the southeast. An equivalent Hebridean scenario would see important centres for late Viking Age Christianity, such as Iona, with a *Pap-* name; if that was the case, it has not survived.[16] Therefore, both linguistic and historical arguments may be levelled against the proposal of twelfth-century retrospective naming.

Another idea to be reckoned with is MacDonald's suggestion of late-ninth- and early-tenth-century retrospective coining of *Pap-* names. He argued that "the restricted range of forms common to all areas, the unspecified nature of the names as place-names, and also their numbers and distribution – make me think … they were coined and applied retrospectively [in the late ninth and tenth centuries]" (MacDonald 2002: 21). Although Viking Age retrospective naming is a possibility, further analysis of the place-name material argues against this. To elaborate, the first names of Scandinavian origin in the north Atlantic area are thought to be major topographical names, containing coastal, headland, and river names such as *-fjörður* "firth, bay", *-ey* "island", and *-nes* "ness, headland", whereas generic settlement names, such as those containing *-býli*, are understood to be marginally later. Over twenty *Pap-* names contain elements denoting major topographical features, and roughly a dozen names denote settlement (the *-býli* names), which suggests that *Pap-* names may be among the earliest Scandinavian names in the north Atlantic area. This apparently robust assumption refutes the idea that these names were "coined and applied retrospectively" (Gammeltoft 2004a: 43). In this way, it is worth noting that my *Viking-Age Communities* catalogue also identifies most of the Norse minor names of the Hebridean *Pap-* islands as topographical, which is consistent with the naming scenario outlined above.

The third hypothesis, that *Pap-* names reflect the character of earliest Norse settlement, is the best fit. Given that *Pap-* names are Norse names and were transformed by the Old Norwegian syncope sometime before 1150, it may be argued on linguistic grounds that these names were coined within the period ca. 800–1100. Given that name elements denoting major topography and settlement are thought to be the first names of Scandinavian origin in the north Atlantic area, the predominance of major topography and settlement-denoting elements in *Pap-* names (and among the catalogued Hebridean *Pap-* island names) points to their origin in the earliest period of Scandinavian settlement. Taken together, then, the linguistic and place-name evidence suggests strongly that *Pap-* names reflect earliest Norse settlement.

Conclusions and Further Problems

This chapter has proposed important refinements to our understanding of the use of *pap*-element place names. *Pap-* names are Norse names and may be among the earliest Scandinavian-origin names in the north Atlantic area. As Norse names, they are not directly related to early Christian settlement *before* the Viking Age. However, an indirect relationship remains possible and may be suggested by potentially early ecclesiastical structures and cross sculpture at or near *Pap-* sites (Lowe 2002; Fisher 2002). Nevertheless, the argument made here is that, on their own, *Pap-* names should not be seen to remember early Christian settlement *before* the Viking Age but should be interpreted as reflecting the earliest Scandinavian colonization of the north Atlantic area. This highlights the poorly understood, yet apparently real, relationship between the area's Norse speakers and early Christian communities. When cast against the backdrop of strong early Christian associations for the Hebrides, future research might consider why *Pap-* names are regularly distributed in the Scottish islands but are rare and clustered in the Faroe Islands and Iceland.

4 Seljaland, Vestur-Eyjafjallahreppur, Iceland

Mér liggur við að efast um, að hellarnir séu frá Íslands bygðar tíma. Mundi ekki hugsanlegt, að þeir gæti verið eldri? Mér hefir dottið í hug, að þeir kunni, ef til vill, að vera eftir papa, eða hina írsku menn, sem hér voru fyrri en vorir norrænu feður.

(I have begun to doubt whether these caves are from Iceland's [Norse] settlement period. Is it not conceivable that they could be older? It has occurred to me that they could have been made by *papar*, or the Irish men who were here before our Norse fathers.)

Brynjúlfur Jónsson, *Rannsókn í Rangárþingi sumarið 1901*[1]

Haustið 1905, 6. okt., 3 árum eftir að grein Brynjúlfs Jónassonar í Árbók Fornleifafél. frá 1902 var komin út, kom í blaðinu "Fjallkonan" fyrri hluti greinar eftir Einar Benediktsson, með yfirskriftinni *Íra-býlin* ... Segir höfundurinn, að hann hafi "lengi haldið það víst, að áður en Norðmenn, feður vorir, fundu eyjuna, sem vér byggjum, hafi mannavist og mannvirki fundizt víðs vegar um Ísland, miklu meiri en sagnir eru enn orðnar ljósar um ..."

Að því er snertir þennan heyhelli á Ægissíðu ræður hann það, að hann sé eftir írska munka, sérstaklega af krossmörkum í honum, sem "eru höggvin á víð og dreif um hvelfingu hellisins," og "krossmarki allstóru" á hellisgaflinum innst, sem hann nefnir í því sambandi kórþil.

(The autumn of 1905, October 6th, three years after Brynjúlfur Jónsson's article in *Árbók hins Íslenzka Fornleifafélagsins* (1902) appeared, Einar Benediktsson published the first half of an article in the newspaper *Fjallkonan* (The Mountain Woman) with the title "Irish-abodes"... The writer said that he had "long held it probable that, from before the Norse (our fathers) found the island that we settled, people's dwellings and structures have been found far and wide in Iceland, more than has become clear in accounts." ...

He concludes, with regards to this hay-cave at Ægissíða, that it is the work of Irish monks, particularly cross-marks in the cave, that "are cut in many places on the cave vaults," and "a rather large cross-mark" in the innermost corner, which he refers to as choir panelling.)

Matthías Þórðarson[2]

Stór hellir er í kletti bak við gamla bæjarstæði á Seljalandi undir Eyjafjöllum. Hellirinn er í röð merkra þjóðminja, alsættur krossmörkum og ristum af ýmsum toga, allt aftan frá miðöldum.

(A large cave is in a crag at the back of the old farm-site at Seljaland under Eyjafjöll. The cave is in a row of national monuments, covered with cross-marks and various carvings, reaching as far back as the Middle Ages.)

Þórður Tómasson í Skógum, *Setið við sagnabrunn*[3]

Since the early twentieth century some scholars have related artificial cave sites in southern Iceland to the earliest settlement of the island by monastic communities of Gaels. These sites present an enigma: artificial caves are the best preserved and most numerous medieval structures to survive as visible monuments in Iceland and yet have received the least attention. Given that the shelter provided by temporary and permanent constructions (such as pithouses, longhouses, or caves) is key to the survival of human populations in the north Atlantic area, cave buildings are long overdue for in-depth study.

Brynjúlfur Jónsson (and subsequently Einar Benediktsson) proposed that these caves, constructed by people and ranging from person-sized shelters to large two-storeyed chambers, housed Iceland's early "Irish" monastic communities. Writing a generation later, Matthías Þórðarson took a more cautious approach, instead stressing the antiquity and uncertain origin of these medieval sites.[4] Despite renewed attention over the last twenty years, these numerous caves, still thought to be early, have yet to be integrated into the island's settlement sequence. As the relationship between these sites and early Irish religious communities is unclear, chapters 4 to 7 seek to achieve some resolution to this question. Specifically, chapters 4, 5, and 7 focus on aspects of the built environment that is characteristic of human occupation, whereas human-induced landscape changes are explored in chapter 6. In short, chapters 4 to 7, the Seljaland section, select a cave group for study and assess the origins and role of these caves in their natural and cultural landscape.

Investigations of cave use elsewhere suggest that one might expect "the distribution of utilised caves… [to] broadly reflect the geology of the country"

(Branigan and Dearne 1992: 38). Iceland's geology makes possible the construction of cave sites in several regions (for example, in the south, southeast, and northeast); however, there is no obvious physical or cultural reason for the extreme concentration of caves in southern Iceland (plotted in figure 4.1). The challenge for the Seljaland section is to put this cave group into context. The present chapter reports the results of a field survey at Seljaland in the Eyjafjallasveit district of southern Iceland, selects the caves at Seljaland for detailed study, and attempts to relate them to their archaeological and physical environments. In southern Iceland nearly two hundred artificial caves have been cut into palagonite tuff or soft sandstone. An important question is the date of these caves. As the chapter epigraphs illustrate, earlier generations of scholarship have related some of the sites to settlements of papar, while more recent workers are cautious of such ideas, instead stressing that the caves are ripe for research.[5] Given that Icelandic cave use is described in the early literature about medieval Scandinavia[6] and that cave use formed an aspect of early Christian settlement in Scotland and Ireland (for example, Ahronson et al. 2006; Ahronson and Charles-Edwards 2010), claims for the antiquity of these sites must be taken seriously. Furthermore, following upon the methodological ideas explored in chapter 2, we might propose that early Christian associations for these caves be addressed holistically – by which I mean in light not only of archaeological materials but also of place names and literature. To elaborate, identifying papar or early Christian Gaels in Iceland has proved to be archaeologically problematic. However, the preceding chapter's toponymic study suggests that the Icelandic occurrences of *Pap-* names result from the interactions of early Christian communities with Viking Age Scandinavian-speaking colonists,[7] and this is a conclusion that may be set against early literature from the Gaelic world that describes journeys to the island by eighth-century clerics, as well as medieval Icelandic literature that identifies Irish papar as Iceland's first settlers. A danger with isolated consideration of the materials of a single field is that it may alternatively encourage the archaeologist to be sceptical of early Christian settlement, encourage the place-name scholar to elaborate a scenario of papar and Norse interaction in the early Viking Age, and encourage the literature scholar to argue for two discrete settlements with minimal interaction: of early Christian Gaels throughout the eighth century and Norse beginning at the end of the ninth. Each of these interpretations is weakened by the others; integrative work is needed to accommodate the results of each field of research. To anticipate, I contend that the fresh research reported in the following pages promises some resolution to the wider problem of integrating the mono-disciplinary perspectives outlined above. Furthermore, by assessing whether southern Iceland's artificial caves could have originated with religious communities of Gaels, research at Seljaland contributes to the thrust of this book (that is, whatever the results may be, the tackling of this question may be expected to inform our understanding of the early medieval relationships between Atlantic Scotland, the Faroe Islands, and Iceland).

Settlement Context

Modern Iceland is generally thought to inherit patterns of settlement and resource exploitation from Scandinavian groups, who are believed to have entered an "empty" landscape under their own pioneering initiative in the late ninth century. The arrival and survival of people in a new environment such as southern Iceland may be identified both from preserved archaeological material and from impacts upon the landscape. Finds from Eyjafjallasveit suggest that the region was settled by the Norse within the *landnám* period (870–930), though the wide date brackets for these artefact types are a problem.[8] *Landnámabók*, whose first version is dated to the twelfth century, also points to Norse colonization of the area at that time, with descriptions of eight early settlement farms (three of which may be located today),[9] and claims that this portion of the island was settled late in this landnám period.[10] Care must be taken when dealing with this source, however, as older data had been reworked with contemporary purpose. In other words, *Landnámabók* locates Viking Age settlements in order to legitimize major landholders in the later medieval period. Intriguingly, the area's place names (as recorded in *Landnámabók*) include a notable concentration of Celtic-element names – more numerous in Eyjafjallasveit than in the rest of Rangárvallasýsla district.

Let us focus on *Seljaland*, which new discoveries indicate is the oldest recorded farm name in its regional unit of Vestur-Eyjafjallahreppur. Thus we may identify, in literature from the late eleventh or twelfth century, that the *Seljaland*-element names *Seljalandsar* ("Seljaland river") and *Seljalandsmúli* ("Seljaland promontory") act as geographical markers in the *Sturlubók*, *Hauksbók*, and *Melabók* texts of *Landnámabók.*[11] These attestations are important discoveries, which suggest that the *Seljaland* name is among the oldest place names in Iceland, probably dating from at least the twelfth century (and potentially earlier). Furthermore, this newly identified early dating for the *Seljaland* name calls for a rethinking of Sveinbjarnardóttir's proposals regarding that place, as it presents a fundamental problem for her analysis.

To elaborate: in her study of settlement in Eyjafjallasveit, Sveinbjarnardóttir identified the first mention of *Seljaland* in a Church deed from 1332 and, unusually, understood that place name as "shieling land" (rather than the plural "shielings land").[12] On these grounds, she proposed Seljaland to have been an early dependency of the nearby Dalur farm (Sveinbjarnardóttir 1991: 76). A serious

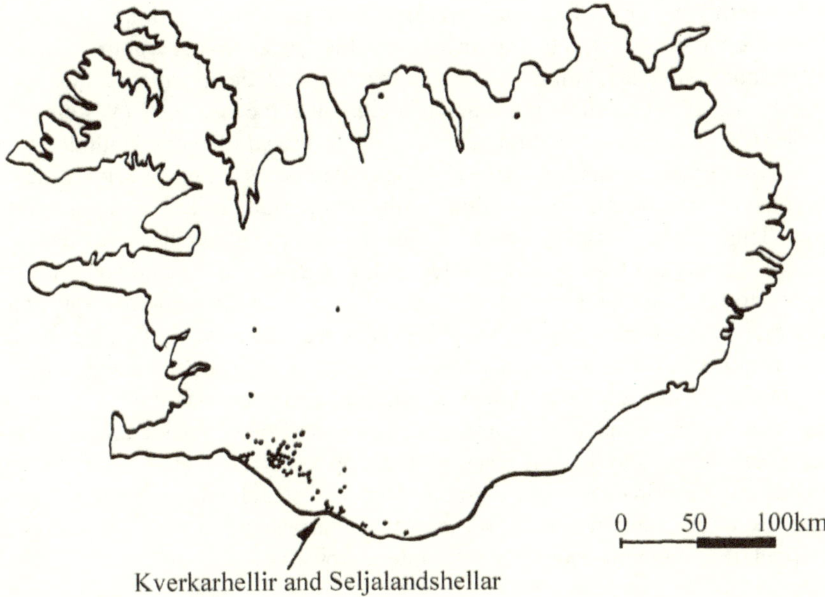

Figure 4.1 Distribution of artificial caves across Iceland. The extreme concentration of caves in southern Iceland is *not* limited by the geology of the island (i.e., the Holocene lithology of southeastern and northeastern Iceland is comparable to that of southern Iceland, yet there is no concentration in the southeast and northeast). Adapted from Hjartarson et al. (1991: 12).

difficulty for this interpretation, however, is that Seljaland can now be identified in the older written materials mentioned above, and these newly discovered attestations of the *Seljaland* name from the century *before* Dalur's first recorded appearance introduce a logical flaw into Sveinbjarnardóttir's argument. In other words, while Dalur first appears in a partial church list written soon after 1200,[13] Seljaland is well attested in literature from the previous century, where the *Seljaland*-element names *Seljalandsar* and *Seljalandsmúli* act as landmarks in multiple *Landnámabók* texts. Furthermore, there are problems with Sveinbjarnardóttir's etymology as, in order for us to accept her analysis of *Seljaland*, we would expect (a) the *sel-* element to be singular (not *selja*, which may instead reflect the plural form "shielings"), and (b) the *sel-* element to be positioned at the end of the word (not the beginning). Therefore, rather than suggesting that Seljaland was a late dependency of Dalur, our reconsideration instead holds that the *Seljaland* name is among the oldest recorded farm names in Iceland.

Projecting patterns of land use and land division described in late medieval literature backwards into the landnám period is one approach commonly used by Icelandic scholars, "on the basis that these late medieval patterns must ultimately derive from choices made at the beginning of the *landnám*" (Vésteinsson 1998: 6). Given this tradition, the use of *Seljaland*-element landmarks in *Landnámabók*'s account of earliest Norse settlement is suggestive, pointing to the place's existence from the initial settlement period, at least as a "marked" area. This would be consistent with the important ecological niches and resources (discussed later in this chapter) that converge at Seljaland and are presumed to have encouraged the site's selection in the early settlement process. The merits of this idea may be suggested by the area's above-ground archaeological material, which certainly testifies to management strategies for these resources. Fortunately, assessment of whether Seljaland was indeed a site of early settlement is made possible by the concentration of visible archaeological features there and the region's enviable tephra sequence, thus corroborating the legacy of environmental and archaeological research that points to the area as an excellent arena for study of the island's earliest archaeological past and, particularly, of human-environmental interactions.

Environmental Context

In comparison to the rest of Europe, Iceland was settled very late, and human settlement triggered transformations of the environment, which were distinct from previous trajectories of natural change. The period of earliest settlement established patterns of social organization, land use, and impacts upon the environment, setting in place historical legacies of landownership and environmental exploitation that are visible in both above-ground archaeological features and in the area's sediments. The island was transformed over these centuries: birch woodland was cleared; domesticated animals and crops were introduced; native mammal, bird, and fish populations were overexploited; natural vegetation cover was stripped; and consequently the soils were destabilized. These human impacts set in motion or accentuated processes that have resulted in an environmental disaster – modern-day Iceland's unstable soils and heavily eroded landscape.

Throughout this period a dynamic natural environment has bounded the Markarfljót and Eyjafjallasveit areas of Iceland (figure 4.2). Hekla lies to the north, while to the east the landscape is dominated by the glaciers Eyjafjallajökull and Mýrdalsjökull as well as the active central volcano of Katla. The escarpment that forms Seljaland is itself a landmark, looking west over the glacial river Markarfljót and the lowland coastal plain (*sandur*), as well as southwest to the nearby Westman Islands. Today constrained to one powerful channel, the

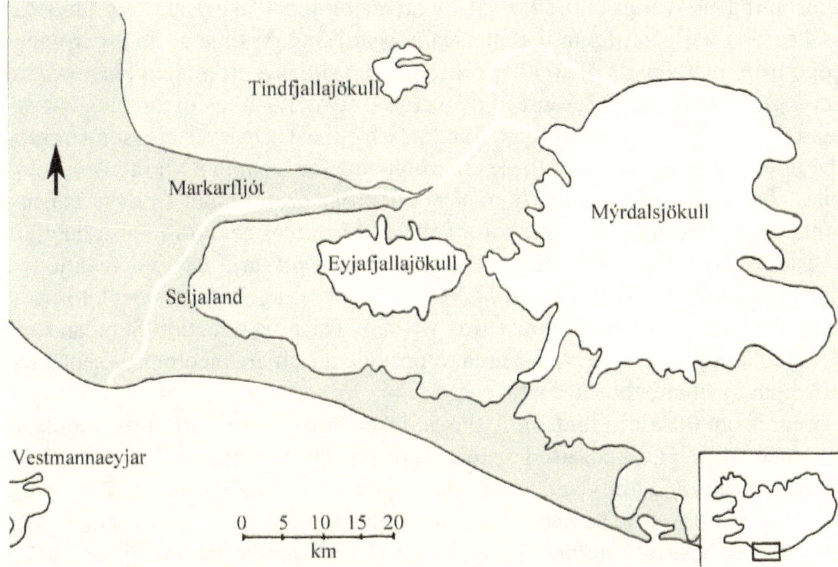

Figure 4.2 Location of Seljaland in southern Iceland. The land above the escarpment edge overlooks the wide sandur plain and coastline. The arrow indicates north. Adapted from Simpson et al. (2001: 178).

Markarfljót exemplifies environmental change over historical time, having flowed through winding and constantly migrating channels across a very large delta at the time of early settlement.

Fortunately chronological precision is possible for many events (archaeological deposits as well as landscape and vegetation change) because of the technique of *tephrochronology*. Tephrochronology uses the layers of ash (*tephrae*)[14] deposited by volcanic eruptions for chronological precision. Discussed at length in chapters 5 and 6, the study of volcanic airfall deposits is a powerful dating tool, particularly applicable to the excellent tephra sequence at Seljaland; within the historic period, tephra deposits there include a sequence of twelve layers from the 1947 Hekla eruption to the ca. 870 Vatnaöldur tephra layer, also known as the landnám tephra – and all clearly separated by wind-blown sediments.

Problem and Context

Chapters 4 through 7 integrate aspects of archaeological and environmental research at Seljaland, a well-constrained study area that is characterized by substantial above-ground survival of archaeological material.[15] Its physical and ecological position in the landscape is striking. Visible as an escarpment edge from many parts of southern Iceland, the site is a prominent place where ecological niches and resources converge – namely, areas of highland, lowland plain, cliff, river, marshland, and nearby coast. Orri Vésteinsson stresses the importance of access to these environments for Iceland's Viking Age colonists; from an early period, human populations are thought to have consistently exploited the concentration of varied resources found in these habitats (Vésteinsson 1998: 6–12). In addition, the *Seljaland* farm name is mentioned indirectly in the medieval *Landnámabók*, suggesting its settlement from at least the time at which that text was written. Thus, in selecting Seljaland for detailed study, one expects the area to provide a rich archaeological sequence in which to situate the cave sites there.

Seen from the air in figure 4.3, the Seljaland area forms part of the highland summer grazing grounds used by local farmers. The vegetation is characterized by low shrubs and grassland and is, except for a sheltered *kverk* (small corrie), without tree cover. (The *kverk* has been fenced off from livestock since 1981 and is now host to a number of well-established trees with thickly vegetated understorey.)[16] A ridge runs across Seljaland, along which lie the cave sites Kverkarhellir and Seljalandshellar,[17] while the Seljalandsá (Seljaland river) runs east-west along the northern edge of the study area until it cascades off the escarpment onto the lowland sandur plain in a spectacular waterfall, Seljalandsfoss (Seljaland waterfall). The eastern boundary is marked by the Hofsá/Veystri-Hofsá, a north-south running river, beyond which the land ascends steeply to higher mountainous ground. The southern boundary is delimited by the escarpment or lowland boundary, the western edge forming a natural border of cliffs within which the Kverkarhellir cave site is located, overlooking the heavily sedimented sandur plain.

The problem for this chapter focuses upon the poorly understood origins of Iceland's cross-marked caves.[18] This rare situation in Atlantic archaeology, of investigating a well-represented site type *yet to be integrated into the settlement sequence*, spurred my field program at Seljaland (for example, Ahronson 2002a: 111, 115; 2003b: 56; 2004: 79).

Hypotheses

The artificial caves at Seljaland, with their enigmatic rock-cut sculpture, do not exist in isolation. Rather, these sites are situated in a human and physical landscape. Correspondingly, understanding the distribution and chronology of archaeological features at Seljaland enables consideration of whether caves

Figure 4.3 Study area. Adapted from aerial photograph (1984 series) of Seljaland, based on data from National Land Survey of Iceland (www.lmi.is/wp-content/uploads/2013/10/License-for-use-of-free-NLSI-data-General-Terms.pdf). Scale 1:10000.

represent a different type of settlement to more "traditional" farm sites or a subset of settlement. Our two competing hypotheses propose that (a) the Seljaland caves are nested within the traditional farm landscape or (b) the Seljaland caves are at odds with (or independent of) the traditional farm landscape.

Method

In order to situate the Seljaland caves within a landscape of settlement, visible archaeological features at Seljaland were surveyed from 17 to 22 September 2001, in particularly wet conditions. Fieldworkers on this aspect of the Seljaland Project were Guðmundur Helgi Jónsson and Florian Huber. Shown in figure 4.3, the boundaries of the study area were selected for a variety of reasons. The river Seljalandsá was chosen as a northern edge on the grounds that this landscape feature acted as a landmark in the island's oldest literature. The western and southern boundaries were delineated by the escarpment edge; this line represents the boundary between the sandur plain and the grassland of Seljaland. Notably, the area of modern farm buildings was not included (see, for instance, figure 4.4), because the migrating route of the Markarfljót – only artificially stabilized in recent centuries – is recorded to have flowed over this area, apparently taking it to the mouth of the Seljalandshellar caves in 1836 and probably destroying or burying older archaeological deposits (Hjartarson et al. 1991: 246). Similarly, twentieth-century road construction involved the dynamiting of the Setberg farm site, at the extreme southwest of the study area (Hálfdan Ómar Hálfdanarson, personal communication), thus providing grounds for choosing the road as a practical boundary. The eastern limit of the study area was chosen along a line defined by the Hofsá/Veystri-Hofsá, with a north-south ridge of higher ground lying eastwards. An aerial photograph of Seljaland formed the basis for the survey, with the entire area being walked in strips 20–30 metres apart. To enable interpretion of each structure, all visible features were photographed, measured, or sketched to scale, and global positioning satellite (GPS) points taken. In the following illustrations the arrow indicates north. All photographs in figures 4.5–4.10 (except 4.6) and 4.14–4.15 were taken by Florian Huber.

Results and Discussion

The merits of selecting the boundaries outlined above may be demonstrated by the distribution of archaeological sites; there is a thinning out of archaeological features in the northern, western, and eastern sections of the study area (figure 4.6). Furthermore, the survey identified the southern section of the area as a focus for activity (which includes the caves), with clusters of secondary sites located on the higher ground overlooking that "ridge" of settlement. In the following pages, the survey sites are summarized in table 4.1, as well as located by GPS coordinates in table 4.2 and by superimposition upon the aerial plan in figures 4.4 and 4.6. Photographs and scaled sketches are presented as figures 4.5 and 4.7–4.15.

At the edge of an escarpment overlooking the sandur plain, the Seljaland area is visually prominent in southern Iceland. The escarpment rises gently to its highest and most exposed point, Krosshóll, where the remains of the eroded small structure SLJ 18 survive (figure 4.16). Bounded by rivers, cliffs, and escarpment edge, this naturally bordered unit has a high concentration of the classic Icelandic farming assemblage of archaeological features, in addition to a number of exceptional structures. The typical assemblage of visible features

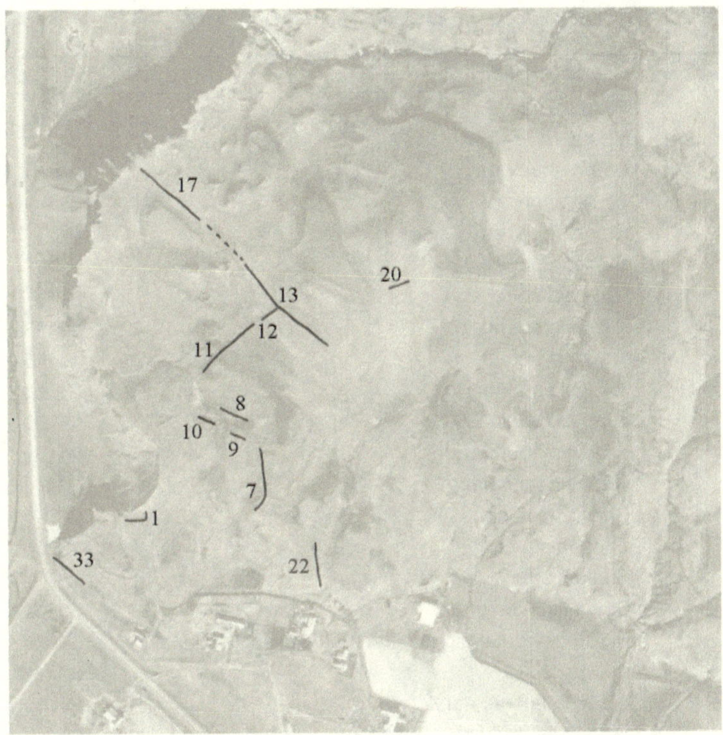

Figure 4.4 Adapted aerial photograph of study area with the following field boundaries located: SLJ 1, SLJ 7, SLJ 8, SLJ 9, SLJ 10, SLJ 11, SLJ 12, SLJ 13, SLJ 17, SLJ 20, SLJ 22, SLJ 33. Based on data from National Land Survey of Iceland (1984 series) (www.lmi.is/wp-content/uploads/2013/10/License-for-use-of-free-NLSI-data-General-Terms.pdf). Scale 1:10000.

relating to farming practices includes many animal houses, such as a possible shieling site (SLJ 29), and a large L-shaped structure (SLJ 14), probably a nineteenth- or twentieth-century *fjárhús* (sheep house) for hay storage and to house sheep during the winter. There is also a network of turf- and stone-walled field boundaries. These walls vary in size, style, material, and, most likely, age. Reuse of older boundaries is a possibility, while heavily eroded examples point to abandonment. In contrast, other large distinct walls still stand as physical boundaries today. Although it would be unusual for prominent, good, and accessible farmland to be subdivided to such an extreme, the concentration of animal houses and field boundaries could suggest shared use of Seljaland's

Table 4.1 List of sites surveyed at Seljaland (SLJ)

Site number	Site description	GPS points
1	Field boundary (?)	1, 2
2	Sheep house (?)	3
3	Stone structure	4
4	Stone structure	5
5	Stone structure	6
6	Stone structure	7
7	Turf field boundary	9–11
8	Turf field boundary	12, 13
9	Turf field boundary	14, 15
10	Turf field boundary	16, 17
11	Turf field boundary	18–20
12	Turf field boundary	21, 22
13	Turf field boundary	23–6
14	Sheep house and hay cellar (*fjárhús?*)	27
15	Sunken structure	28
16	Sunken structure	29
17	Stone field boundary	30, 31
18	Sub-rectangular stone structure (Krosshóll "chapel")	32
19	Cairn	33
20	Stone field boundary	34–5
21	Small turf structure	36
22	Turf field boundary	37, 38
23	Small turf and stone structure	40
24	Large turf and stone structure	41, 42
25	Three-chambered artificial cave (Seljalandshellar)	39
26	Sunken feature (possible structure?)	43
27	Three stone, turf, and concrete structures	44
28	Three related turf and stone structures	45
29	Turf and stone as well as turf structures (*shieling?*)	46
30	Structural features	52
31	Wood fragment nailed to rock-face	53
32	Stone structure	54
33	Turf field boundary	55–6
34	Artificial cave (Þrasahellir)	57
35	Artificial cave (Kverkarhellir)	61
36	Redirected (?) stream	47–51
37	Cairn	58
38	Cairn	59
39	Cairn	60

Table 4.2 GPS points and coordinates for Seljaland survey sites

GPS point	GPS coordinate	GPS point	GPS coordinate
1	N 63 36 35.6" W 19 59 37.1"	32	N 63 36 45.6" W 19 59 05.4"
2	N 63 36 35.6" W 19 59 35.5"	33	N 63 36 45.6" W 19 59 05.2"
3	N 63 36 33.7" W 19 59 30.3"	34	N 63 36 43.6" W 19 59 10.1"
4	N 63 36 33.7" W 19 59 26.8"	35	N 63 36 43.8" W 19 59 09.2"
5	N 63 36 34.4" W 19 59 24.7"	36	N 63 36 31.4" W 19 59 17.4"
6	N 63 36 34.0" W 19 59 24.2"	37	N 63 36 31.7" W 19 59 20.7"
7	N 63 36 38.5" W 19 59 23.9"	38	N 63 36 33.6" W 19 59 20.2"
8	N 63 36 37.8" W 19 59 23.8"	39	N 63 36 30.5" W 19 59 17.7"
9	N 63 36 36.9" W 19 59 23.5"	40	N 63 36 30.3" W 19 59 17.8"
10	N 63 36 36.3" W 19 59 23.2"	41	N 63 36 30.6" W 19 59 18.5"
11	N 63 36 35.7" W 19 59 24.0"	42	N 63 36 30.8" W 19 59 18.7"
12	N 63 36 39.5" W 19 59 24.7"	43	N 63 36 33.6" W 19 59 22.0"
13	N 63 36 39.8" W 19 59 25.8"	44	N 63 36 30.3" W 19 59 08.0"
14	N 63 36 38.8" W 19 59 25.3"	45	N 63 36 29.6" W 19 58 58.7"
15	N 63 36 38.7" W 19 59 24.7"	46	N 63 36 46.7" W 19 58 38.7"
16	N 63 36 39.4" W 19 59 27.5"	47	N 63 36 34.3" W 19 59 13.4"
17	N 63 36 39.6" W 19 59 28.7"	48	N 63 36 33.8" W 19 59 16.1"
18	N 63 36 41.2" W 19 59 28.1"	49	N 63 36 32.6" W 19 59 18.0"
19	N 63 36 41.7" W 19 59 26.8"	50	N 63 36 31.6" W 19 59 18.3"
20	N 63 36 42.6" W 19 59 24.3"	51	N 63 36 31.2" W 19 59 18.7"
21	N 63 36 43.9" W 19 59 18.6"	52	N 63 36 36.7" W 19 59 40.2"
22	N 63 36 43.3" W 19 59 21.3"	53	N 63 36 34.9" W 19 59 42.4"
23	N 63 36 46.2" W 19 59 19.6"	54	N 63 36 33.8" W 19 59 43.5"
24	N 63 36 44.7" W 19 59 18.0"	55	N 63 36 35.0" W 19 59 43.1"
25	N 63 36 41.8" W 19 59 15.3"	56	N 63 36 32.1" W 19 59 40.7"
26	N 63 36 40.1" W 19 59 13.3"	57	N 63 36 30.4" W 19 59 11.6"
27	N 63 36 44.5" W 19 59 26.4"	58	N 63 36 48.2" W 19 59 21.2"
28	N 63 36 44.6" W 19 59 27.1"	59	N 63 36 48.5" W 19 59 22.1"
29	N 63 36 45.1" W 19 59 28.2"	60	N 63 36 48.5" W 19 59 22.6"
30	N 63 36 50.4" W 19 59 31.2"	61	N 63 36 40.4" W 19 59 49.4"
31	N 63 36 48.6" W 19 59 24.5"		

Figure 4.5 SLJ 17: Stone field boundary. Barbed wire and fallen post indicate modern use or reuse of this boundary. Looking northwest.

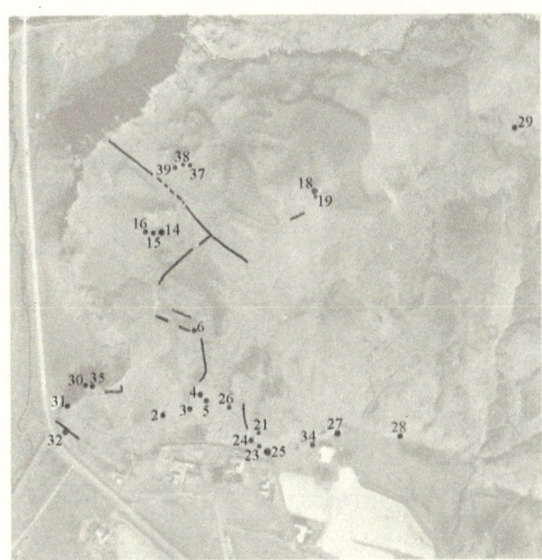

Figure 4.6 Adapted aerial photograph of study area, locating all surveyed features. Field boundaries (the subject of figure 4.4) are unnumbered, while all other features are identified by their SLJ number. Based on data from National Land Survey of Iceland (1984 series) (www.lmi.is/wp-content/uploads/2013/10/License-for-use-of-free-NLSI-data-General-Terms.pdf). Scale 1:15000.

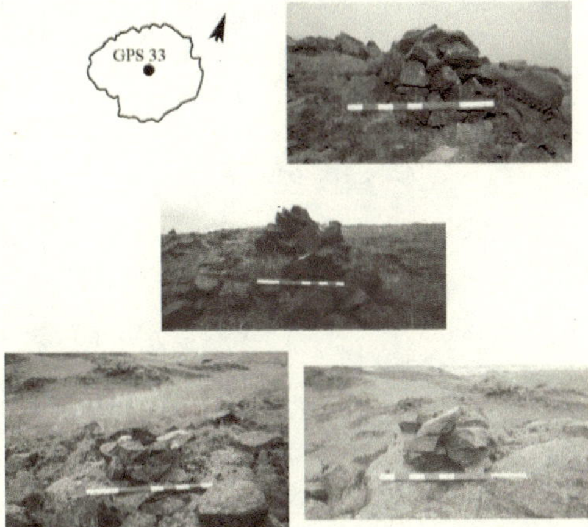

Figure 4.7 *Above left.* SLJ 19: Cairn; 0.8 m in height; scale 1:120. *Above right.* SLJ 19: Looking north. *Middle.* SLJ 37: Cairn, looking north. *Below left.* SLJ 38: Cairn, looking north. *Below right.* SLJ 39: Cairn, looking north.

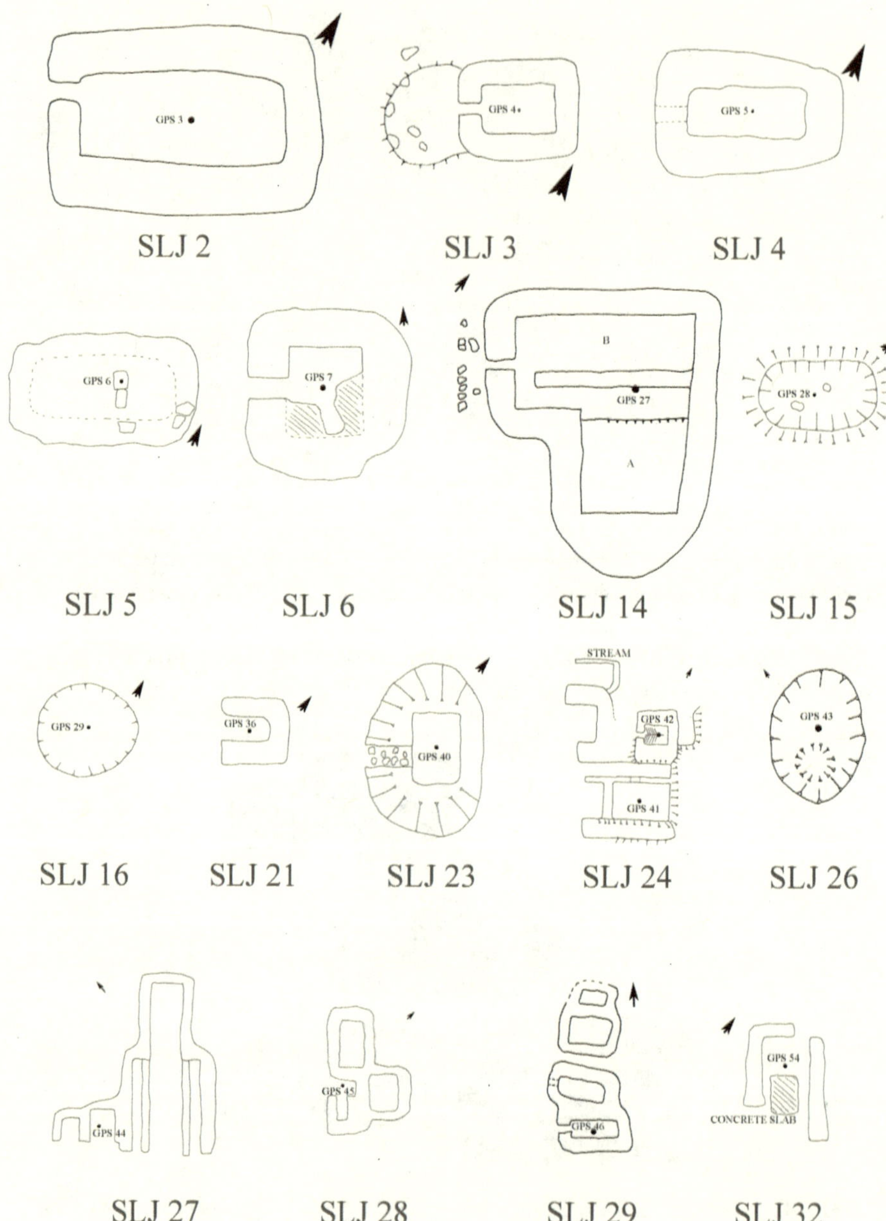
GPS 3
GPS 4
GPS 5
SLJ 2
SLJ 3
SLJ 4
GPS 6
GPS 7
B
GPS 27
A
GPS 28
SLJ 5
SLJ 6
SLJ 14
SLJ 15
STREAM
GPS 29
GPS 36
GPS 40
GPS 42
GPS 41
GPS 43
SLJ 16
SLJ 21
SLJ 23
SLJ 24
SLJ 26
GPS 44
GPS 45
GPS 46
GPS 54
CONCRETE SLAB
SLJ 27
SLJ 28
SLJ 29
SLJ 32

Figure 4.8 SLJ 2: Possible sheep house; stone walls survive up to a height of 1.5 m; inside of structure is filled with collapsed stone, wooden beams, and occasionally corrugated iron, probably from roof; scale 1:320. SLJ 3: Stone structure; walls survive up to a height of c. 1 m; overgrown with a few visible stones; the area in front of the entrance is raised and contains some stones; scale 1:320. SLJ 4: Stone structure; walls survive up to a height of 1 m; very overgrown; because of collapsed stones, entrance is unclear; scale 1:320. SLJ 5: Stone structure; walls survive up to a height of 0.30–0.40 m; visible stones are planned; very overgrown and difficult to identify extent of inner walls (shown by dotted line); scale 1:320. SLJ 6: Stone structure; walls survive up to a height of c. 1 m; overgrown with visible stone walls; occasional corrugated iron; southern half of structure contains possible collapse or some kind of division within the structure; scale 1:320. SLJ 14: Sheep house and hay cellar (*fjárhús*?); walls survive up to a height of 3.3 m; area A is deeper than the rest of the structure; area B is divided by a 0.50 m high stone wall; scale 1:400. SLJ 15: Sunken structure; feature reaches a depth of 1 m; completely overgrown; no visible wall structure but "wall mound" is in line with SLJ 14 and 16 (and lies directly to the northwest of SLJ 14); scale 1:320. SLJ 16: Sunken structure; shallow sunken feature completely overgrown and aligned with SLJ 14 and 15; no visible stones; scale 1:320. SLJ 21: Small turf structure; turf walls survive up to a height of c. 0.45 m; scale 1:320. SLJ 23: Small turf and stone structure; wall constructed of stone with turf on outside; collapsed entrance; scale 1:320. SLJ 24: Large turf and stone structure; walls surviving up to a height of 1.8 m; scale 1:400. SLJ 26: Sunken feature; scale 1:160. SLJ 27: Three stone, turf, and concrete structures; walls survive up to a height of 1.8 m; scale 1:800. SLJ 28: Three related turf and stone structures; walls survive up to a height of 1.5 m; scale 1:800. SLJ 29: Turf and stone as well as turf structures (*shieling*?); overgrown walls survive up to a height of 0.6 m; southern structure is of turf and stone, and the northern three structures are of turf; scale 1:800. SLJ 32: Stone structure; stone walls survive up to a height of 0.7 m; large concrete block sitting in middle of the structure, probably not result of collapse; scale 1:400.

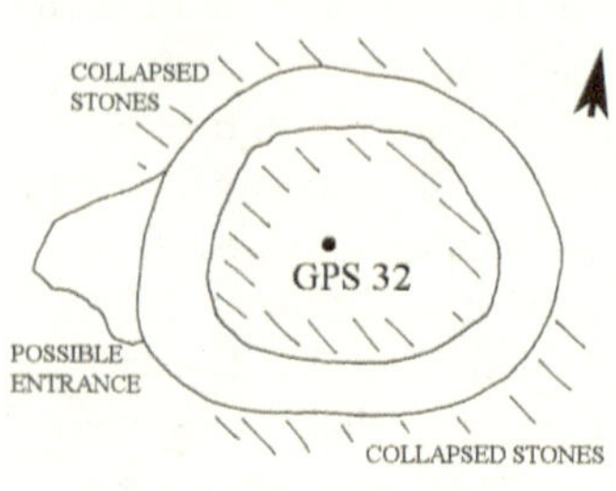

Figure 4.9 SLJ 18: Sub-rectangular stone structure (Krosshóll "chapel"). Stone walls surviving up to a height of 0.50–0.60 m (1–2 rows of stones). Mostly collapsed. Some rocks, present before construction, may have been incorporated into the structure. Scale 1:160. Photograph looking east.

Figure 4.10 SLJ 30: Structural features. Located immediately outside Kverkarhellir cave. Difficult to interpret structural details. Possible steep worked pathway linking the structure with the plain below. Scale 1:220. Photograph looking north.

resources by the local community, and the *Seljaland* place name, if indeed derived from "shielings land," may support this interpretation. Certainly, Kverkarhellir cave was used for communal purpose between 1872 and 1895, when the site (otherwise a sheep house) served as *þingstaður*, housing local parliamentary meetings in the spring, once the winter's accumulation of sheep manure had been removed (Tómasson [í Skógum] 1997: 151).

Exceptional sites include the caves Seljalandshellar/Papahellir (SLJ 25), Kverkarhellir (SLJ 35), and Þrasi/Þrasahellir (SLJ 34). These caves were dug into palagonite tuff (tool markings on the Kverkarhellir and Seljalandshellar wall surfaces are illustrated in figures 4.17 and 4.18, respectively). The

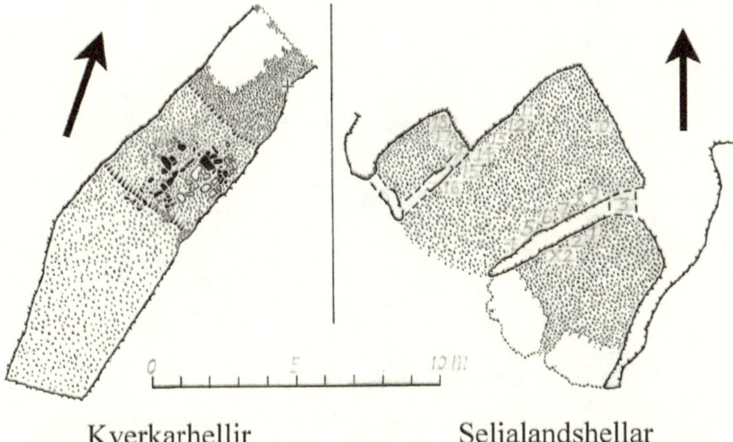

Figure 4.11 SLJ 25 (Seljalandshellar) and SLJ 35 (Kverkarhellir) plans. The crosshair at the eastern wall of the Kverkarhellir cave mouth indicates the site of cross KV, and the numbers on the Seljalandshellar plan indicate crosses SLJ 1–19 as well as the four mid-sized crosses represented by X2. The cross sculpture is discussed in chapter 7. The ground surface inside Kverkarhellir has been cleaned, recorded, and planned, while the Seljalandshellar plan is drawn from the published illustration in Hjartarson et al. (1991: 246). Drawn by Ian G. Scott.

Figure 4.12 SLJ 25: Three-chambered artificial cave (Seljalandshellar). Photograph looking northwest.

Figure 4.13 SLJ 35: Artificial cave (Kverkarhellir). Potentially two (or three) phases of construction, the oldest being a small chamber (height 2 m, width 3 m, depth 3 m). In the foreground a path runs from SLJ 30 (from which the photograph was taken) to the mouth of the cave, in shadow at the base of the left side of the rock outcrop. Note the steep descent from the cave mouth. Photograph looking southeast.

Figure 4.14 SLJ 34: Artificial cave (Þrasahellir). Entrance height is 1 m and width is 1.5 m, widening into a large low-roofed chamber. Sediments have accumulated to a substantial depth (perhaps 1+ m). Photograph looking north.

Figure 4.15 SLJ 31: Wood fragment nailed to rock face, 0.15 m in length. Nails are modern. Photograph looking east.

Figure 4.16 With its small eroded structure, Krosshóll is the highest point in the photograph (though to the east of the study area the land rises steeply and reaches greater elevation).

Figure 4.17 Tool markings from the east wall in the oldest section of Kverkarhellir (SLJ 35).

Figure 4.18 Tool markings from the east corner of the north wall of the Seljalandshellar (SLJ 25) middle chamber. Scale divided into 0.01 m and 0.05 m increments.

Seljalandshellar caves in particular are of interest, with their three distinct rooms, chimney, and 105 cross carvings on the surviving walls. Some antiquity is claimed for Kverkarhellir; this cave features in Jón Árnarson's collection of nineteenth-century folklore, where folk tradition describes human habitation there in the 1500s (Árnarson [1993] 1856: 200–2). If occupied at the same time, the multiple chambers of the Seljalandshellar (one with two floors), with the prominent cross sculpture cut into the walls, would presumably have been a primary site, and Kverkarhellir a secondary. Interpreting Þrasahellir, currently a low-roofed chamber, is difficult as sediments have accumulated to substantial depth (perhaps 1 m or more).

Another exceptional feature is the small west-oriented sub-rectangular stone structure (SLJ 18) at the prominent and exposed point known as Krosshóll (cross hill). Its size, shape, and west orientation have some similarity to early Christian drystone cell architecture, such as that found on North Rona and Canna in the Hebrides (Fisher 2001: 101, 114–16), while the site has religious associations; folklore describes the eroded Krosshóll structure as a "Catholic" chapel (Tómasson [í Skógum] 1997: 152). One possibility, difficult to assess given the thin soil cover, is that the structure indeed acted, at some period, as a cell or chapel. This is a priority for further excavation.

The hypotheses under consideration propose the Seljaland caves to be either coherent with or at odds with more traditional farm sites. The survey focused attention upon a line or "ridge" of features including all three cave areas, with the concentration of surveyed features found in the area of the Seljalandshellar, Þrasahellir, and modern farm buildings (seen in figure 4.6). Modern settlement may thus be noted as consonant with the Seljalandshellar and Þrasahellir but not coherent with Kverkarhellir. If these cave sites are contemporary, it is possible there has been a shift of focus in settlement (that is, from the line or ridge including the three cave sites to the cluster focused on the modern farm buildings). As the presence of Kverkarhellir has been key in formulating this idea, excavation of that site would be a critical test of the proposal that there was a shift in focus. Aside from location, the cave sites themselves lend some support to the hypothesis that they were primary sites in themselves. In other words, although these caves have acted in the modern period as a subset of more traditional farm settlement (that is, as sites to shelter animals, store goods, or dry or smoke foods), they have been used for purposes outside of the traditional farming landscape (that is, to house an outlaw in the sixteenth century and as a nineteenth-century *þingstaður*, or local parliament place). Furthermore, the prominence of cross sculpture in these caves suggests that use was made of already existing sites and that they were originally constructed for other purposes. To be precise, the cross sculpture points to the significance of the

Seljalandshellar caves as a Christian religious site, and detailed study of this sculpture should enable assessment of cultural affinities for these rock-cut crosses. Therefore, in seeking to resolve the competing hypotheses regarding the role of the cave sites, study of the cross sculpture is called for, while Kverkarhellir is of highest priority for excavation and may prove key in relating Seljaland's caves to the classic farm features revealed by the survey. In particular, dating the site using the local tephra sequence will be an important first step in the process.

Conclusions and Further Problems

The Seljaland archaeological survey revealed a good representation of a typical assemblage of human and animal house structures as well as field boundaries, many of which relate to farming practices. This "classic" assemblage is made exceptional in that structure types (such as shieling, fjárhús, and field boundaries) are well represented and survive well as visible features – and occur in an area provided with a powerful dating tool, an enviable tephrochronological sequence. This survey noted the special potential of the area for investigating human exploitation of the natural environment and continuity of land use. The unusual features such as the Krosshóll "chapel" and the Seljaland caves (Kverkarhellir in particular) warrant further investigation in their own right, as they are difficult to relate to the classic landscape of settlement (as revealed by the survey).[19]

The subdivision of land at Seljaland and the possibility of community use may be significant, especially in light of the potential derivation of the place name as "shielings land." Given its prominence in the landscape, good land, access to various habitats, and attestation in the island's earliest literature, one expects Seljaland to have been consistently exploited by human populations from an early period. If the Seljaland area was instead avoided in the initial process of Norse colonization and therefore found itself outside the early Norse farming landscape, then maybe the area could have been subdivided later as shielings between competing land owners, with the place name coined at this later point and subsequently incorporated into the medieval *Landnámabók* texts. One tantalizing possibility, which the Seljalandshellar's alternative (and potentially late) *Papahellir* name points to, is that the area may already have been occupied at the time of Norse land-taking. The archaeological invisibility of both Ari fróði's papar and Dicuil's eighth-century Gaelic clerics, however, is a problem for this suggestion.

In summary, archaeological survey of Seljaland has raised the possibility that the caves there were originally constructed as primary sites with a different focus of settlement to the traditional farming landscape revealed by survey. Excavation of Kverkarhellir was identified as a critical test of this idea. Fortunately the local tephra sequence may help date that site and additionally provide palaeoenvironmental data with which to assess land use changes over time. Furthermore, study of the cross sculpture in the Seljalandshellar and in Kverkarhellir should permit consideration of cultural affinities for these sites by comparison with the sculpture of Scandinavia as well as Britain and Ireland. Therefore, in order to understand the Seljaland caves better, these sites warrant further investigation by excavation (chapter 5), study of human-environmental interactions (chapter 6), and detailed examination of cross sculpture (chapter 7).

5 Dating the Cave

The sedimentary pile at any one place … is nothing more than a tiny and fragmentary record of vast periods of earth history.

Derek V. Ager, *The Nature of the Stratigraphical Record*[1]

For the archaeologist, the location of discard within a settlement is of great importance.

Michael B. Schiffer, *Formation Processes of the Archaeological Record*[2]

As discussed in the previous chapter, the Icelandic artificial cave sites are thought to be old (Holt and Guðmundsson 1980: 16–17), but their origins and history are enigmatic. As part of the Seljaland Project, test trenches at the mouth of Kverkarhellir cave identified debris from cave construction within a dated sequence of volcanic ash layers, or tephrae. Locating an episode of construction within the excellent chronological framework provided by these tephrae is an important step for understanding the caves.

Hjartarson and Gísladóttir describe the southern Iceland caves as including a number of "the oldest *housebuildings* in Iceland" (Hjartarson and Gísladóttir 1983: 133). Many caves are listed in 1709 land registers, while a late-twelfth-century description of Bishop Þórlakur's miracles mentions the collapse of a cattle cave.[3] It is noteworthy that cave use is described at such an early date, for the twelfth century is the period of the oldest Icelandic writing. Still earlier and from a Continental perspective, Adam of Bremen provides the first known description of Icelandic cave use in his eleventh-century account, where he writes of the island's inhabitants that "*in subterraneis habitant speluncis, communi tecto et strato gaudentes cum pecoribus suis*/they live in underground caves, glad to have roof and food and bed in common with their cattle" (*Adam*: bk. 4, ch. 36, skol. 153; Schmeidler 1917: 272; Tschan 1959: 217). Peculiar to many of these caves, as well as some Westman Island rock alcoves, are stylistically distinctive cross carvings that, taken together, form a coherent body of sculpture. These rock-cut crosses have some similarities to early Christian sculpture from other Atlantic areas. Furthermore, the modern ideas locating early Christian papar communities across the north Atlantic region are of significant antiquity and longevity. In southern Iceland, certain artificial caves are the subject of papar folklore, and *Pap-* names are sometimes associated with these places.[4] As mentioned in chapters 3 and 4, the Seljalandshellar caves are one such example, holding early Christian associations for the local community[5] and carrying the alternative name *Papahellir* (cave of papar), which was used as a child's name for that place (Hálfdan Ómar Hálfdanarson, personal communication). Although such associations certainly merit consideration, at present these caves remain a tantalizing enigma.

Investigations at Seljaland initially sought to contextualise the caves alongside the landscape of settlement there. Archaeological survey noted the possibility that the Seljaland caves had been constructed as primary sites independent of the modern settlement pattern, and called for the critical test of targeted excavation at Kverkarhellir in order to constrain cave use chronologically. For establishing a chronological framework, tephrochronology is particularly suitable. This dating technique uses tephra layers within the sedimentary record as time-parallel marker horizons, in other words as horizontally continuous units that represent an instance in time within the sedimentary record of a region. A regional chronology can be developed by tracing these tephra layers across an area, and independent ages can be obtained for these layers by using written materials, ice core data, and radiometric dating techniques. The stratified sequence of dated tephra layers can then provide a chronological framework within which to place events identified from the sedimentary record. As a chronological technique, tephrochronology produces remarkable results for southern Iceland generally, while a strong focus of research centres on Seljaland itself. Researchers have been drawn to the area because throughout the Holocene (approximately the last ten thousand years) a number of very active volcanic systems in close proximity to Seljaland have produced many visually and geochemically distinctive tephra layers. As centimetre-scale deposits clearly separated by wind-blown (or aeolian) sediments, these layers are particularly suitable for stratigraphy-based tephrochronology. This is a key point for the use of tephra layers at Seljaland: high rates of aeolian sediment accumulation have produced a sequence of deposits in which there is a real separation between tephra from 920 and from 935 (or even 1500 and 1510). The local historical tephra sequence has been well studied (Dugmore 1987) and comprises fall-out from the following eruptions (accompanied by AD dates):

Hekla, 1947 (Þórarinsson 1954); Katla, 1918 (Þórarinsson 1975); Eyjafjallajökull, 1821 (Larsen 1979); Katla, 1755 (Þórarinsson 1975); Katla, 1721 (Þórarinsson 1975); Hekla, 1597 (Þórarinsson 1967); Hekla, 1510 (Þórarinsson 1967); Katla, 1500 (Larsen 1984); Hekla, 1341 (Þórarinsson 1967); Eldgjá, 935 (Zielinski et al. 1995); Katla, ca. 920 (Hafliðarson et al. 1992); and Vatnaöldur, ca. 870 (the landnám tephra) (Grönvold et al. 1995; Zielinski et al. 1997). In short, the very detailed and well-constrained record of tephra layers developed for the region makes the Seljaland area ideally suited for the application of tephrochronology (Dugmore 1987; Larsen et al. 2001).

Problem and Context

Although suggested by medieval literature to be early, the period in which artificial caves were first constructed is uncertain. Dating of construction is thus crucial for understanding these sites. Applying tephrochronology is an important step and develops the earlier efforts to date human activity at another southern Icelandic cave site, Kolholtshellir (Holt and Guðmundsson 1980). Survey of the Seljaland area identified three caves: Þrasahellir, the Seljalandshellar, and Kverkarhellir. That survey called for excavation of Kverkarhellir as a critical test of the proposal that settlement at Seljaland shifted from a ridge including all three caves to the cluster defined by the modern buildings. As well as being an outlier to this modern settlement cluster, Kverkarhellir is the most practical of the cave sites at Seljaland to excavate. Both Þrasahellir and the Seljalandshellar, for instance, pose special challenges for targeted excavation of early historic deposits.[6] Þrasahellir, accessible through the partly infilled entrance, has experienced substantial accumulation of sediments, and the depth of this material presents practical difficulties for an exploratory program of excavation. In addition, the proximity of modern farm buildings suggests that Þrasahellir and the Seljalandshellar have experienced serious disturbance both inside and in the immediate vicinity of the caves. The three chambers of the Seljalandshellar, for example, have until recently been used as outbuildings that were shared among the nearby farms (Tómasson [í Skógum] 1997: 148–9). A further challenge for excavating the Seljalandshellar is posed by the wetness of the immediate area, though these water-logged soils also promise special possibilities for preservation. Kverkarhellir, however, is situated some distance from the modern settlement cluster, and, despite the cave interior having use that has been recorded since the early modern period,[7] high sediment accumulation rates on the well-drained slope outside the cave suggest that early historic sediments may lie beneath disturbed upper sediments. As mentioned in the survey, the reworking of surface material is described in the period from 1872 to 1895, when Kverkarhellir served alternatively as seasonal sheep house and local parliament site (*Þingstaður*) for the district. During this time the accumulated sheep dung from each winter was removed in preparation for the local parliamentary meeting (Tómasson [í Skógum] 1997: 151). The shovelling probably removed some depth of underlying cave deposits, and, in addition to depositing material, these events may have reworked surface sediments on the exterior slope. Perhaps more important, however, was the landscaping in the 1980s of Kverkin (the corrie in which Kverkarhellir lies) and the unfortunate "clearing out" of surface material from Kverkarhellir in the late 1990s. This work included significant disturbance of the upper sediments in the vicinity of the cave for the laying of stone pathways and extensive tree planting (Hálfdanarson, personal communication). In spite of these difficulties, Kverkarhellir nevertheless presents the most straightforward site for a program of excavation targeting the deeper early historic deposits (presumably those associated with earliest cave use).

Kverkarhellir is presented in figures 5.1–5.2. As I have noted elsewhere, two phases of construction may be suggested by floor heights (Ahronson 2002a: 114). To elaborate, the floor surface of the two metres nearest the cave mouth appears to be set lower than the floor surface of the rest of the cave, with sediments having accumulated on this lower surface to the level of the rest of the cave. The proposal is that the lower stone floor defines the original construction phase of the cave and that this younger "extension" was dug out after a period in which sediments had accumulated to a certain depth, and thereby keeping level with the sediments in the older phase. Excavation of the cave floors is necessary to assess the merits of this idea.

The cave fabric is a palagonite tuff and would have been dug out by iron-headed tools. The earliest phase may have expanded upon a relict sea-cut notch, and involved the digging of an area with approximate dimensions of 2 m (height) × 2 m (length) × 3 m (width) – and producing at least 12 m^3 of debris. It is possible that a rock-cut cross on the eastern wall is associated with this phase of construction. Assessing the necessary time and potential methods for the digging out of the cave would be a fruitful avenue for experimental research. In anticipation of such work, Edinburgh stonemason Gardiner Molloy as well as Chris Doherty of the Research Lab for Archaeology and the History of Art (Oxford) suggest that the construction of Kverkarhellir may be expected to have produced palagonite debris consisting largely of angular medium pebbles to small cobbles (roughly 10–120 mm), accompanied by substantial amounts of finer pebbles (2–10 mm) and later infilled with aeolian material (Molloy, personal communication; Doherty, personal communication).[8] Debris

Figure 5.1 Kverkarhellir cave mouth, looking south from site SLJ 30. Photograph by Tom McGovern.

Figure 5.2 Structural features inside cave, looking towards rear.

could include artefacts associated with construction such as damaged iron tools; however, considering the importance of recycling iron and the general rarity of artefacts from archaeological investigations in Iceland, the recovery of such material is unlikely. As a rule, the expected lithic debris (especially that produced by construction on this scale) should be dumped nearby, but avoiding access routes and activity areas (Schiffer 1987: 58–64). In the case of Kverkarhellir, topography presents limited possibilities, suggesting that an apron of waste would have been deposited on the slope outside the cave mouth. This depositional model is sketched in figure 5.3. The search to locate this construction debris poses the following question, tackled in this chapter: when was Kverkarhellir's earliest phase of construction?

Hypothesis

As touched upon earlier, Holt and Guðmundsson undertook limited excavation at Kolsholtshellir in 1975. Having surveyed eighteen artificial caves and completed a preliminary study of rock-cut crosses found at these sites, they selected the land of Kolsholtshellir, in the Villingaholtshreppur district of Árnessýsla, for field excavation. Instead of excavating the cave interior, their approach was to test trench an "*allstór öskuhaugur*" (fairly large ashheap) related to the cave. Their work recovered artefactual material from a stratified deposit that included a tephra layer suggested to be from Katla in 1500. They also identified a small oval-shaped lens of the landnám tephra (Vatnaöldur, ca. 870) near the base of the deposit and used this to imply that cave use began at this site sometime before ca. 870 (Holt and Guðmundsson 1980: 19–25).

These 1975 investigations highlighted the uncertain chronology for artificial caves and attempted to tackle the question of dating the earliest phase of construction. Their application of tephrochronology, however, could have been more fully described were it to have been undertaken today. Specifically, the reasoning behind their identification of the Katla 1500 tephra is unclear, while they appeal to expert authority for the landnám tephra without explaining the basis for this identification. Furthermore, if this isolated deposit is indeed landnám tephra, the potentially complex provenance for a single lens must be remembered; in addition to primary deposition as airfall, possible sources also include reworking of older material or even preservation within a later turf cutting. In short, Holt and Guðmundsson's limited excavation produced preliminary results, which call for further work. Nonetheless, this small-scale research holds significance, first because they identified artificial cave sites as suitable for excavation, and second because they called attention to material located *outside of* a cave structure but *associated with* cave use. Most important, however, was that this early study triggered later work, including the substantial inventory that Guðmundsson undertook with Hjartarson and Gísladóttir.

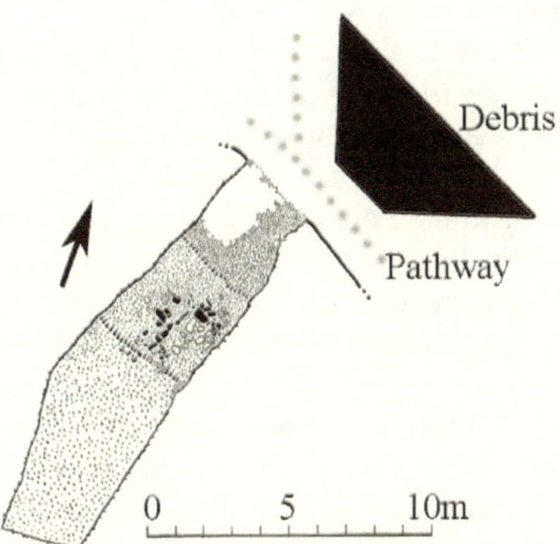

Figure 5.3 Kverkarhellir cave and proposed apron of waste. The debris in this model has been offset to avoid the pathways associated with Kverkarhellir (one running upslope to the southeast, another to the nearby feature SLJ 30 to the west, and another downslope to the north). In this model an average thickness of 0.6 m was assumed, though one would expect thickening in the central area of deposit and thinning at the edges. Furthermore, this average thickness must be an underestimate as this waste material would be loose rather than compacted as solid rock. Additionally, the proposed sub-triangular shape for the waste deposit is only one of the possible debris forms. As a simple calculation, the depositional model illustrated here nevertheless permits quantification of the sorts of results to be expected. Plan of Kverkarhellir drawn by Ian G. Scott.

Building upon Holt and Guðmundsson's small-scale field study, my Seljaland investigations have been the first to apply a robust methodology to constrain cave use chronologically. In 2001 and 2002 I undertook assessment excavation alongside rigorous application of tephrochronology (Ahronson 2002a; 2003b; Smith and Ahronson 2003). With the selection of Kverkarhellir for targeted study, my goal was to locate debris produced by cave construction within a well-stratified sequence of tephra deposits. Figure 5.3 outlines a depositional model for the estimated 12 m^3 of primary construction debris. Previous work on sediment accumulation rates at Seljaland suggests such material should be stratified within an aggrading sequence of deep sediments (Dugmore and Erskine 1994).

The hypothesis under consideration is that if a well-stratified sequence of sediments exists in the vicinity of Kverkarhellir, and includes prehistoric and historic tephrae (which may be identified through stratigraphic and geochemical analyses), then locating a dump of debris-type material within this sequence and in areas generally predicted by our depositional model will date an episode of construction at Kverkarhellir. In other words, a deposit identified as construction debris should be in *both* the right sort of location (that is, the area loosely predicted by the apron model) *and* be of the predicted character (that is, a thick deposit of predominantly pebbles and small cobbles infilled with aeolian material). As mentioned earlier, debris could incorporate artefacts associated with construction, but this should be considered unlikely. In considering potential construction debris, an important concern is establishing that natural processes were not responsible. Overlooking the Markarfljót flood plain at thirty-two metres above sea level, Kverkarhellir's situation midway up an escarpment precludes a flood event there. Eroded material from the escarpment face, however, must be considered a possibility. Correspondingly, in considering the hypothesis above, our method must assess whether a deposit of palagonite "debris" could have been produced by a natural erosion episode.

Method

Tephrochronology is a stratigraphy-based technique that sometimes uses geochemical analysis in order to resolve ambiguities in field identifications. It must be stressed, however, that geochemical analysis alone is insufficient for application of this technique; the stratigraphic sequence of tephrae in a section is the basis for interpretations. The first concern was whether a well-stratified sequence of tephra deposits, intercalated with aggrading sediments, could be identified near Kverkarhellir. In order to resolve this question, I excavated trench D3 to reveal a sedimentary profile, from which tephra samples were taken in September 2001 and geochemically analysed over the following months. The trench is located east of Kverkarhellir in figure 5.4. Tephra layers were logged, and a north-facing profile (or *section*), 1 m in width, was recorded to a depth of 2.2 m. Layers, or contexts, were identified according to a system combining trench number (for example, D3) and context (for example, A, B); thus, D3G expresses trench D3, context G. For this section the sequence of sedimentary layers was recorded by scale diagram, based on measurements and observations of grain size, colour, layer thickness, continuity of units, and layer composition. Context descriptions are presented, and a scale diagram summarizes a sedimentary log for comparison with reference profiles recorded at Seljaland (Dugmore 1987). This reference profile is a complete sequence of undisturbed tephra layers consistent with wider records in the Markarfljót, Seljaland, and Sólheimar areas. Geochemical analyses of samples from tephra layers D3F and D3G were carried out by electron microprobe analysis using a Microscan V instrument, following procedures summarized by Dugmore, Larsen, Newton, and Sugden (Dugmore et al. 1992).

After the establishment of the local stratigraphy the second concern was to locate a deposit of debris-type material, anticipated to contain angular palagonite pebbles and small cobbles. Trench D1 was opened in pursuit of this concern.

Located in figure 5.4, trench D1 was excavated in September 2001 and August 2002 and sited within the predicted apron of waste, immediately in front of Kverkarhellir. West-facing and north-facing sections (2 m and 1 m in width, respectively) were recorded to a maximum depth of 2 m. In order to relate the tephra stratigraphy of this trench to that of D3, the logging was done in the same manner for each, and geochemical analyses were undertaken of tephra layers D1E and D1G.

As the analysis described above called for further work, another trench (D4) was opened. Located in figure 5.4, trench D4 was sited east of Kverkarhellir within the predicted apron of waste. Excavated in August 2002, west-facing and north-facing sections were recorded as above, 1.5 m in width and to a maximum depth of 2 m. Crucially, a thick context of angular palagonite pebbles and cobbles lay below tephrae produced by the eruptions Hekla 1597, Katla 920, and Vatnaöldur 870 (these last two were identified through comparison to the geochemically confirmed D3 sequence). Following guidelines outlined for Quaternary researchers (Jones et al. 1999: 30; Russell and Marren 1999: 191–5), the stratigraphic sequence relating this debris-type context to the Katla 920 and Vatnaöldur 870 tephrae is presented through annotated photographic overlays to the west-facing section.[9] Angular cavities were noted in a number of pebbles and cobbles from the debris-type deposit, and specialist morphological analysis of a very angular palagonite small cobble was undertaken by Chris Doherty at the Research Lab for Archaeology and the History of Art (Oxford); this study is presented in full below. In addition, samples were taken of the potential debris deposit (context N/O), and the particle-size distribution was quantified. Excavation of trench D4 included the removal of a 0.25 m x 0.25 m sample column, and data from context N/O was obtained as part of this exercise. Jones et al. observe that "sieving is the most commonly used method in the laboratory for sorting sediment into grain-size classes and determining grain-size distribution" (Jones et al. 1999: 13). This method was followed in the work outlined here. In the processing of the sample column each context and spit was weighed before and after dry sieving through a 5 mm mesh (shown in figure 5.7). At this point, the weight of cobbles with one

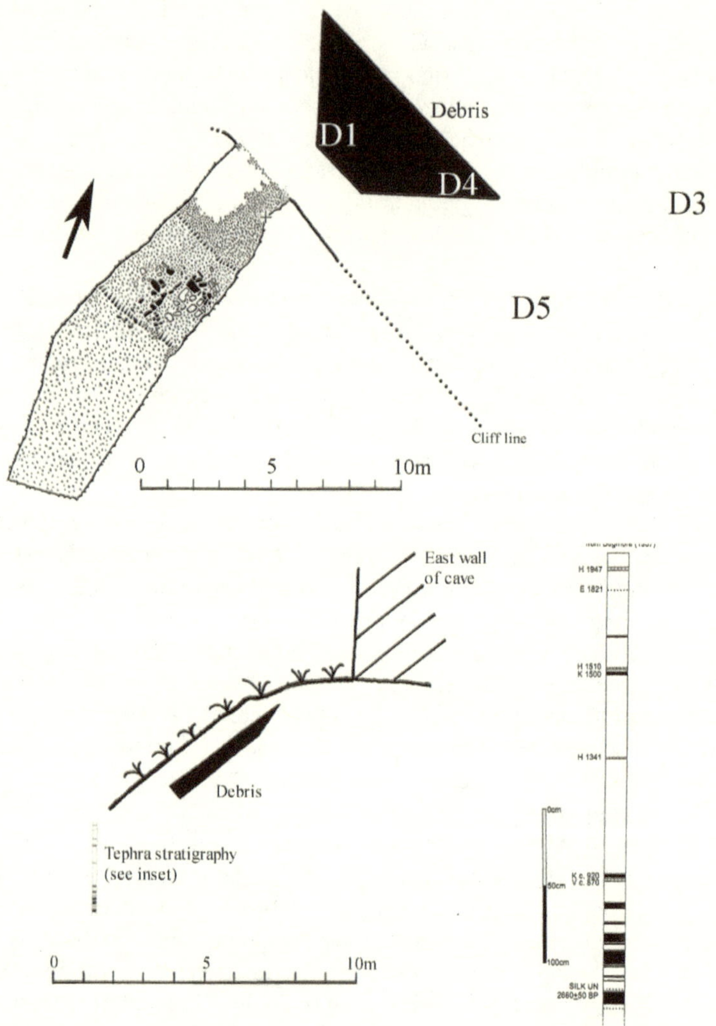

Figure 5.4 *Above*. Location of trenches near Kverkarhellir. *Below*. Sketch profile of northwest-facing section showing the mouth of Kverkarhellir and the steep descent (which leads to the sandur plain), as well as the predicted apron of waste and a generalized stratigraphic profile for tephra layers at Seljaland. The inset diagram is the expanded reference profile (note the different scale) for Seljaland area tephra layers (Dugmore 1987). Compare the idealized model illustrated here with the results presented in figures 5.6 and 5.7.

dimension greater than 100 mm was recorded in order to account for a potential error in sampling smaller portions of this material. One hundred grams of each dry-sieved sample younger than the landnám tephra (deposited ca. 870), and the entire sample of older deposits (including a further 10 L sample from the context of angular palagonite pebbles and small cobbles), were then removed to the University of Iceland Research Centre in the Westman Islands for further study. There the sampled material was wet sieved through a 5 mm mesh, air dried, and then dry sieved through 19.00 mm, 12.50 mm, 9.50 mm, and 5.00 mm meshes (with bronze frame and stainless steel mesh). Each fraction was examined and weighed using a Metler PE 3600 electronic scale, distinguishing between cobbles with one dimension over 100 mm and coarse pebbles and small cobbles ranging between 19.00 and 100 mm.[10] Data collected from the debris-type context N/O is presented in tabular form and analysed graphically because of the nature of the difference between samples.

Investigating whether a potential construction deposit might have been produced by a natural erosion episode is vital. As outlined in the hypothesis section, eroded material from the escarpment face would be expected to deposit palagonite debris along the cliff base, including the immediate area of Kverkarhellir. Correspondingly, trench D5 was sited along the cliff base, upslope from Kverkarhellir, and is located in figure 5.6. Excavated in August 2002, 1.5 m wide east-facing and north-facing sections were logged to a depth of 1.5 m and correlated with the geochemically confirmed D3 tephra stratigraphy. Deposits of cobbles and smaller pebbles were revealed and interpreted to result from prehistoric first millennium AD erosion events. The stratigraphic interpretation of this material is presented in text, and two 5–10 L samples were taken. These samples were studied in their entirety following the method described above. The resulting data was tabulated, analysed graphically, and compared to the "debris-type" context N/O from trench D4. Trench D5 was sited below a similar part of the cliff face as trench D4, and the samples studied from both trenches are close in age. In other words, trenches D4 and D5 are located beneath the same geological formation, and material produced by erosion events should be comparable between these trenches because of the expected continuity of erosion processes acting upon this cliff face throughout the first millennium AD.

Results and Discussion

Tephra Stratigraphy and Geochemical Analyses

Figures 5.5–5.6 show Kverkarhellir trenches D3 and D1 as well as Seljalandsheiði tephra stratigraphies. The Seljalandsheiði profile shows that in this area

Figure 5.5 Detail of the north-facing section of trench D3. From top down, including tephrae produced by the following eruptions: K920 (black), V870 (upper grey is mixed and perhaps slopewash; lower grey is airfall), and a pre-historic Katla (?) deposit (thick black). Photograph taken in September 2001.

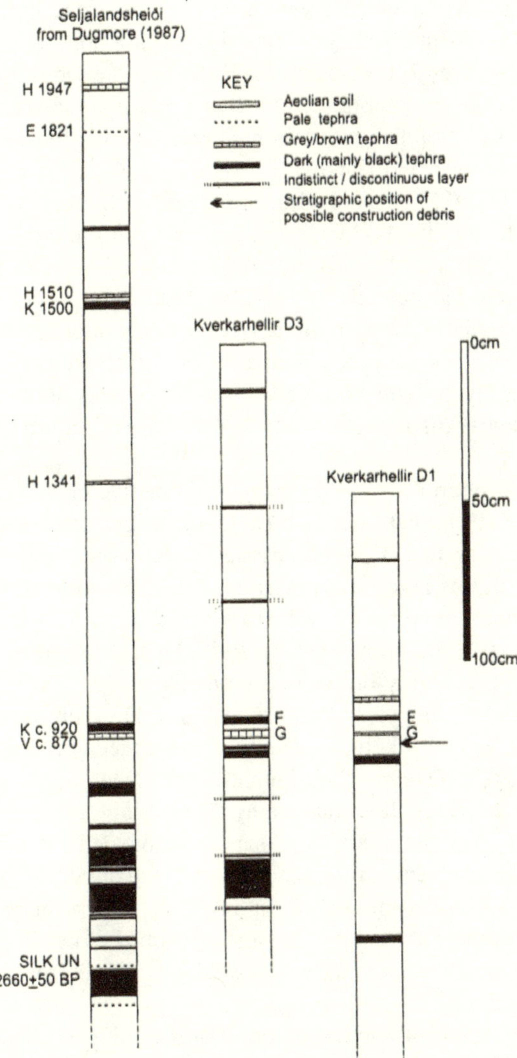

Figure 5.6 Stratigraphy of Kverkarhellir trenches D3 and D1, and a reference profile for Seljalandsheiði from Dugmore (1987). The tephra layers are labelled with a two-element system: volcanic system and date (H1947 for Hekla AD 1947). Volcanic systems are abbreviated to K (Katla), H (Hekla), E (Eyjafjallajökull), and V (Vatnaöldur). The SILK prefix refers to a silicic tephra layer from Katla (Larsen et al. 2001). Tephra layers from historical time have calendar ages, and prehistoric dates are stated in ^{14}C years BP (Þórarinsson 1954, 1975, 1967; Dugmore 1987; Grönvold et al. 1995; Zielinski et al. 1997).

very few black Katla tephra layers have been recorded in the soils during historic time. The distinctive key historical layers are predominantly from Hekla:[11] H1947 (coarse grey-brown pumice), H1510 (coarse grey-brown pumice), and H1341 (fine blue-grey tephra). K1500 is a relatively coarse black tephra layer from Katla. A pair of distinctive tephra layers is found near to the time of Norse settlement of the island (landnám): V870 and K920. The Vatnaöldur ca. 870 tephra layer (V870) is from the Barðarbunga-Veiðivötn system and is generally understood to seal the prehistoric sequence from the Norse settlement period (Vésteinsson 1998: 3–4). This greenish brown tephra with a small pale silica-rich component has been dated to 871 ± 2 and 877 ± 4 (Grönvold et al. 1995; Zielinski et al. 1997). Approximately fifty years later (c. 920), Katla erupted, producing the black Katla R tephra.[12] Thick (often greater than 10 cm), coarse black tephra layers from the Katla central volcano dominate the prehistoric sequence, clearly distinguishable from the series of tephra deposits post-dating landnám.

Initial field interpretation identified a distinctive pair of tephra layers as the K920 and V870 couplet; in trench D3 this stratigraphic interpretation was convincing, whereas in D1 the stratigraphic data was only suggestive (certain problems with this layer, such as compaction and potential reworking, called for geochemical analysis to evaluate a V870 identification). All contexts are described in table 5.1. Contexts D3F and D1E are composed of fine black tephrae, while D3G is a grey-brown unit with pale grains, and D1G may be comparable to it. Below this pair of tephra layers in D3 there are a number of thick coarse black tephrae likely to have been deposited prior to ca. 870, based on comparisons with Dugmore's Seljaland profile (Dugmore 1987). This interpretation of the Kverkarhellir stratigraphy depends upon removal of the upper part of the profile, that above K1500. As a consequence of the rich record of earth working at the site, removal or disturbance of the upper soil and tephra deposits above K1500 is easily envisaged. In trench D1 a deposit characterized by angular palagonite pebbles was identified 10 cm below the potential landnám tephra; one possibility is that this material was debris from initial construction of Kverkarhellir.

Our stratigraphic interpretation correlates the Kverkarhellir layers with the K920 and V870 couplet and was tested by analysing the geochemistry of samples from both trenches (tables 5.2 and 5.4). Geochemical analyses of material from trench D3 support our identification of the ca. 920 Katla R and ca. 870 landnám tephrae there, while trench D1 is less straightforward, pointing to D1E as a Katla tephra and calling for further work on D1G.

The tephra layers D3F and D1E are attributed to an eruption within the caldera of the volcano Katla. This is based on stratigraphy-based field identification, supported by comparisons of the Kverkarhellir geochemical data pre-

Table 5.1 Contexts from trenches D1 and D3

Layer	Description	Layer	Description
D1 A	very dark brown clay with sand and angular palagonite pebbles		
D1 M	black coarse sand tephra	D3 S	black coarse sand tephra
D1 B	dark brown clayey silt with sand and angular pebbles	D3 C	dark-brown silt with little sand
D1		D3 A	grey coarse silty sand tephra (?)
D1		D3 D	brown clayey silt with some sand
D1 C	intermittent grey silty sand	D3 B	intermittent grey silty sand tephra
D1 D	brown silty clay with sand and angular palagonite pebbles	D3 E	brown silt
D1 E	black fine sand tephra (Katla tephra, potentially K920?)	D3 F	black fine sand tephra (K920) (possible tree casts)
D1 F	light grey-brown very silty clay with sand and angular palagonite pebbles	D3 I	light-brown silt
D1 G	grey fine sandy silt tephra (V870?)	D3 G	grey fine silty sand tephra (V870)
D1 H	grey-brown silty sand with angular palagonite pebbles (oldest construction debris-type material)	D3 K	red-brown silt
D1 I	grey pumacious tephra (or pumice)	D3 L1	intermittent black fine sand tephra
D1 J	light-brown clay with sand and pebbles (occasionally angular)	D3 J	black fine sand tephra
D1 K	grey coarse pumice (?)	D3 N1	brown silt
D1 L	very compact brown to grey sandy pebbles	D3 L2	intermittent black fine sand tephra
		D3 O	light-brown silt
		D3 P	intermittent black fine silt tephra
		D3 N2	brown silt
		D3 M	black fine silty sand tephra
		D3 Q	brown sandy silt
		D3 T	black fine silty sand tephra
		D3 R	brown silty clay

Table 5.2 Chemical analyses of layer E from section D1 (selection from 14 analyses) and layer F from D3 (selection from 12 analyses) from Kverkin, Seljaland. Total iron is expressed as FeO.

	SiO_2	TiO_2	$Al2O_3$	FeO	MnO	MgO	CaO	Na_2O	K_2O	Total
(D1)	47.73	4.76	12.59	14.27	0.24	4.79	9.61	3.16	0.77	97.91
	47.68	4.66	12.66	14.77	0.22	4.73	9.56	3.06	0.80	98.15
	47.54	4.77	12.66	14.78	0.23	4.86	9.60	3.09	0.82	98.35
	47.38	4.35	12.60	14.73	0.28	4.83	9.33	3.17	0.80	97.47
	47.30	4.80	12.63	14.63	0.29	4.86	9.61	3.22	0.80	98.14
	47.30	4.61	12.62	14.50	0.25	4.85	9.52	3.31	0.89	97.85
	47.29	4.85	12.63	14.46	0.25	4.82	9.44	3.21	0.87	97.83
	47.20	4.68	12.59	14.25	0.20	4.76	9.25	3.23	0.86	97.01
	47.16	4.57	12.53	14.42	0.26	4.84	9.43	3.25	0.75	97.21
	47.15	4.73	12.66	13.96	0.28	4.93	9.43	3.10	0.80	97.02
	47.09	4.70	12.57	14.59	0.22	4.96	9.22	3.18	0.74	97.28
	46.85	4.77	12.75	14.65	0.29	4.89	9.66	3.13	0.79	97.78
Mean	*47.31*	*4.69*	*12.62*	*14.50*	*0.25*	*4.84*	*9.47*	*3.18*	*0.81*	*97.67*
(D3)	47.53	4.64	12.57	14.50	0.21	4.77	9.34	3.20	0.75	97.50
	47.31	4.72	12.50	14.40	0.23	4.81	9.38	3.15	0.81	97.29
	47.28	4.63	12.46	14.37	0.22	4.75	9.35	3.21	0.83	97.11
	47.24	4.59	12.46	14.55	0.27	4.82	9.26	3.25	0.78	97.22
	47.20	4.60	12.52	14.31	0.30	4.75	9.36	3.10	0.84	96.98
	47.19	4.51	12.40	14.54	0.27	4.78	9.45	3.20	0.82	97.16
	47.17	4.49	12.47	14.28	0.26	4.66	9.41	3.13	0.77	96.64
	47.09	4.65	12.62	14.61	0.23	4.83	9.31	3.29	0.81	97.44
	47.08	4.53	12.33	14.32	0.22	4.71	9.36	3.22	0.79	96.57
	46.96	4.58	12.47	14.49	0.27	4.65	9.13	3.16	0.81	96.52
Mean	*47.21*	*4.59*	*12.48*	*14.44*	*0.25*	*4.75*	*9.34*	*3.19*	*0.80*	*97.04*

sented here (table 5.2) with analyses of Katla ca. 920 from the nearby coastal plain of Landeyjar (Duncan 2001), and a typical basaltic Katla tephra discussed by Larsen (Larsen 2000) (see table 5.3). However, the basaltic tephrae produced during intra-caldera eruptions of Katla are difficult to differentiate through analysis of major element chemistry (Larsen 2000). Katla has erupted approximately every forty-seven years during the historic period. This under-

Table 5.3 Summary of published chemical analyses of basaltic tephrae from Katla: (1) Katla 920 analysis from Skíðbakkavatn, Landeyjar (selection from 13 analyses), data from Duncan (Duncan 2001); (2) Katla 1625 (mean of 7 analyses), data from Larsen (Larsen 2000: 7). Total iron is expressed as FeO.

	SiO_2	TiO_2	$Al2O_3$	FeO	MnO	MgO	CaO	Na_2O	K_2O	Total
(1)	47.70	4.58	12.41	14.82	0.21	4.68	9.36	3.10	0.89	97.75
	47.30	4.56	12.48	14.73	0.26	4.77	9.51	2.98	0.82	97.41
	47.23	4.70	12.59	14.49	0.22	4.75	9.41	3.16	0.78	97.33
	47.15	4.39	12.50	13.92	0.22	4.78	9.46	3.04	0.80	96.26
	47.12	4.72	12.39	13.43	0.24	4.84	9.35	3.21	0.74	96.04
	47.01	4.48	12.52	14.57	0.21	4.90	9.26	3.25	0.79	96.99
	46.81	4.52	12.61	14.31	0.19	4.78	9.63	3.21	0.84	96.90
	46.77	4.63	12.70	14.50	0.23	4.81	9.22	3.17	0.82	96.85
	46.75	4.55	12.15	14.32	0.17	4.98	9.51	3.12	0.79	96.34
	46.75	4.66	12.53	14.13	0.18	4.79	9.42	3.14	0.79	96.39
	46.74	4.62	12.66	14.43	0.21	4.77	9.47	3.16	0.89	96.95
Mean	*47.03*	*4.58*	*12.50*	*14.33*	*0.21*	*4.80*	*9.42*	*3.14*	*0.81*	*96.84*
(2) Mean	*46.28*	*4.56*	*12.62*	*14.75*	*0.23*	*4.89*	*9.97*	*2.72*	*0.71*	*97.44*

scores the general point that the identification of tephrae from geochemical analyses alone (in this case a basaltic Katla tephra) cannot allow us to allocate a date to these layers. In the present example, identifying which Katla eruption produced these tephrae necessitates the stratigraphic relation of these layers to a visually or chemically distinctive layer (or sequence of layers), such as the landnám tephra.

Layer G from trench D3 (table 5.4) has strong geochemical similarities to landnám tephra analyses from Landeyjar (Duncan 2001) and those published in Larsen et al. (Larsen et al. 1999) (see table 5.5). Initial analysis of layer G from D1, however, was problematic and called for more work. The landnám tephra has two components, one basaltic and the other silicic. Basalt, with silicon dioxide (SiO_2) content around 49% and low potassium oxide (K_2O) levels around 0.2%, is the main component of the landnám tephra layer in Eyjafjöll and the sole component farther east (Guðrún Larsen, personal communication). The silicic component is characterized by high levels of K_2O, typically greater than 4% where SiO_2 content is greater than 70% (Larsen et al. 1999). These traits make the landnám tephra chemically distinctive. Sample D3G, though difficult to analyse with few silicic grains in it, shows similar chemical characteristics to this pattern. The analyses in table 5.4 show a distinct basalt component, similar to the published data, and a number of silicic grains with SiO_2 above 70% and K_2O around or above 4%. It should be noted that the iron oxide (FeO) content of the silicic component appears somewhat higher than in previously published data, particularly that of Larsen et al. (Larsen et al. 1999). However, the similarities between this analysis of D3G and the data from Duncan and Larsen et al. confirm the stratigraphy-based field interpretation that this layer is likely to be the landnám tephra (Larsen, personal communication).

Integrating geochemical analyses of the paired layers F and G from trench D3 with the observed tephra stratigraphy presents a good case for identification of a Katla tephra and the landnám tephra, confirming the initial field interpretation that these layers correlate with the K920 and V870 couplet. Thick, coarse black tephra layers below this pair of tephrae, and the lack of such layers above this couplet, also support this proposal. Geochemical analyses on material from trench D1, however, are inconclusive and call for further excavation; the composition of layer D1E is comparable to Katla tephrae, but layer D1G, the deposit noted by initial field interpretation as potentially landnám tephra, remains problematic.

Sample Column Analyses

Although lacking the predicted thickness, a deposit of debris-type material was identified in trench D1. The difficulties outlined above, however, called for the siting of another trench within the predicted apron of waste in the hopes of constraining deposits within a robust tephra sequence. Trench D4 was therefore opened and found to realize these hopes; stratified tephrae were identified through comparison with the geochemically confirmed D3 sequence, including H1597, K920, and V870. Identifications were based upon grain size, colour, layer thickness, continuity of units, layer composition, and stratigraphic position. In figure 5.7, a 50–75 cm thick deposit of angular pebbles and small cobbles (context N/O) was discovered to lie up to 25 cm beneath the ca. 920 Katla and landnám couplet, with the K920 and V870 tephrae running intermittently across the trench and therefore interpreted as in situ airfall deposits. Context N/O thus was understood to significantly predate the ca. 870 Vatnaöldur tephra layer. Uncertainties remain, however, on just how long before ca. 870 this debris-type material was deposited, as the tephra stratigraphy in this trench did not include older layers; very local factors, including those linked to human agency, may have affected sediment accumulation rates for this trench and pose a challenge to precise dating. Certainly, the 25 cm of aeolian sediments sealed by the

Table 5.4 Chemical analyses of (a) silicic part and (b) basaltic part of the D3G tephra layer from Kverkin, Seljaland (selection from 21 analyses). Three sporadic grains, which may be xeno-glasses (volcanic glass acquired from the walls of the eruption conduit) or contamination from surrounding tephra-rich soil, are shown at the base of the table. Total iron is expressed as FeO.

	SiO_2	TiO_2	$Al2O_3$	FeO	MnO	MgO	CaO	Na_2O	K_2O	Total
(a)	71.81	0.27	14.78	2.72	0.10	0.24	0.92	4.46	4.67	99.96
	71.60	0.35	13.16	3.58	0.17	0.16	1.08	4.31	3.95	98.36
	71.07	0.24	12.77	3.35	0.16	0.12	0.87	4.17	4.00	96.77
	70.85	0.24	12.47	3.06	0.12	0.12	0.88	4.00	4.06	95.80
	69.89	0.44	14.43	2.97	0.10	0.42	1.22	4.16	4.44	98.07
Mean	*71.04*	*0.31*	*13.52*	*3.14*	*0.13*	*0.21*	*1.00*	*4.22*	*4.22*	*97.79*
(b)	49.64	1.75	13.32	12.35	0.24	6.55	11.40	2.50	0.20	97.95
	49.51	1.73	13.38	12.69	0.22	6.42	11.19	2.66	0.19	97.99
	49.45	1.81	13.23	12.63	0.24	6.52	11.38	2.56	0.19	98.03
	49.42	1.75	13.28	12.29	0.24	6.51	11.36	2.55	0.24	97.65
	49.29	1.85	13.15	12.74	0.23	6.39	11.16	2.51	0.27	97.60
	49.20	1.92	13.17	12.75	0.23	6.57	11.12	2.56	0.24	97.76
	49.17	1.87	13.08	12.52	0.25	6.29	11.11	2.56	0.25	97.10
	49.16	1.87	13.35	12.68	0.27	6.43	11.11	2.56	0.22	97.66
	49.05	1.90	13.25	12.68	0.22	6.34	11.17	2.56	0.21	97.37
	49.01	1.84	13.09	12.71	0.26	6.33	11.02	2.50	0.22	96.98
	48.80	1.90	13.23	12.50	0.28	6.43	11.17	2.50	0.22	97.03
Mean	*49.25*	*1.84*	*13.23*	*12.60*	*0.24*	*6.43*	*11.20*	*2.55*	*0.22*	*97.56*
	47.49	4.30	12.09	14.46	0.25	4.57	9.34	3.14	0.83	96.46
	47.07	4.58	12.41	13.85	0.29	4.83	9.60	3.21	0.85	96.68
	46.86	4.37	12.45	14.57	0.24	4.84	9.43	3.18	0.83	96.76

landnám tephra suggest a date well before ca. 870 – probably several decades earlier, if not a century or more.[13] As an estimate then, context N/O should be not much younger than ca. 800 and is potentially of greater antiquity.

Upon field examination, material from N/O was found to be of comparable fabric to that of the cave interior. Two samples of this context were taken and analysed: one from the sample column described in the method section, and a further 10 L sample (labelled D4 N/O "special") from the section face

Table 5.5 Summary of published analyses of the V870 *landnám* tephra: (1a) silicic part of the landnám tephra from Skíðbakkavatn, Landeyjar (selection from 14 analyses); (1b) basaltic part of the landnám tephra from Skíðbakkavatn, Landeyjar (selection from 8 analyses), data from Duncan (2001); (2a) lower silicic part of the landnám tephra from áfangagil (mean of 12 analyses); (2b) upper basaltic part of the landnám tephra from áfangagil (mean of 6 analyses), data from Larsen et al. (1999: 468). Total iron is expressed as FeO.

	SiO_2	TiO_2	$Al2O_3$	FeO	MnO	MgO	CaO	Na_2O	K_2O	Total
(1a)	71.93	0.24	14.53	2.52	0.10	0.21	0.90	4.27	4.90	99.60
	71.90	0.24	14.59	2.49	0.03	0.23	0.88	4.25	4.90	99.51
	71.58	0.26	14.62	2.31	0.01	0.21	0.80	4.23	5.06	99.08
	71.19	0.31	14.43	2.20	0.05	0.18	0.60	4.25	5.12	98.33
	71.16	0.31	14.68	2.56	0.05	0.27	0.90	4.19	4.95	99.07
	71.15	0.26	14.34	2.34	0.04	0.27	0.83	4.50	4.73	98.46
	71.12	0.32	14.44	2.44	0.03	0.23	0.79	4.76	4.66	98.79
	71.12	0.25	14.40	2.45	0.04	0.25	0.84	4.67	4.78	98.80
	71.11	0.35	14.37	2.46	0.08	0.28	0.84	4.90	4.74	99.13
	70.99	0.26	14.14	2.32	0.05	0.23	0.87	4.38	4.72	97.96
	70.74	0.32	14.35	2.43	0.04	0.28	0.92	4.45	4.73	98.26
	70.03	0.28	14.58	2.38	0.08	0.22	0.81	4.48	4.71	97.57
Mean	*71.17*	*0.28*	*14.46*	*2.41*	*0.05*	*0.24*	*0.83*	*4.44*	*4.83*	*98.71*
(1b)	49.62	1.84	13.41	12.48	0.21	6.65	11.32	2.40	0.23	98.16
	49.23	1.79	13.24	12.35	0.19	6.46	11.19	2.41	0.21	97.07
	49.09	1.86	13.23	12.35	0.14	6.48	11.17	2.38	0.21	96.91
	49.01	1.96	13.10	12.48	0.18	6.47	11.29	2.48	0.27	97.24
	48.61	1.92	13.28	12.42	0.22	6.40	10.87	2.45	0.22	96.39
Mean	*49.11*	*1.87*	*13.25*	*12.42*	*0.19*	*6.49*	*11.17*	*2.42*	*0.23*	*97.15*
(2a) Mean	*70.97*	*0.25*	*14.46*	*2.32*	*0.09*	*0.24*	*0.89*	*4.78*	*4.64*	*98.63*
(2b) Mean	*49.27*	*1.83*	*13.73*	*12.19*	*0.23*	*6.85*	*11.55*	*2.36*	*0.21*	*98.22*

photographed in figure 5.7. In the excavating and sampling of context N/O, thirty-two very angular, very coarse pebbles and small cobbles were found to share a common morphology of angular cavities, possibly produced by an iron digging tool. In order to assess whether an iron digging tool was indeed responsible for these features, Molloy examined the "best" example (the small cobble in figure 5.8), and later Doherty subjected it to morphological analysis.

Doherty's analysis cannot establish exact origin but did suggest that the angular cavity on that cobble was not directly created by tooling or hammering and that it appears to match angular basalt clasts found within the palagonite fabric. In other words, the cavity in figure 5.8 appears to have been formed around a now-absent basalt clast. Several lines of investigation suggest that this angular cavity (and potentially the comparable cavities in all thirty-two examples from context N/O) is from such a clast:

- First, this cavity has an improbable geometry for a tool or nail (given concave *and* convex planes of cavity) but is an exact match for the angular frost-shattered basalt clasts.
- Second, the cavity is bounded by extensive fractures that run (in some cases) to other clasts. These fractures are annealed and are not planes of weakness (as expected if derived from tooling or hammering). In addition, the concave form of fractures, such as that labelled A in figure 5.9, is in agreement with a slumped sub-glacial or non-sedimentary origin.
- Third, there is an absence of striations (or tooling marks) along the cavity walls (though these are not universally visible on stone-working debris).
- Finally, there is a lack of metal staining along cavity walls. (Although metal staining is present as iron-manganese at the apex of the cavity, this is natural and occurs elsewhere on the object. Again, however, we need not expect metal staining on stone-working debris.)

The conclusions of Doherty's study are clear: cavities such as the one in this small cobble are not tooling marks. An unresolved question, however, is why these cavities are present in such numbers in context N/O and yet largely absent from other sample column contexts. If context N/O was indeed construction debris, one possibility suggested by Molloy is that the act of digging out a cave from this palagonite fabric caused fragments to loosen from the walls along fault lines defined by basalt clasts, thus producing the notable number of pebbles and cobbles with these angular cavities (Molloy, personal communication). This idea may have some merit, but until it is tested by further work, these tool markings must be set aside as inconclusive on their own.

As outlined in the hypothesis section, it was expected that the digging out of Kverkarhellir might have produced palagonite debris characterized by large amounts of angular medium pebbles to small cobbles (roughly 10–120 mm), accompanied by substantial quantities of finer pebbles (2–10 mm) and infilled with later aeolian material. In addition, the construction debris model predicts a thick deposit of material within an apron of waste, perhaps between 0.5 m and 1 m in thickness. Excavation of context N/O, itself 0.50–0.75 m in

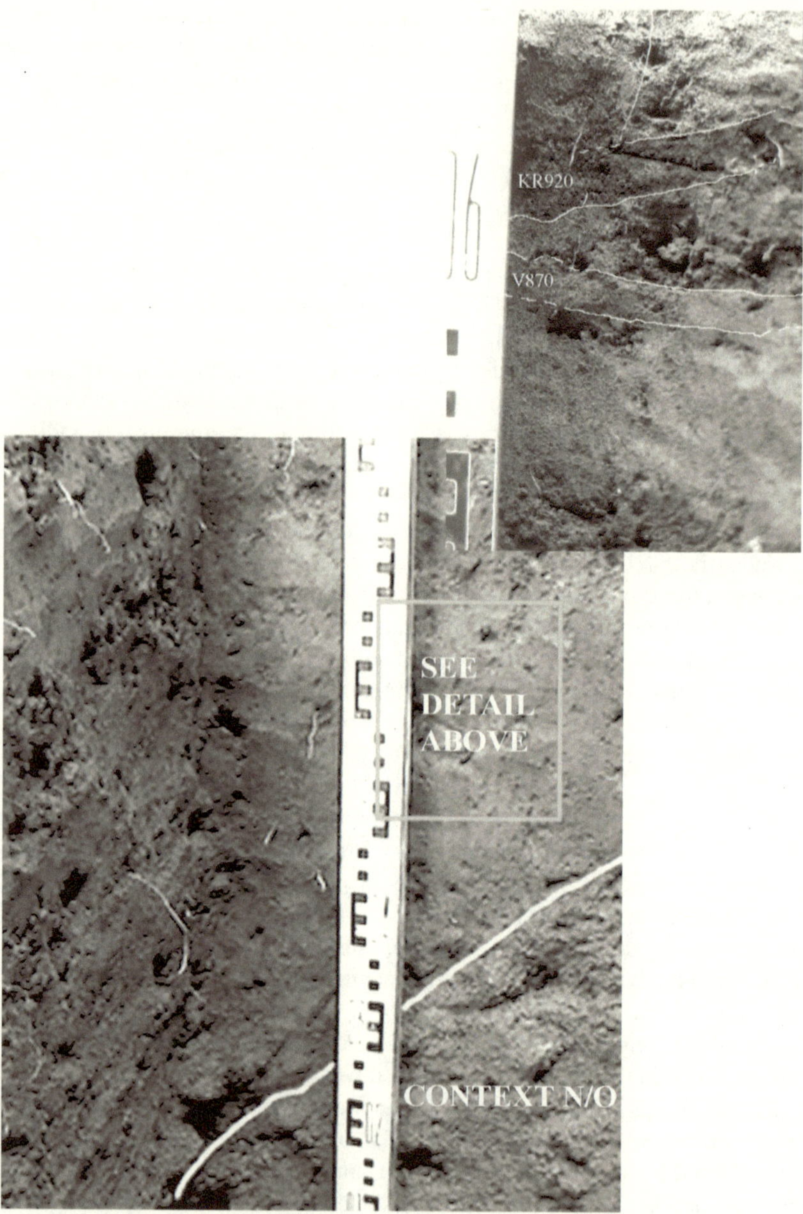

Figure 5.7 Trench D4 west-facing section, including debris-type context N/O. Original photograph by Paul Klotz. *Detail*: K920/V870 couplet in the west-facing section. Photograph with overlay.

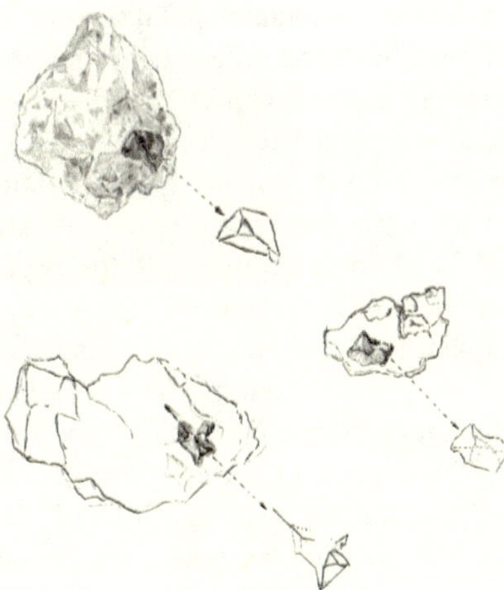

Figure 5.8 Sketches of very angular, very coarse pebbles and small cobbles sharing comparable angular cavities from the debris-type context N/O, labelled *a* (*top left*), *b* (*top right*), and *c* (*bottom*). Scale 1:6. Drawn by Kerry-Anne Mairs.

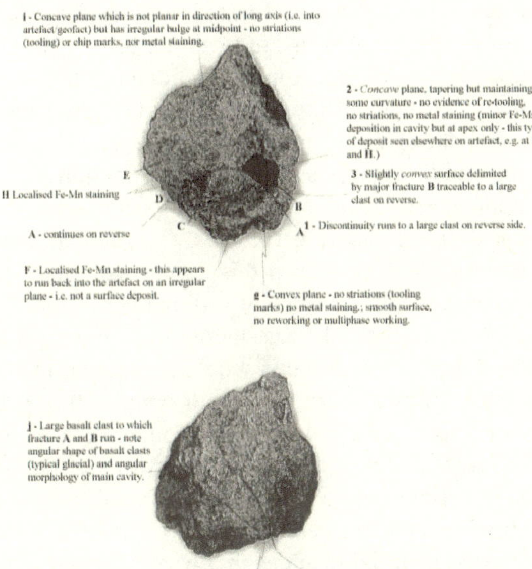

Figure 5.9 Chris Doherty's analysis of a "tool marked" very angular, small cobble. Scale 1:4.

thickness, revealed a deposit of angular palagonite within the predicted area that matched these expectations. As noted earlier, a sample column was excavated in trench D4. Figure 5.10 compares the raw context weights from this column and complements the recorded thickness of 0.50–0.75 m by demonstrating just how massive N/O is alongside other contexts. In addition, sampling this context permitted precise quantification of particle size distributions. Table 5.6 and figure 5.11 define a deposit with the expected substantial quantities of finer pebbles and aeolian material (the < 5.0 mm and 5.0–9.5 mm fractions) and large quantities of medium pebbles to small cobbles (the 9.5–12.5 mm, 12.5–19.0 mm, 19.0–100.0 mm and > 100.0 mm fractions). This is a good case for the application of the principle of *Occam's razor*:[14] identifying this context as having the expected debris-type character, thickness, and location presents a strong case for interpreting context N/O as debris from a construction episode of Kverkarhellir. One final concern, however, is whether this debris-type material could have been deposited by an event of natural erosion from the escarpment face overlooking the study area.

In order to assess the character of natural erosion deposits, trench D5 was sited upslope from Kverkarhellir, along the escarpment base. This trench included deposits of palagonite cobbles and smaller pebbles within a matrix of aeolian material interpreted to be eroded from the cliff face. Thick, coarse black tephra layers provided a chronological framework for these natural erosion deposits. As noted earlier and illustrated in figure 5.6, thick (often greater than 10 cm), coarse black tephra layers from the Katla central volcano dominate the prehistoric sequence preceding the landnám ash. The trench D5 tephrae are comparable to those at the base of the D3 sequence and were thus interpreted on these stratigraphic grounds as prehistoric erosion events – probably dating to the middle centuries of the first millennium AD. This interpretation depends upon the removal of the upper portions of the profile, those younger than ca. 870. Considering the record of human disturbance in this area, and the steep slope upon which this trench was sited, erosion is easily envisioned to account for the absence of sediments younger than ca. 870 (including the V870 tephra). From the east-facing section two samples were taken of naturally eroded deposits within this sequence, and particle size distribution is quantified in table 5.7 and figure 5.13. Both samples (no. 1, from 1 m below ground surface, and no. 2, from 1.4 m below ground surface) are dominated by coarse pebbles to large cobbles (the 19–100 mm fraction) as well as fine pebbles and aeolian material (the < 5 mm fraction). Notably, only a small proportion of these samples included pebbles ranging between 5 mm and 19 mm. Crucially, this eroded material (such as that photographed in figure 5.12) was perceived upon excavation to be of radically different character to context N/O (photographed in figure 5.7); the results of particle size analyses quantify some

Table 5.6 Data from D4 N/O samples. N/O is a combined context and was sampled in six spits, each roughly 10 cm in depth. N/O "special" was a sample taken from the section face photographed in figure 5.7. Weight is given in grams.

Trench, context, and (spit)	Unsieved weight	> 5.00 mm weight, dry sieved	< 5.00 mm weight	5.00–9.50 mm weight	9.50–12.50 mm weight	12.50–19.00 mm weight	19.00–100.00 mm weight	> 100.00 mm weight
D4N(1)	6510.00	1990.00	5373.09	524.68	131.37	150.10	330.76	0
D4N(2)	7020.00	3370.00	5677.67	702.90	244.33	229.80	165.30	0
D4N(3)	6800.00	3000.00	5019.40	721.50	243.70	347.80	467.60	0
D4O(1)	9170.00	4330.00	6042.65	708.30	307.03	238.42	1241.90	631.70
D4O(2)	11280.00	7540.00	4429.56	825.80	293.00	478.64	2927.50	2325.50
D4O(3)	9810.00	5890.00	7362.65	664.80	271.55	381.10	1129.90	0
D4N/O totals	50590.00	26120.00	33905.02	4147.98	1490.98	1825.86	6262.96	2957.20
N/O 'special'	14100.00	7030.00	9568.22	1032.20	459.040	638.00	1920.90	481.64

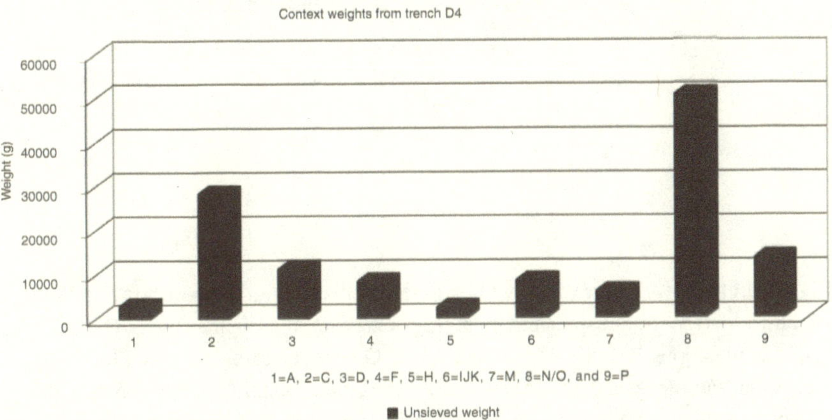

Figure 5.10 Context weights from trench D4 sample column (0.25 m x 0.25 m). Note how context N/O, the debris-type deposit, stands out as massive alongside other contexts from the sample column.

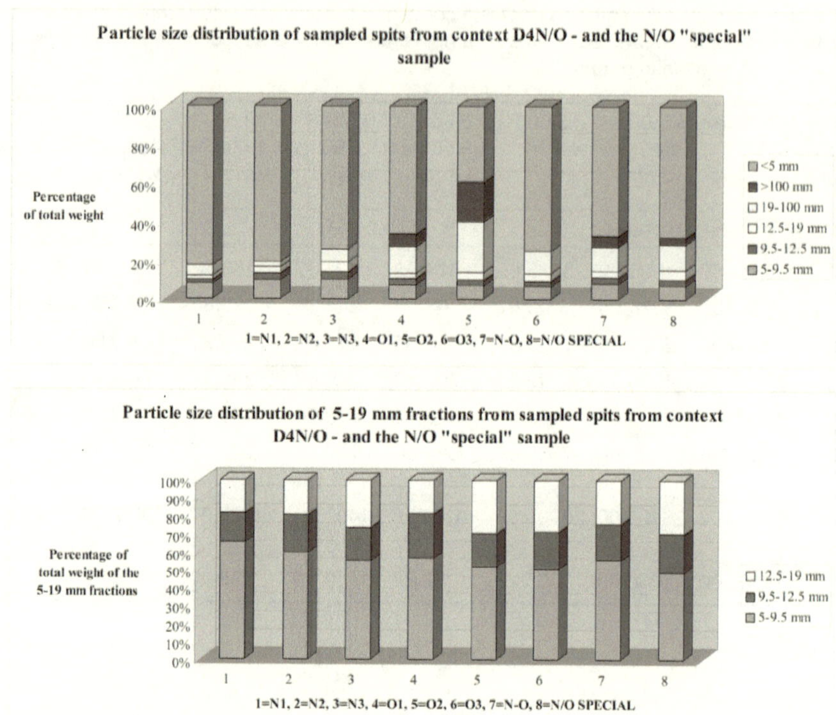

Figure 5.11 *Above.* Context D4 N/O particle size distribution by percentage of total weight, sorted by 10 cm spits and including context total as well as the N/O "special" sample. Note the coherency of context N/O between sample column totals and the special sample, especially in the values for particles ranging between 5 mm and 19 mm as well as, to a lesser degree, for particles greater than 19 mm (see below for further demonstration of the coherency of this fraction throughout context N/O). *Below.* Context N/O particle size distribution of the 5–19 mm fraction, sorted by 10 cm spits and including context total as well as the N/O special sample. Graphing this fraction is only made meaningful since the 5–19 mm fractions from all these samples are of comparable proportions of each *entire* sample. This graph reinforces the conclusion of coherency for context N/O arrived at above.

Table 5.7 Data from D5 erosion deposits 1 and 2, with weight given in grams

Trench and sample number	Unsieved weight	> 5.00 mm weight, dry sieved	< 5.00 mm weight	5.00–9.50 mm weight	9.50–12.50 mm weight	12.50–19.00 mm weight	19.00–100.00 mm weight	> 100.00 mm weight
D5 #1	6640.00	4970.00	1049.99	128.92	83.26	152.63	2832.30	2392.90
D5 #2	2910.00	2720.00	2023.01	86.55	43.22	45.02	712.20	0

of these differences. Figure 5.13 demonstrates key differences in the values for particles ranging between 5mm and 19mm: these are only a small proportion (5–6%) of the naturally-eroded samples, but a large proportion of the N/O samples (15%). Thus we may conclude that this debris-type deposit was not produced by a natural erosion episode from the escarpment face.

Conclusions and Further Problems

In exploring the problem of Kverkarhellir's earliest phase of construction, this chapter articulated the hypothesis that, if a well-stratified sequence of sediments exists in the vicinity of Kverkarhellir and includes prehistoric and historic tephrae (which may be identified through stratigraphic and geochemical analyses), then locating a dump of debris-type material within this sequence and in areas generally predicted by our depositional model will date an episode of construction at Kverkarhellir.

This proposal was tested by excavating a number of trenches and by assessing particle size distribution for individual contexts. The tephra sequence in the immediate area of Kverkarhellir was found to include key historical tephrae, such as the landnám and K920 couplet, and a number of thick prehistoric tephrae. Dated by this sequence to ca. 800 (or earlier), a deposit of debris-type thickness and character was identified within the predicted apron of waste from the early digging out of Kverkarhellir. This thick debris-type context appears to be part of a dump of construction debris because comparable material was not found elsewhere (except in trench D1, which may include a thinner deposit of similar material). Given the scale of work outlined here, the case for this thick debris-type deposit being part of a construction dump is a good one. Although expectations of location, thickness, and particle size distribution were satisfied, a continuing concern was that this deposit could have been produced by a natural erosion episode from the escarpment face.

Figure 5.12 D5 north-facing section, including thick coarse black tephra layers deposited in the centuries preceding the *landnám* eruption of the Barðarbunga-Veiðivötn system. "Eroded" material, similar in character and age to samples 1 and 2, may be seen in the upper left corner of the image. Photograph taken in August 2002.

Correspondingly, excavation revealed the local character of erosion deposits, and samples were processed to provide particle size distributions (apparently of limited range). Crucially, the debris-type context was *unlike* erosion-origin material and was thus interpreted as construction debris from the digging out of Kverkarhellir.

The outlined hypothesis has so far withstood testing, and the resulting date for construction at Kverkarhellir raises important questions. As noted earlier, the Norse settlement period of Iceland is generally understood to post-date the

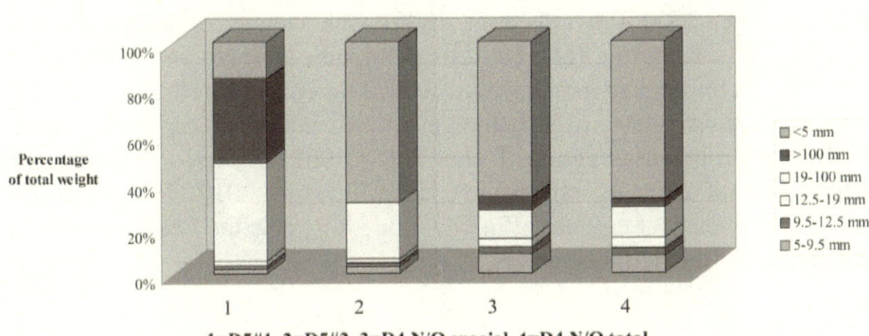

Figure 5.13 Particle size distribution by percentage of total weight of erosion deposits from trench D5 and debris-type context N/O from trench D4. Key differences between eroded and debris-type samples may be seen in the values for particles ranging between 5 mm and 19 mm.

landnám ash of ca. 870. Although suggestions for early cave use in southern Iceland have been previously made, this chapter contains the most comprehensive investigation yet undertaken. A strength of this work was the robust tephrochronological techniques used to date Kverkarhellir. Care must be taken with these results, however, as they identify what may be the earliest human presence on the island, in ca. 800 (or earlier). The Seljaland investigations are thus far the clearest indicator of people in Iceland at such an early period, but problematic or tentative work in the Westman Islands and Reykjavík suggests complementary dates.[15] Perhaps more relevant, however, is the local palaeoenvironmental change identified as taking place in ca. 800 at Seljaland and potentially related to human activity in the landscape (that is, woodland clearance and the introduction of domesticates) (Dugmore and Erskine 1994: 69–73; Ashburn et al. 2003: 88). In exploring these early environmental changes at Seljaland, chapter 6 develops and applies a new technique, *tephra contouring*, to questions of ninth- and tenth-century deforestation. If Kverkarhellir was indeed constructed in the eighth century, immediate questions arise as to *who did so*. In light of the place name and the folklore associating the Seljaland caves with early Christian Gaels or papar, one bold idea is that these cave sites were built by early Christian communities as a *díseart*, or "desert place in the Ocean" – potentially comparable to settlements on North Rona and elsewhere in Atlantic Scotland and Ireland. Recent work, for instance, considers similarly early dates for cereal pollen along these lines, suggesting early Christian monastic settlement and farming in the Faroe Islands (Jóhansen 1985; Hannon and Bradshaw 2000; Edwards et al. 2005). One avenue for assessing cultural affinities is to study the rock-cut cross sculpture in southern Iceland's caves and alcoves. Such an approach would be well timed, considering that the sculpture and cave use related to early medieval Christianity in Atlantic Scotland has profited from recent attention (Fisher 2001; 2002; 2005; Tolan-Smith 2001; Ahronson et al. 2006; Ahronson and Charles-Edwards 2010). In order to elaborate and test ideas of cultural affinity and identity, chapter 7 looks to the rock-cut crosses of the Seljaland caves.

6 Three Dimensions of Environmental Change

A considerable problem in sedimentological descriptions is that recognition of most sedimentary structures occurs in two dimensional sections, but almost all sedimentary structures are three dimensional.

A.P. Jones, M.E. Tucker, and J. Hart (eds.), *The Description and Analysis of Quaternary Stratigraphic Field Sections*[1]

Whilst the tephra horizons mean that extensive areas are sealed and it would theoretically be possible to excavate and reconstruct entire plant communities, an effective sampling strategy ... would not only need skills more appropriate to the archaeologist but also require an investment of time."

Paul C. Buckland, *Tephrochronology and Palaeoecology*[2]

Let us explore vegetation changes in the centuries surrounding Norse settlement in order to contextualize human activity better in that landscape. As mentioned in previous chapters, the island was transformed over those centuries: human populations appeared; woodland was reduced; domesticated animals and crops were introduced; native mammal, bird, and fish populations were over-exploited; natural vegetation cover was altered; and the soils were destabilized.

At Seljaland the oldest of these palaeoenvironmental changes has been detected in early-ninth-century sediments and has been claimed to be related to human activity in the landscape (that is, woodland clearance and the introduction of domesticates). In order to assess ideas regarding ninth- and tenth-century deforestation at Seljaland, this chapter introduces tephra contouring as a new technique for investigating the tephra record of past land surfaces. As a new method for environmental studies, tephra contouring provides unexpected results, suggesting structural changes in vegetation cover both before ca. 870 and again in the decades leading up to ca. 920.

Problem and Context

Iceland plays a key role in our understanding of the north Atlantic world, partly because of its tephra deposits and consequent chronological markers for archaeological and environmental study. In studying stratigraphical sections across the Markarfljót sandur area, Hreinn Haraldsson observed sedimentological changes beginning before the landnám tephra had been deposited (c. 870) (Haraldsson 1981). Applying the local tephra stratigraphy from a series of profiles at Seljaland to build upon Haraldsson's wider observations, Andrew J. Dugmore and Camilla C. Erskine argue that "the stratigraphically sharp and geographically extensive nature of this change indicates an abrupt and major regional change in geomorphological process … [which] points to a large scale mobilisation of aeolian sediment" (Dugmore and Erskine 1994: 73–4). In other words, they propose that wind-blown sediments started moving around the landscape at this time, eroding in one place and accumulating elsewhere. At Seljaland this geomorphological change is revealed by a distinctive lightening of colour in the post-landnám sediments, while earlier occurrences of this change have been identified by Dugmore and Erskine as well as by Donald Ashburn et al. in early-ninth-century sediments at sites situated between 100 and 200 metres above mean sea level (figure 6.1) (Dugmore and Erskine 1994: 72; Ashburn et al. 2003: 83). Furthermore, Ashburn et al. studied the magnetic susceptibility of the lighter deposits that are characteristic of this new geomorphological process; they favour the idea that the consistently low susceptibility values resulted from human impacts upon these soils, namely from "the addition of organic matter from both animal waste and decaying vegetation after initial disturbance by non-indigenous herbivores" (Ashburn et al. 2003: 92). Ashburn et al. link these wind-blown sediments to domesticated animals because of the high organic content of the sediments. It is possible that we are seeing the effect of domesticated animals on a fragile woodland ecosystem, and the consequent breaking up of the soil cover.

Regionally, two ecological zones are understood to have characterized the landscape around Seljaland prior to human settlement: one zone of raised woodland dominated by birch (*Betula*) and willow (*Salix*), and another zone of vegetation without raised woodland, which Dugmore et al. subdivide into lowland coastal plain and upland components (Dugmore et al. 2000: 29). Amanda Thomson elaborates the expected distribution and vegetative character cover for the lowland sandur component and raised woodland zones in the centuries

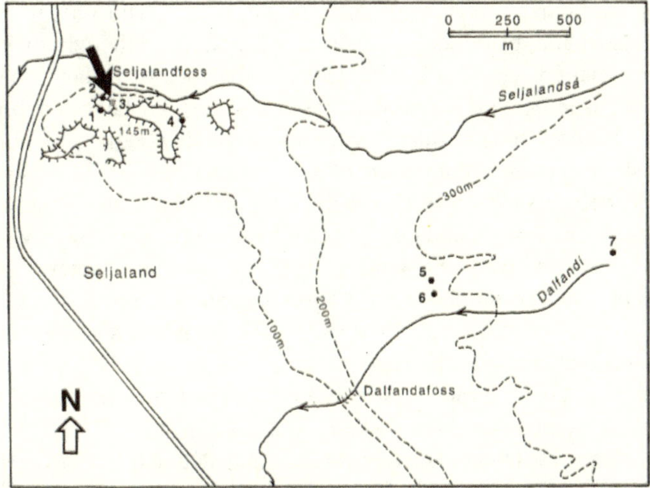

Figure 6.1 Map locating Ashburn et al.'s profiles 1–7. Adapted from Ashburn et al. (2003: 83). Those profiles within the 100–200 m contour lines (i.e., 1–4) were found to have a distinctive lightening of colour in early ninth-century sediments; this colour change is widespread in post-*landnám* sediments and associated with human impacts upon the environment. Indicated with an arrow, tephra contouring trenches A1 and A2 were sited adjacent to Ashburn et al.'s profile 3.

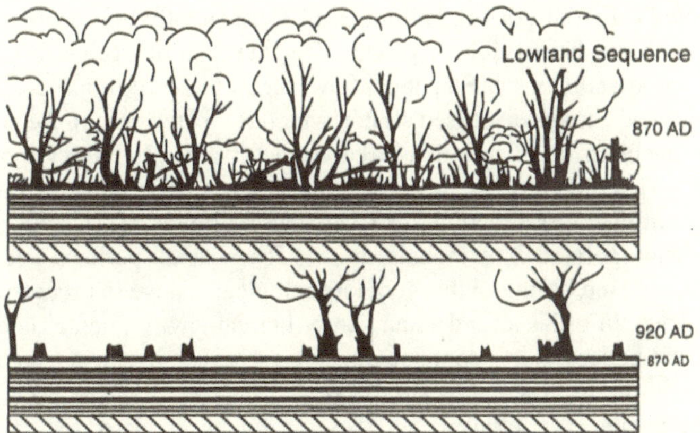

Figure 6.2 Modelled vegetation structure for lowland areas of Seljaland at the time of the deposition of the V870 and K920 tephrae. Detail from Dugmore and Simpson's composite presentation of historic vegetation models (Dugmore and Simpson, forthcoming: fig. 6).

preceding the human colonization of Eyjafjallasveit:[3] "The *sandur* plain[4] between the coast and the uplands at the time of *landnám* is thought to have been covered by marshy grassland, with scattered patches of birch woodland on raised areas, as indicated by peat deposits and macro-fossils found throughout the region … Above the marshland, up to 300 m, birch woodland predominated, with a lush understorey composed of grasses and herbs" (Thomson 2003). Situated on well-drained slopes between 10 and 300 metres above mean sea level, this latter area of woodland may be quantified as covering roughly 300 hectares – an area effectively the same as that surveyed in chapter 4 (Amanda Thomson, personal communication).[5] This scenario of a "pre-settlement" landscape dominated by woodlands is supported by the island's earliest literature, which claims that Norse settlers encountered "*viði vaxit á miðli fjalls ok fjøru*" (*Íslendingabók*: ch. 1; Benediktsson 1968: 5; woods between mountains and shore). It is presumed that this woodland was quickly reduced by human populations, in some cases to create arable land, as attested in the later *Grágás* legal code (Finsen 1852 [1974]: 448). Figure 6.2 models vegetation cover for those landscapes sealed by the K920 and V870 tephra layers.

Careful examination of the character of local tephra horizons supports this idea of a wooded landscape. Northeast of Seljaland, "holes" in the landnám and older prehistoric tephra layers have been suggested as tree casts, and thus evidence for forest cover (Mairs 2003). In addition, undulating and discontinuous soil-tephra contact surfaces have also been noted for the landnám and prehistoric layers and would be expected for tephra deposited in birch woodland with lush understorey. A reminder that this area of Iceland is capable of sustaining woodland is provided by Kverkin; in the last thirty years this corrie has been sealed off from grazing animals, and subsequently tree populations and undergrowth are flourishing. A problem for the idea of extensive late-ninth-century woodland areas at Seljaland, however, is the early-ninth-century geomorphological change discussed earlier, which is most visible in the postulated heart of this birch woodland (that is, between 100 and 200 metres above mean sea level). This record of geomorphological change suggests structural changes in vegetation cover and an influx of aeolian sediment that has not been sufficiently incorporated into models of past landscapes, perhaps because the precise nature and timing of this geomorphological change in process is poorly known. Thus, in order to understand early human-environmental interactions at Seljaland better (and to contextualize the early date for cave use), we shall grapple with the following questions: When was tree cover reduced (or lost) from forested areas at Seljaland, and was this reduction related to human activity in the landscape (such as that implied by the episode of cave construction discussed in chapter 5)?

Hypotheses

In response to the questions, we may formulate hypotheses that relate the structure of vegetation cover at Seljaland to human impacts upon the landscape. A prior assumption for these proposals is the association of tree cover with people; this point will be returned to below. That said, three alternative hypotheses are proposed: (1) tree cover was reduced between 870 and 920; (2) tree cover was reduced later; or (3) tree cover was reduced earlier.

All of these hypotheses assume that reduction of woodland in the ninth and early tenth centuries would have been determined by intensive human use. This assumption is a potential problem, but, considering the relative stability of the north Atlantic climate throughout the ninth, tenth, and eleventh centuries (Ogilvie et al. 2000), the relating of tree-cover reduction to human activity has gained widespread support among palaeoecology researchers in southern Iceland. Haraldsson, for instance, concludes that birch woodland on raised areas of the Landeyjar coastal plain experienced steady growth in extent and trunk diameter between 800 and 900, with reduction and extinction of that woodland by 950; this is a period coincident with Norse settlement there (Haraldsson 1981: 41–2). Thus what Haraldsson identifies as the background trend of steady growth in woodland areas throughout the ninth century for the coastal plain (which Seljaland overlooks) points to the robustness of this assumption that people were instrumental in the destruction of forest environments. In other words, since a natural trajectory of woodland *growth* is widespread prior to human colonization, then the *reduction* of woodland at the same time that people arrive in the landscape suggests people to be a major cause of woodland loss. Another possibility, more difficult to assess, however, is that forest cover might also be *fostered* by human land management strategies, in other words that a stand of woodland could be maintained or fostered as a result of human use, rather than despite human use. A key way to accommodate this latter concern is to relate models of forest loss to complementary studies, such as the magnetic susceptibility studies of Ashburn et al., in order to achieve a more holistic (and thus more secure) grasp of human-environmental interactions and subsequent landscape change.

Method

The merits of using tephra to study human-induced deforestation have come to be widely appreciated in recent years, not only by Icelandic researchers but also by teams investigating the earliest horizon of human impact on the vegetation of northern New Zealand (Newnham et al. 1998). In the majority of this work, however, tephra layers have been used *indirectly* in order to chronologically constrain sedimentary records, such as deposits of pollen. I propose that this indirect use of tephra layers may be complemented by the realization that tephra layer morphology[6] may also provide *direct* fossil records of vegetated landscapes. A classic example of this possibility is the tephra deposited by Vesuvius in AD 79 on Herculaneum and Pompeii; this tephra preserved not only "casts of men and other vertebrates ... in the deposit but also insects, and plants" (Buckland 1981: 382).

At Seljaland the models of landscape change discussed earlier suggest that we should anticipate key differences between ninth- and tenth-century tephra layers; in other words, we expect variation in vegetation cover to be reflected by the morphology of tephra horizons. Thus a heavily wooded environment with lush understorey (such as that predicted for 870 by the landscape model in figure 6.2) should produce an undulating and discontinuous tephra layer with holes where tree trunks stood at the time of the ash fall. Open grassland, however, should produce an evenly distributed and well-defined tephra layer. I suggest that by studying the morphology of both the V870 and K920 tephra layers at Seljaland, we might perceive the clearance of woodland areas and consequently growth of open grassland (which could in turn support populations of grazing animals).

One way to study the *form* of tephra layers is to contour its three-dimensional surface. Three-dimensional contouring of open areas is common in archaeological research (where it is a fundamental technique) but rare in palaeoenvironmental studies (cf. this chapter's epigraphs by Jones and Buckland). At Seljaland the sedimentary sequence of centimetre-scale tephra airfalls intercalated with aggrading aeolian sediments is well suited to three-dimensional contouring, with these tephrae forming discrete, layered "photographic negatives" of successive land surfaces. This chapter explores the question of woodland cover at Seljaland, and we may propose that excavation of the contours of K920 and V870 tephrae will expose photographic negatives of land surfaces from ca. 920 and ca. 870, thus allowing woodland cover and change in vegetation structure between these times to be quantified. In other words, after recording the surface of these tephrae over a given area, one can quantify the density and trunk thickness of tree cover over the area by looking to the holes in the tephra where ground-level vegetation, such as tree trunks, prevented deposition. Furthermore, the excavation of a small number of these open areas should permit the statistical significance of such studies to be assessed in relation to a larger area, such as the 300 hectares of woodland cover proposed by Thomson to lie between the 10 metre and 300 metre contour lines at Seljaland.[7]

Thus, since other techniques such as section profiling and pollen sampling are not able to quantify woodland directly, the tephra contouring technique may be anticipated to provide a unique contribution to studies of landscape change in southern Iceland (and also for other places with comparable tephra and sediment sequences, such as New Zealand).

The viability of applying tephra contouring was first assessed in July 2001, and preliminary results were published elsewhere (Ahronson 2003b: 63–7). This test involved the excavation of a rectangular 1.5 m x 1.5 m area (trench A1) at the site of Ashburn et al.'s profile 3 (at an elevation of 128 m above mean sea level; see figure 6.1). The surfaces of three stratigraphically identified volcanic airfall layers were contoured and recorded by photograph and scale diagram, and clearly defined circular holes in the deposits were noted as probable tree casts (figure 6.3). These contoured tephrae were correlated with a number of previously studied stratigraphies and thus identified as in situ tephrae from the eruptions of 1500 Katla, 920 Katla , and 870 Vatnaöldur (Dugmore, personal communication). Two circular, 9 cm diameter features were interpreted as tree casts, one in the K1500 tephra layer (figure 6.3) and another in the K920 tephra layer. This early trial established the feasibility of contouring the surfaces of the K1500, K920, and V870 tephra layers and demonstrated that the presence of ground-level vegetation may be identified by the morphology of these tephra layers.

Therefore, in August 2002 a rectangular 3 m x 2–3 m area (trench A2) was excavated immediately northwest of trench A1 (that is, the southeast corner of trench A2 was identical to the northwest corner of trench A1). The ground surface and the surfaces of the K1500, K920, and V870 tephra horizons were contoured, recorded by photograph and scale diagram, and elevation was recorded to the centimetre by theodolite. Application of the tephra contouring technique raised many topics for discussion. However, as we are presently concentrating on ninth- and tenth-century vegetation structures, treatment of those points outside our remit (for example, the morphology of the K1500 tephra) will be undertaken elsewhere. Thus only data for the surfaces of the K920 and V870 tephra horizons are presented in the next section.

Results and Discussion

The technique worked. Contours were obtained for centimetre-scale and continuous tephra layers identified as in situ airfall deposits from eruptions of Katla in 1500 and ca. 920, as well as Vatnaöldur in ca. 870. Discussion here will concentrate on these last two layers. As stressed earlier in the chapter, the

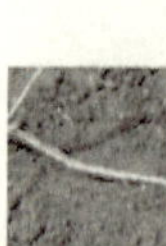

Figure 6.3 Detail of a feature in the K1500 tephra layer (area A1) interpreted to be the trunk cast of a tree.

small scale of the tephra contours excavated at Seljaland presents significant statistical limitations to wider interpretations. Nevertheless, our results were clear and may be summarized simply (and presented visually in figures 6.4, 6.5, 6.6, 6.7, and 6.8). In the K920 tephra layer two 5–9 cm circular holes[8] were interpreted to be trunk casts of thin trees, while, considering Thomson's suggestion that vegetated understorey should have flourished in this area (and which can be seen flourishing in Kverkin today), a number of medium-sized irregularly shaped gaps in the tephra layer were interpreted to be the result of a lush understorey of vegetation, which prevented deposition of tephra within these features (figures 6.4 and 6.9). In addition, Ashburn et al.'s work at this location identified a spike in the magnetic susceptibility of sediments ca. 920; they suggest this spike may have resulted from the burning of woodland at that time (Ashburn et al. 2003: 92–3). Furthermore, since tephra contours for the K920 layer have "photographed" what appears to be a small area of young woodland with lush understorey, consideration of Ashburn et al.'s results lead to the suggestion that it was this woodland that later burned.

In contrast with K920, the contoured surface of the V870 tephra layer suggests a different vegetative structure for that landscape. The contouring of this

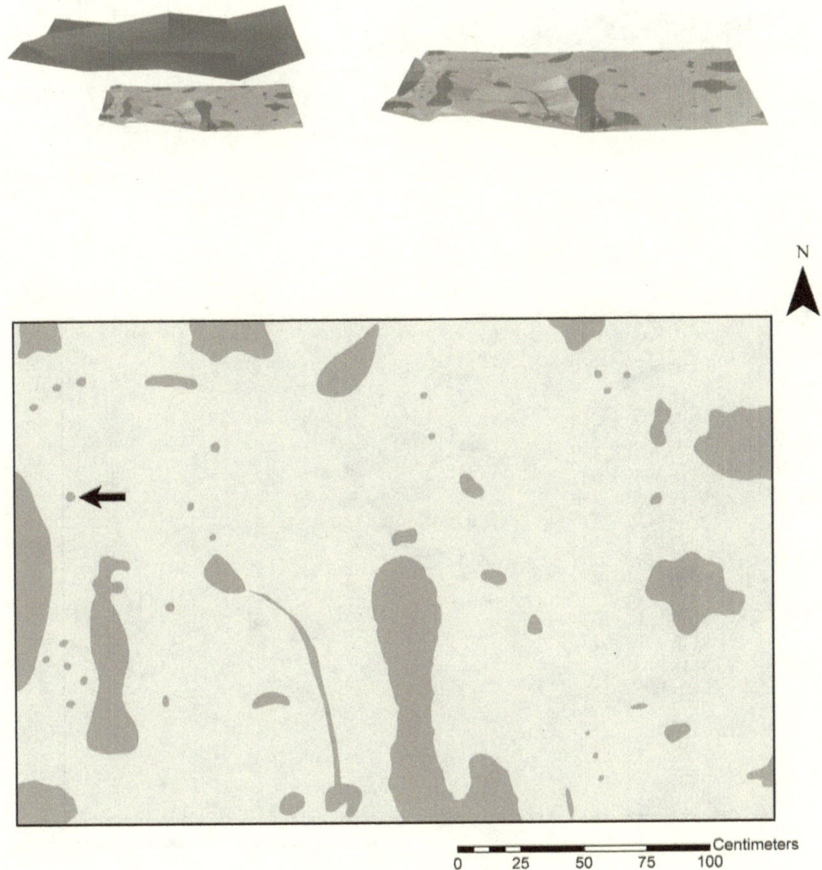

Figure 6.4 *Above left and right.* Oblique images of modern grassed land surface and of the surface of the K920 tephra layer, using interpolated points. "Holes" in the tephra horizon are identified in grey; a ground-level understorey of vegetation probably prevented the deposition of K920 tephra within these features. Looking north. Drawn by John Higdon. *Below.* Surface of K920 tephra layer. A single 5 cm diameter tree cast is identified by an arrow. Drawn by John Higdon.

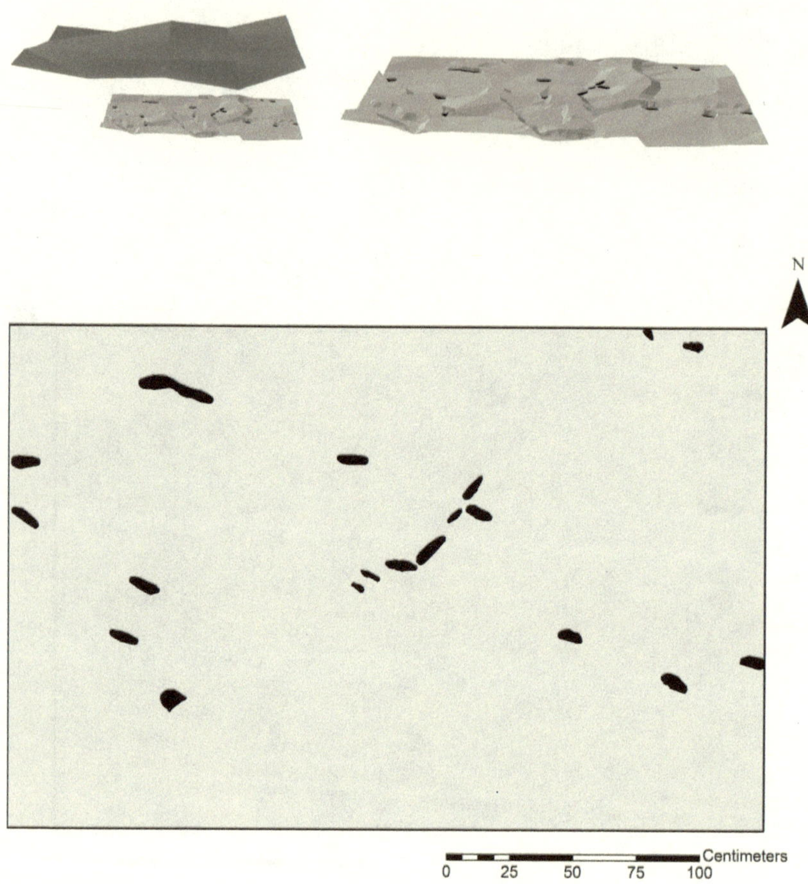

Figure 6.5 *Above left and right.* Oblique images of modern grassed land surface and of the surface of the V870 tephra layer, using interpolated points. "Depressions" in the tephra horizon are infilled in black and were found to form linear patterns running across the excavation area. Since they are regularly spaced and arranged in linear patterns, these features may be preserved animal tracks. Looking north. Drawn by John Higdon. *Below.* Surface of V870 tephra layer. Drawn by John Higdon.

Figure 6.6 Section and oblique views of the modern land surface, K1500 tephra layer and K920 tephra layer. Looking south.

Figure 6.7 Oblique views of the K1500 tephra layer (1 m x 3 m) and K920 tephra layer (2 m x 3 m). Looking west.

Figure 6.8 Oblique views of 1 m x 3 m areas of the K1500 tephra layer, K920 tephra layer, and V870 tephra layer. Looking southwest.

Figure 6.9 Detail of a feature in the K920 tephra layer interpreted to be the trunk cast of a tree. This tree cast is identified by an arrow in figure 6.4.

Figure 6.10 Detail of "depressions" in the V870 tephra. In the section, note how the K920 tephra layer is broken at this location (perhaps by post-depositional reworking of tephra into soils). Looking west.

Figure 6.11 Tracks made by modern farm animals at Seljaland in 2002.

landnám layer, deposited ca. 870, revealed a continuous and well-defined surface without holes or irregular gaps in the tephra layer (figure 6.5). Interpretation of the data suggests an open grassland environment without tree cover. As these results run counter to the vegetation cover predicted by Thomson in the preceding sections (and apparently well established for this area of southern Iceland), two main possibilities present themselves: first, that we have contoured a natural clearing in woodland cover; and second, that this 3 m x 2 m area was cleared of birch trees by people before the landnám tephra was deposited. This second possibility could also help explain the change in sedimentation processes identified at this site by Ashburn et al., in sediments dated to ca. 800, and proposed to reflect the impact of people on the local environment and the introduction of non-indigenous herbivores into the landscape (Ashburn et al. 2003). If this latter possibility were the case, such clearance would probably have occurred several decades before 870 in order to produce such an open and well-defined tephra layer. In addition, unexpected linear "depression" features were found in this tephra layer; their size, shape, and distribution hold out the possibility that they were created by medium-sized herbivores, such as sheep or small- to medium-sized cows, treading upon the freshly deposited tephra (figures 6.5, 6.10, and 6.11). Although land mammals of this size are not native to Iceland, the idea of early herbivore tracks in the landnám tephra is made plausible by the recent discovery of a field boundary (indicative of farm animals) in Reykjavík dated to ca. 850 (Roberts et al. 2002: 35–9). Furthermore, this interpretation of the features might in turn strengthen the second possibility – that we have excavated a landscape that was cleared of tree cover by people, and was not a natural open area in woodland. These ideas would profit from further excavation of tephra contours trenches at Seljaland and the statistical quantification of our results. Correspondingly, in the assessment of our three hypotheses, the data provided by our trial of the tephra contouring technique support the third hypothesis that tree cover at Seljaland was reduced before 870–920 and that intensive use of the landscape was underway by that time. Intriguingly, the growth of a young woodland with lush understorey by ca. 920 may suggest either abandonment of Seljaland in the 870–920 period or a change in land management at that time. Crucially, however, the area excavated was small, and further work is needed to develop these initial interpretations.

Conclusions and Further Problems

This chapter explored vegetation changes in the centuries surrounding Norse settlement in order to contextualize human activity in the landscape. To assess ninth- and tenth-century deforestation, tephra contouring was introduced as a new technique for investigating the tephra record of past land surfaces. Results from application of tephra contouring suggest early- to mid-ninth-century clearing of woodland at Seljaland to create an open grassland environment (suitable for grazing) and potentially identified the presence of non-indigenous herbivores by ca. 870. Unexpectedly, land use at Seljaland appears to have changed by ca. 920, with the growth of a young woodland with lush understorey; if sustained by later work, this change might relate to the area's abandonment during the Norse landnám period or to a change in land management strategies at that time. In other words, these results may be set alongside the early date for activity at Kverkarhellir cave (which may be the earliest human activity in Iceland).

Importantly, however, the small scale of our excavated area limits the initial results from the tephra contouring technique, and further work is called for. In addition, efforts at defining the *representativeness* of the tephra contours have asked fundamental questions of the commonly used technique of recording an exposed vertical profile, or section (Jones et al. 1999: 27–33). A *section* is a freshly exposed (roughly) vertical face, which is sometimes stepped. To create a one- or two-dimensional log of such a vertical section is a basic technique employed by Quaternary researchers, including tephrochronological workers active in Iceland (Jones et al. 1999: 27–33). Instead of the excavation and recording of what is essentially a two-dimensional snapshot of a layer, the tephra contouring technique has the advantage of exposing the quantifiably representative three-dimensional surface of that layer. For instance, the ca. 870 Vatnaöldur tephra may be exposed over a 3 m x 2 m surface within a 100 m x 100 m area in order to consider the land surface that was across this area at the time (assuming similar elevation, microclimate, et cetera). Crucially, the confidence with which results produced by contouring the small tephra surface may be related to the larger area is quantifiable. This means that the tephra contours technique is suitable for investigating questions of representativeness over a landscape. In addition, applying tephra contours in this way has the potential to clarify the practice of two-dimensional vertical profile recording, suggesting, for instance, that the *section* is appropriate for investigating the presence of features in deposits (such as tree trunks) but not the questions of the representativeness of these features over a landscape.

7 The Crosses of a Desert Place?

Cros Chríst tarsin ngnúisse, tarsin gclúais fon cóirse. Cros Chríst tarsin súilse. Cros Chríst tarsin ṣróinse.

Cros Chríst tarsin mbélsa. Cros Chríst tarsin cráessa. Cros Chríst tarsin cúlsa. Cros Chríst tarsin táebsa.

Cros Chríst tarsin mbroinnse (is amlaid as chuimse). Cros Chríst tarsin tairrse. Cros Chríst tarsin ndruimse.

Cros Chríst tar mo lama óm gúaillib com basa. Cros Chríst tar mo lesa. Cros Chríst tar mo chasa.

Cros Chríst lem ar m'agaid. Cros Chríst lem im degaid. Cros Chríst fri cach ndoraid eitir fán is telaig.

Cros Críst sair frim einech Cros Chríst síar fri fuined. Tes, túaid cen nach n-anad, cros Chríst cen nach fuirech.

Cros Chríst tar mo déta nám-tháir bét ná bine. Cros Chríst tar mo gaile. Cros Chríst tar mo chride.

Cros Chríst súas fri fithnim. Cros Christ sís fri talmain. Ní thí olc ná urbaid dom chorp ná dom anmain.

Cros Chríst tar mo shuide. Cros Chríst tar mo lige. Cros Chríst mo brig uile co roisem Ríg nime.

Cros Chríst tar mo muintir. Cros Chríst tar mo thempal. Cros Chríst isin altar. Cros Chríst isin chentar.

O mullach mo baitse co ingin mo choise, a Chríst, ar cach ngábad for snádad do chroise.

Co laithe mo báisse, ría ndol isin n-úirse, cen ainis do-bérsa crois Críst tarsin ngúisse.

Christ's cross over this face, and thus over my ear. Christ's cross over this eye. Christ's cross over this nose.

Christ's cross over this mouth. Christ's cross over this throat. Christ's cross over the back of this head. Christ's cross over this side.

Christ's cross over this belly (so is it fitting). Christ's cross over this lower belly. Christ's cross over this back.

Christ's cross over my arms from my shoulders to my hands. Christ's cross over my thighs. Christ's cross over my legs.

Christ's cross to accompany me before me. Christ's cross to accompany me behind me. Christ's cross to meet every difficulty both on hollow and hill.

Christ's cross eastwards facing me. Christ's cross back towards the sunset. In the north, in the south unceasingly may Christ's cross straightway be.

Christ's cross over my teeth lest injury or harm come to me. Christ's cross over my stomach. Christ's cross over my heart.

Christ's cross up to broad (?) Heaven. Christ's cross down to earth. Let no evil or hurt come to my body or my soul.

Christ's cross over me as I sit. Christ's cross over me as I lie. Christ's cross be all my strength till we reach the King of Heaven.

Christ's cross over my community. Christ's cross over my church. Christ's cross in the next world; Christ's cross in this.

From the top of my head to the nail of my foot, O Christ, against every danger I trust in the protection of thy cross.

Till the day of my death, before going into this clay, I shall draw without … Christ's cross over this face.

Mugrón (*comarba* Coluim Chille AD 965–81)[1]

Simple crosses cut into artificial caves and alcoves in southern Iceland form a coherent and largely unrecorded sculptural tradition. In our final study let us look to the rock-cut crosses at Seljaland and, as one way to explore the diffusion of culture and movements of people, seek to contextualize these cross forms through comparison with sculpture from other Atlantic areas.

Problem and Context

Where are the Seljaland rock-cut crosses best paralleled?

A feature of numerous southern Iceland caves as well as some Vestmannaeyjar (Westman Islands) exposed alcoves is rock-cut crosses that, taken together, form a coherent sculptural tradition. Although significant in number and in spite of this tradition's clearly productive influence on modern-day Iceland, the rock-cut crosses have yet to achieve widespread recognition as an art-historical movement. At Seljaland, for instance, innovative local custom prompts the marking of crosses upon plastic-wrapped hay (to ward off ravens; figure 7.1). The form of Iceland's rock-cut crosses includes characteristic features, a number of which are recognizable by Icelanders today; some crosses are named, and their cross-forms replicated as meaningful symbols. For example, the Heimaey "stave church" in the Westman Islands is decorated with a cross form taken from the nearby Papakross, and the Pentecostal Church in Iceland has adopted this cross form as its own (Torfason 2000: 7–8; figures 7.2 and 7.3). Furthermore, the Krossaþrenning Blindrafélags (tripartite cross of the Society for the Blind) is derived from the tripartite *krossaþrenningar* at Efri-Gegnishólar (Hjartarson et al. 1991: 30). In popular imagination, a Celtic identity is ascribed to these crosses, and the fascination with this "Celtic inheritance" may have inspired Reykjavík's Scottish- and Irish-themed pub, "The Celtic Cross" (figure 7.4).

Despite the evidently popular interest in cross forms from these sites, however, rock-cut crosses have only recently featured in academic studies, and fundamental questions have yet to be posed. Thus, in recognizing cave and "exposed alcove" cross sculpture as a coherent tradition, the question that this chapter confronts may be expressed as follows: what are the origins and cultural affinities of these crosses?

When situating Iceland's cave crosses within a wider context, it is crucial to recognize that this question is related to (but *distinct* from) the dating of cave construction discussed in chapter 5; in other words, if a date of ca. 800 is maintained for human settlement at Seljaland, this early date does not necessarily carry through to the sculpture. A cross may be cut at any time in a cave's lifespan – and possibly on several independent occasions. This point is illustrated by St Molaise's Cave on Holy Island off the coast of Arran (North Ayrshire, western Scotland). The cave's cross sculpture may be divided into two phases: an initial phase of large simple crosses accompanied by small graffito crosses associated with early Christian religious use, and a later phase of thirteenth-century Norse runic inscriptions and graffito crosses[2] (Fisher 2001: 61–5). Analysis of rock-cut sculpture from artificial caves, then, should be careful to allow for multiple episodes of carving at any time after the construction of these caves.

Chapter 4 mentioned the long history of southern Iceland's artificial cave sites in the textual tradition, the earliest reference being Adam of Bremen's eleventh-century description of the inhabitants of Thule (his usage signifying Iceland): "in subterraneis habitant speluncis, communi tecto et strato gaudentes cum pecoribus suis" (Adam: bk. 4, ch. 36, skol. 153; Schmeidler 1917: 272). (They live in underground caves, glad to have roof and food and bed in common

Figure 7.1 Cross-marked bales at Seljaland. Photograph by Florian Huber.

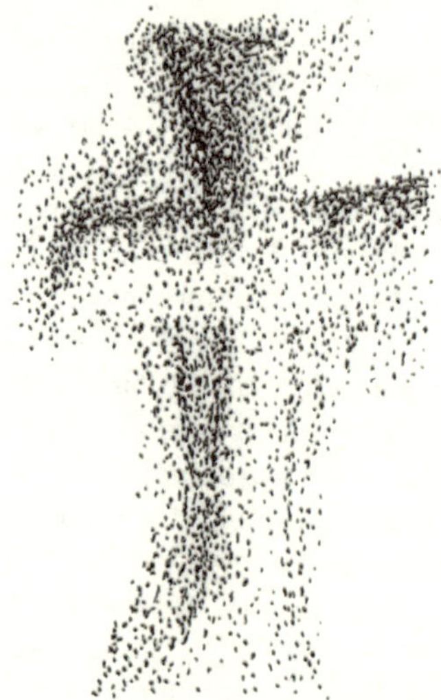

Figure 7.2 Illustration of cross VE1 (*Papakross*) from Hetta, Heimaklettur, Westman Islands. Scale 1:10. Drawn by Ian G. Scott.

Figure 7.3 Modern stave church on Heimaey.

Figure 7.4 The Celtic Cross pub in Reykjavík.

with their cattle; Tschan 1959: 217.) Although it is occasional, reference to cave use continues throughout the medieval and later periods. Only recently, however, have writers turned their attentions to markings cut into cave walls, but focusing largely upon runic and modern lettering rather than rock-cut crosses.[3] The reason for this approach to cave study may be straightforward: without regional catalogues and modern typologies for the Atlantic area, such as that produced by Ian Fisher for Scotland's west highlands and islands, the task of contextualizing southern Iceland's simple cross sculpture encounters substantial difficulties. One author articulates these difficulties with the caution that "crosses are probably the most common symbol to have survived through the perpetual changes in the history of thought in Europe" (Friðriksson 1994: 26). Advances are being made, however, and in their survey of cave sites Hjartarson et al. incorporate the most substantial catalogue of Icelandic rock-cut crosses to date.[4] The following excerpt from an emergency archaeological assessment[5] demonstrates the impact of Hjartarson et al.'s catalogue: "Seljalandshellar – 3 hellar hlið við hlið. Mikið af ristum í veggjunum, þmt. krossmörk sem eru gömul." (Seljalandshellar – 3 caves side by side. Many carvings in the walls, including cross-marks that are old.) In this brief passage the author shies away from discussing the character and historical place of the sculpture but (unlike earlier scholars) *includes* the cross marks in the inventory.

As mentioned in chapter 4, Brynjúlfur Jónsson was the first to introduce southern Iceland's cave sites into modern scholarship (Jónsson 1900; 1902; 1906; Friðriksson 1994: 24). Jónsson, however, ignored the cave sculpture, as did Matthías Þórðarson in his 1931 study. In fact, the minimal attention that Þórðarson gives to rock-cut crosses is largely in reference to the writings of Einar Benediktsson, poet and businessman:[6]

> Haustið 1905, 6. okt., 3 árum eftir að grein Brynjúlfs Jónassonar í Árbók Fornleifafél. frá 1902 var komin út, kom í blaðinu "Fjallkonan" fyrri hluti greinar eftir Einar Benediktsson, með yfirskriftinni Íra-býlin; siðari hlutinn kom í næsta tölublaði, 13. s. m. Segir höfundurinn, að hann hafi "lengi haldið það víst, að áður en Norðmenn, feður vorir, fundu eyjuna, sem vér byggjum, hafi mannavist og mannvirki fundizt víðs vegar um Ísland, miklu meiri en sagnir eru enn orðnar ljósar um" ...
>
> Að því er snertir þennan heyhelli á Ægissíðu ræður hann það, að hann sé eftir írska munka, sérstaklega af krossmörkum í honum, sem "eru höggvin á víð og dreif um hvelfingu hellisins" og "krossmarki allstóru" á hellisgaflinum innst, sem hann nefnir í því sambandi kórþil. (Þórðarson 1931: 57)

> (The autumn of 1905, October 6th, three years after Brynjúlfur Jónsson's article in *Árbók hins Íslenzka Fornleifafélagsins* (1902) appeared, Einar Benediktsson published the first half of an article in the newspaper *Fjallkonan* (The mountain woman) with the title "Irish-abodes"; the second half appeared in the next edition on the 13th of the same month. The writer said that he had "long held it probable that, from before the Norse (our fathers) found the island that we settled, people's dwellings and structures have been found far and wide in Iceland, more than has become clear in accounts" ...
>
> He concludes, with regards to this hay-cave at Ægissíða, that it is the work of Irish monks, particularly cross-marks in the cave, that "are cut in many places on the cave vaults," and "a rather large cross-mark" in the innermost corner, which he refers to as choir panelling.)

Though Þórðarson was doubtful of Benediktsson's interpretations, Benediktsson was nevertheless the first *in print* to struggle with cross sculpture (Benediktsson 1905a; 1905b). He mounted the first expedition to map artificial caves in 1915 (Hjartarson and Gísladóttir 1993), published *Thules beboere* (Benediktsson 1918), and wrote a series of newspaper articles in 1929.[7] His interest was taken up by a friend, the famed painter Jóhannes S. Kjarval, who ca. 1920 illustrated a number of cave features (Hjartarson and Gísladóttir 1983; 1985). It may be that Þórðarson's own substantial cave study was a reaction to Benediktsson's work. If so, Benediktsson occupies a crucial role in Icelandic cave scholarship.

Rock-cut crosses next receive attention in the 1945 edition of *Skírnir*,[8] in which Einar Ól Sveinsson mentions southern Iceland's artificial caves and cites the scholarship of Jónsson, Benediktsson, and Þórðarson (Sveinsson 1945: 200n1). A further brief reference is made by T.C. Lethbridge, where he records and illustrates a cross cut into a small exposed alcove on Heimaklettur in the Westman Islands (Lethbridge 1950: 83–5). Lethbridge's arguments are at times overly ambitious; what is crucial, however, is that he introduced a comparative methodology by illustrating the Heimaklettur cross alongside Shetland, Hebridean, and Argyll crosses.

Guðrún Sveinbjarnardóttir published her 1972 University of Iceland bachelor of arts thesis on papar. In this review of multidisciplinary materials associated with papar, she touches upon southern Iceland's artificial caves, mentioning Benediktsson's work on the crosses as well as Þórðarson's catalogue (Sveinbjarnardóttir 1972: 17). Sveinbjarnardóttir concludes her section by noting the lack of current research into the caves: "En það er með fyrrnefnda hella, sem fleira hér, að lítið hefur verið gert til að varpa ljósi á þá. Síðustu rannsóknir á þeim voru gerðar í kringum 1930" (Sveinbjarnardóttir 1972: 17; But [it can be said] that the said caves, as with other things here, that little has been done to cast light upon them. The latest research on them was carried out around 1930).

Anton Holt and Guðmundur J. Guðmundsson elaborate Lethbridge's comparative method in a discussion "Um krossana í hellunum" (About the crosses in the caves) and categorize the open-air, rock-cut crosses at Dyrhólaey and Heimaklettur alongside sculpture from artificial caves (Holt and Guðmundsson 1980: 16–8, 23). Holt and Guðmundsson tentatively date the large tripartite Efri-Gegnishólar cross (mentioned earlier) to 500–1000 and see parallels in sculpture from Birtley (Northumberland), Whithorn (Galloway), Inishmurray (County Sligo) and Aird a'Mhòrain (North Uist, Outer Hebrides).[9]

The 1980s and early 1990s saw a flourishing of publication on cave sculpture in the work of the trio Árni Hjartarson, Hallgerður Gísladóttir, and Guðmundur J. Guðmundsson. Hjartarson and Gísladóttir progressed from the preliminary comparative approach outlined above. First, they introduced an archaeological inventory methodology with their article on Skollhólahellir cave (Hjartarson and Gísladóttir 1983),[10] and, second, they explored the historiography of cave research through their rediscovery of Kjarval's early illustrations and their discussion of Benediktsson's 1915 expedition (Hjartarson and Gísladóttir 1993; Hjartarson and Gísladóttir 1985). Most significant, however, was the trio's inventory of artificial caves, *Manngerðir Hellar á Íslandi* (Hjartarson et al. 1991). In *Manngerðir Hellar* they provide a lengthy historical discussion of cave research in Iceland, catalogue *all* artificial cave sites (illustrated with simple sketches), and use this robust material to further refine application of the comparative method – here applied to contextualize *both* artificial cave sites and cross sculpture. Their work has been a crucial resource for detailed research at Seljaland. Owing to Hjartarson's, Gísladóttir's, and Guðmundsson's success in promoting Icelandic cave sites, these caves have begun to be integrated into wider scholarship beyond Iceland.[11]

Research published throughout the 1980s and early 1990s was thus pivotal in bringing attention to rock-cut crosses. Recent cave discussions now include cross sculpture. Þórður Tómasson, for instance, incorporates cross sculpture into his 1997 description of the Seljalandshellar caves:

> Stór hellir er í kletti bak við gamla bæjarstæði á Seljalandi undir Eyjafjöllum. Hellirinn er í röð merkra þjóðminja, alsættur krossmörkum og ristum af ýmsum toga, allt aftan frá miðöldum …
>
> Austurhellirinn (gapinn) fyldi vesturbænum, stúkan austurbænum. Meginhellinum var skipt milli býlanna. Vesturbærinn hafði innri hlutann. Þar vóru höggvin spor í berginu, beggja vegna, ætluð fyrir planka sem var í marki. Krossmark er þar beint uppi yfir, vestanmegin. Þarna innan til í hellinum eru fleiri bitaför frá þeim tíma er fiskur var þurrkaður á slám í hellinum. (Tómasson [í Skógum] 1997: 148–9)
>
> (A large cave is in a crag at the back of the old farm site at Seljaland under Eyjafjöll. The cave is in a row of national monuments, covered with cross marks and various carvings, reaching as far back as the Middle Ages …
>
> The eastern cave (*gapi*) belonged to the western farm, and the compartment cave (*stúka*) to the eastern farm. The main cave was divided between the farms. The western farm has the inner part. There were recesses cut into the rock surface, on both sides, meant for beams that were in position.[12] A cross mark is there directly over on the west side. There inside the cave are many beam cuts from the time that fish was dried on racks in the cave.)

Similarly, Ólafur H. Torfason, in his 2000 publication *Nokkrir Íslandskrossar* (A few Icelandic crosses), supports a suggestion first made by Lethbridge to group both cave crosses and the Westman Islands Papakross[13] as a single class of monument:

> Fyrstu kristnu krossarnir sem litu dagsins ljós á Íslandi hafa trúlega verið krossar papanna, keltneskra munka sem Ari fróði segir að hafi búið hér við landnám norræna manna, og e.t.v. anarra keltneskra íbúa. Krossmörk á veggjum hella á Suðurlandi telja sumir að megiskýra með búsetu papa eða anarra kelta. Ekkert er sannað í því efni.

"Keltakross" nefnist krossmark klappað í móberg milli Neðri- og Efri-Kleifar í Heimakletti í Vestmannaeyjum, þarna verða menn að fara um til að nytja eyna og full ástæða til að óska eftir vernd eða kannski minnast slyss. Bænastaðir eru víða í klettum í Vestmannaeyjum og annars staðar. Ekki er vitað um aldur krossins en hann er af keltneskri gerð. Hvítasunnusöfnuðurinn í Vestmannaeyjum gerði hann að merki sínu og svo Hvítasunnuhreyfingin á Íslandi. Nokkrir krossana sem ristir eru í veggi í manngerðum hellum á Suðurlandi eru svipaðir Keltakrossinum í Heimaey að lögum. (Torfason 2000: 7–8)

(The first Christian crosses that saw the light of day in Iceland were probably the crosses of papar, Celtic monks that Ari fróði said lived here at the time of Norse settlement, and perhaps other Celtic inhabitants. Cross marks on cave walls in southern Iceland may be explained, some believe, by the residence of papar or other Celts. No one has resolved the matter.

The cross mark named "Keltakross" was cut into tuff [palagonite] between Neðri- and Efri-Kleifar on Heimaklettur in the Westman Islands, there where people pass to make use of the islands and have every reason to wish after protection or perhaps remember accidents. There are prayer areas in many places in the Westman Islands and elsewhere. The age of the cross is not known, but it is of Celtic manufacture. The Pentecostal following in the Westman Islands made the cross their symbol, and so too did the Pentecostal movement in Iceland. A few of the crosses that are cut into artificial cave walls in southern Iceland are rather similar in form to the Keltakross in Heimaey.)

Torfason entertains the idea of anchoring the medieval tradition of papar to the rock-cut crosses, an association first articulated by Benediktsson and tentatively considered by Lethbridge, Sveinbjarnardóttir, Hjartarson, Gísladóttir, Guðmundsson, Holt, and Friðriksson. In seeking to identify the artists behind rock-cut crosses, Torfason demonstrates what I suggest is a widespread willingness to engage with the cross sculpture – a willingness frustrated by an undated and anonymous artistic tradition and the provision of only a preliminary catalogue.[14]

Turning to a general discussion of the cross itself, this symbol of Christianity came to peninsular and insular northwest Europe[15] from a number of overlapping directions. Christianity came to the region's Roman parts early, first as a secret and persecuted mystery cult.[16] Following official patronage in the fourth century, the chi-rho, the cross, and the marigold were widely taken up across the Christian world to symbolize the resurrection and continuing presence of Christ. With an eye to the relevance of typologies for Scotland, Fisher surveys the use of the cross in this early period:

> Notable examples survive in the murals of Egyptian church apses and in the mosaics of their Italian counterparts, often bedecked with wreaths or jewels or accompanied by birds. Stone sculpture was particularly favoured for funerary monuments, and the cross appeared on inscribed gravestones from Egypt and Gaul, and on Italian and Gaulish sarcophagi. Free-standing crosses marked places of particular sanctity, and the pilgrim Arculf described to Adomnán the silver-plated wooden cross which stood at Golgotha, on the site of one erected by Constantine in the early fourth century. This cross and others were represented on small flasks in which pilgrims carried oil from the Holy Places, and on Byzantine coins and medallions. Wood covered with metal plates was favoured for altar or processional crosses and ivory plaques for book-bindings, while small metal or jewelled crosses were used for personal devotion or as votive offerings. In manuscript painting, an interlaced cross appeared in a Coptic psalter attributed to the early fifth century, and similar initial crosses in Italian works of the late sixth century, while cruciform designs dominate the "carpet pages" of the great insular manuscripts. (Fisher 2001: 8)

Fisher continues to contemplate the range of Mediterranean and Gaulish models behind the earliest cross sculpture of Britain and Ireland. Noting poor survival of imported models, he calls attention to cross forms from western Britain that were stamped into fifth- or sixth-century North African or eastern Mediterranean pottery (Fisher 2001: 8; Campbell 2007). Charles Thomas suggests that "little double-outline expanded-arm crosses" stamped into pottery bases at Tintagel (Cornwall) inspired early stone work at the same site (Thomas 1971: 116–17). Jeremy Knight sees Gaulish prototypes for cross forms cut into stone slabs in western Britain and Ireland in this period (Knight 1999: 176–7), whereas Lloyd and Jennifer Laing note parallel chi-rho forms in Spain as well (Laing and Laing 1990: 175).[17] Fisher contextualizes the influence of Mediterranean and Gaulish models: "Bede records the embellishment of Northumbrian churches in the seventh century with painted panels and manuscripts from Rome and Gaul, and Irish travellers were also familiar with these areas. The Gaulish pilgrim Arculf, who came to Iona about 690, described not only the large crosses erected at pilgrimage sites in the Holy Land but also the elaborate Holy Week ceremonial for the Veneration of the Cross at the Byzantine court" (Fisher 2001: 8).

Particularly, however, cross sculpture shared many features throughout the Breton and insular[18] areas in this period (Davies et al. 2000: 3). The cross was a powerful symbol for early Christian monastic communities, eloquently expressed by Mugrón's *crossradhach* (quoted in full at the beginning of this chapter). Although largely a feature of ecclesiastical sites, certain crosses in western Scotland "offered protection and invited prayer at boat-landings or beside tracks, or marked holy wells" (Fisher 2001: 9). Knight proposes that the prominence of the cross at this time is related to monasticism in late sixth- and seventh-century Britain and Ireland (Knight 1999: 179).

The spread of Christianity to Scandinavia came later, incorporating influences from both the insular and Frankish worlds. The earliest missionaries appear in trading towns such as Birka (Lake Mälar, Sweden), perhaps as early as the eighth century. Ansgar led missions from Saxony to Birka twice in the ninth century (829–31 and 852–5) (Trillmich 1961). Florian Huber relates this period's pagan "hammer" and cross amulets to the historical context (Huber 2000; 2002):

> Several hammer rings have been identified … and we may speculate that these hammer rings represent a manifestation of pagan religion when the local population was confronted with a new Christian ritual and belief – perhaps carried by Ansgar's mission (Staecker 1999a; 1999b). In essence, the argument notes the coincidence of both Thor's hammer rings and the early documented Christian missions to Sweden … Hammer rings occur largely in the ninth and tenth centuries with a clustering around the trading centre of Birka, the site of Ansgar's early ninth-century mission. If such a straightforward scenario is to be imagined, however, one must account for the first appearance of the Thor's hammer rings in eighth-century Sweden prior to Ansgar's mission (Huber 2002).[19]

The coincidence of ninth- and tenth-century hammer rings in the area of Ansgar's mission could suggest a connection between the hammer rings and early Christianity in the Mälar area (though the identification of these amulets with Þór's hammer remains hypothetical). The existence of eighth-century hammer rings, however, is problematic for Staecker's suggestion of these rings as a reaction to a new Christian ritual and belief unless one accepts the idea of eighth-century Christian missions to Sweden.

For eighth-century Scandinavia, Staecker points to Willibrord's visit ca. 700 to the Danish King Ongendus, and Alcuin's discussion with Willehad (bishop of Bremen) in 789 on the subject of converting the Danes (Staecker 1999b). Noting the prominence in the region of historical figures from the insular tradition, Staecker proposes unremembered monastic missions to Scandinavia by communities educated in the Gaelic schools and active across Europe at this time (Huber 2002). Miriam Zeiten notes similar suggestions in Mackeprang and Olsen (Zeiten 1997: 26; Mackeprang 1938: 179–80; Olsen 1966: 119), though she follows Schwarz-Mackensen (1978: 85) and Ström (1984: 140) to challenge a Christian inspiration for Þór-dedicated amulets (Schwarz-Mackensen 1978: 85; Ström 1984: 140).

Both scenarios are plausible. To the south and southwest of Scandinavia, great changes were taking place in these centuries: the Frisians were Christian by ca. 800, and the Old Saxons were violently drawn into the Carolingian empire. Across the empire, conversion and the monastic impulse was strong; foundations were established in newly incorporated Frisia and Saxony at Ramelsloh, Bremen, Bassum, Bücken, Hamburg. and Welenao.[20]

Archaeologically, the first appearance of the cross symbol occurs in areas of ninth-century Christian mission, and a cross amulet from Hedeby is Denmark's oldest. In Denmark a handful of such amulets may be dated to the ninth and tenth centuries, though the majority of cross amulets appear in eleventh-century contexts (Zeiten 1997: 29–30).

Cross forms are also found alongside runic inscriptions cut into stones in the Mälar region of Sweden (Lager 2000: 131). Indeed, crosses may be identified on roughly half of Scandinavia's surviving rune stones, with three-quarters of Sweden's stones incorporating Christian symbolism or prayers (Lager 2000: 120–1). Birgit Sawyer sees that "these monuments reflect the transition from pagan to Christian burial customs" (Sawyer 2000: 17). The earliest stones are dated to ca. 975–1050[21] and incorporate a simple cross and restrained runic band – both cross and band being elaborated throughout the runic period (ca. 970–1130). Late Viking Age decoration becomes very elaborate; for example, a stone from Uppland in Sweden (U735) demonstrates a complex cross form and intricate runic band (illustrated in Lager 2000: 122).

Christian influence from Britain was substantial in Sweden during the conversion period, especially so in the Mälar region (Lager 2000: 130). Lager identifies an insular character in the Scandinavian stones:

> There are considerable similarities between the cruciforms on these runestones, and Viking Age coins and erected stone-crosses from the British Isles. There are also considerable English linguistic influences on these runestones as well as in other early written Swedish sources. Since the erection of runestones in the Mälar region continued for such a long period of time in the presence of British-influenced Christians (whether "missionaries" or not), runestones were probably considered an appropriate expression of Christian faith, perhaps even encouraged by the clerics. (Lager 2000: 130)

Lager outlines a scenario in which the Frankish Church, dominant in Denmark and southern Sweden, may not have tolerated the rune stone as a productive tradition; certainly the erection of these stones ended in Denmark and southern Sweden earlier than elsewhere in Scandinavia (Lager 2000: 130). Sawyer, however, cautions against a straightforward association of Christianity with rune-stone production: "Even if the erection of rune-stones answered religious and social needs in a period of transition, the change of faith and the abandonment of traditional burial customs, however, cannot alone explain the origins, distribution, and uniformity of the fashion" (Sawyer 2000: 19).

In Norway the first bishopric was established at Selja ca. 1070 for Bjarnharðr hinn saxlenzki (Bernhard the Saxon) after his work and travels in Iceland, Rome, and Saxony. Selja, on the extreme northwestern tip of the Norwegian coast, was already host to a Christian community (Nyberg 2000: 69), and we may wonder whether the Seljaland name may be linked to this place in some way. The tradition of the "Holy men of Selja" tells of an Irish monastic settlement on the island taking refuge in a cave that divine intervention sealed with a landslide, leaving them to die as martyrs. Adam of Bremen may refer to Selja in his skolia (nos. 129 and 145),[22] in which he writes of the *septem dormientum* slumbering in a cave in the far north, awaiting the end of the world in order to rise and preach. Adam has Olaf (whether Tryggvason, Haraldsson, or Kyrre) building a church at this site (Nyberg 2000: 69–73; Hommedal 1996).

Fridtjóf Birkeli has studied the roughly sixty standing stone crosses of Norway, though his work may need reassessment in light of clear advances in the study of the insular corpus (Fisher 2005; Birkeli 1973). Standing crosses from the Stavanger area may be related to a neglected cross type common on the northeastern Shetland islands of Yell and Unst in the eleventh centuries. Furthermore, this cross form is found elsewhere in the Atlantic area. Recently discovered near-perfect parallels of the Yell and Unst type may also be identified in three locally made standing crosses from the grounds of the eleventh-century church at Þórarinnstaðir in Seyðisfjörður, eastern Iceland[23] (Fisher 2005; 2002: 55–6; Kristjánsdóttir 2003: 123–4).

In the Faroe Islands, encircled linear, shallow sunken, and outline cross-marked stones have been recovered from Skúvøy; a lost stone from Svinøy was illustrated in 1828; and an unprovenanced (but Faroese) stone is held in the National Museum of Denmark's collection. Many of these stones' cross forms probably demonstrate a connection to the Gaelic Christian sculptural traditions; their similarity in technique and close concentration at the island's earliest *Norse* Christian site suggest they may remember "a Hebridean contribution to the Norse conversion of the islands" (Fisher 2005).

In the above discussion of the Stavanger, Shetland, eastern Icelandic, and Faroese sculpture, Fisher compares cross forms across the north Atlantic area and provides the sculpture with a historical context. His approach is valid. Careful application of typologies developed for simple cross forms demonstrates the potential strengths of sophisticated comparative studies. Ewan Campbell's work on the expanded-terminal form in Argyll illustrates the point. It has long been recognized that expanded-terminal crosses, incised into stone, were characteristic of the early Church in western Scotland and Ireland (Fisher 2001: 12–13). In 1987 Campbell set about a detailed and comprehensive examination of Argyll crosses. This investigation enabled him to identify the expanded-terminal cross form as a coherent group, a group he linked with areas in which the monastic community of St Columba, based in Iona, was active (Campbell 1987: 111). This is consistent with Charles Thomas's view of simple incised crosses:

> In regions of Britain and Ireland where the tradition of the inscribed memorial tombstone was absent, physical commemoration of the Christian dead in stone begins only at the end of the sixth century … The "primary" stones, which are for the most part pre-Norse, are small and plain … this is essentially a western and north-western facet of post-Roman Britain, the source being apparently Ireland, and the spread a reflection of the work of Irish monastic missions. The crosses themselves are of a limited range of linear forms, and are usually incised with a knife or point. (Thomas 1973: 28)

The expanded-terminal cross form central to discussion here belongs to what Campbell describes as a "larger group of simple incised crosses which are commonly found on recumbent slabs, upright pillars, boulders and rock faces throughout the Celtic west" (Campbell 1987: 106). Thomas describes this larger group as *primary cross-marked stones* (Thomas 1971: 112–14), and Isabel Henderson prefers *class IV early Christian monuments* (Henderson 1987: 46). Although they are probably the earliest form of stone crosses, scholars agree that this group has often been ignored because of its simplicity. It nonetheless appears that such simple crosses form a distinctive stage in the development of early Christian decoration in northern Britain and Ireland.

Thomas understands primitive cross-marked stones as emerging in late-sixth- and seventh-century Britain from ultimately Mediterranean models of the fifth and sixth centuries (Thomas 1971: 112–16; Campbell 1987: 107). Looking to Pictland, Henderson has previously suggested simple cross markings as seventh-century phenomena logically preceding the eighth-century relief cross slabs (Henderson 1987: 48). Henderson posited that, in fact, seventh-century Columban activity is responsible for simple cross forms in Pictish areas of eastern Scotland.[24]

Campbell operates from the following basic premise: "While it is possible that the very simplest of these crosses, consisting of plain vertical and horizontal lines, are not amenable to any analysis, the slightly more complex forms may reflect changing fashions in particular regions" (Campbell 1987: 107).

Originally suggested by Hamlin, this premise has proven a valid one, for a pattern does emerge in Argyll (Hamlin 1982: 290).

Argyll, because of its excellent and comprehensive inventory of early Christian monuments, provides a good geographic distribution from which significant archaeological information can be recovered (Campbell 1987: 107). Campbell maps the roughly fifty sites from which one hundred and fifty cross-marked stones have been identified, and a discrete clustering of expanded-terminal crosses is revealed (Campbell 1987: 108; figures 7.5 and 7.6). This clustering of crosses is significant and reinforced by a strong similarity of form and dimension among the expanded-terminal group members. The clustering is important for two reasons. First, these crosses can now be associated in time and space with areas in which the Columban *familia* was active. Second, the cross form is shown *not* to be persistent or recurring, at least not in early Christian Argyll; in other words, if the expanded-terminal form were long lived, then a wide distribution would be expected (Campbell 1987: 107–8). The seventeen expanded-terminal crosses in Campbell's study were recorded from seven sites: Hynish on Tiree; Iona, Nun's Cave, and Scoor Cave on the Ross of Mull; Eileach an Naoimh in the Garvellachs; Barnakill near Dunadd; and at Dunadd itself. Campbell characterizes the collection thus:

> These sites lie in an east-west group running from Tiree to Dunadd. There is a concentration of the crosses on Iona which has one of the largest collections of early Christian monuments in Britain and Ireland with over 100 stones recorded. The Iona collection includes six crosses with expanded terminals and 11 with other forms of elaboration. The other five sites, except Dunadd, would also appear to be religious rather than secular in nature. The two caves on the Ross of Mull have many religious carvings and could be interpreted as retreats or *deserta* for anchorites or penitents. The stone from Hynish, Tiree was found in the make-up of a barn floor, but could possibly have come from the daughter house of Iona, *campus Lunge*, which existed on Tiree. However, there were several other monasteries on Tiree at this time and *campus Lunge* is not securely identified. The group of crosses on the Garvellachs at Eileach an Naoimh is associated with the well-known monastic site traditionally founded by St Brendan. In the past, this has been identified with the Iona daughter house on *Hinba*, but the Royal Commission on the Ancient and Historical Monuments of Scotland (RCAHMS) reject this identification. The cross at Barnakill was found only two kilometres from Dunadd … The –kil place-name may signify the former presence of a religious site. (Campbell 1987: 108–9)

The Columban association with the expanded-terminal cross form is reinforced by an analysis of Adomnán's *Life of St Columba*. Textual study reveals that,

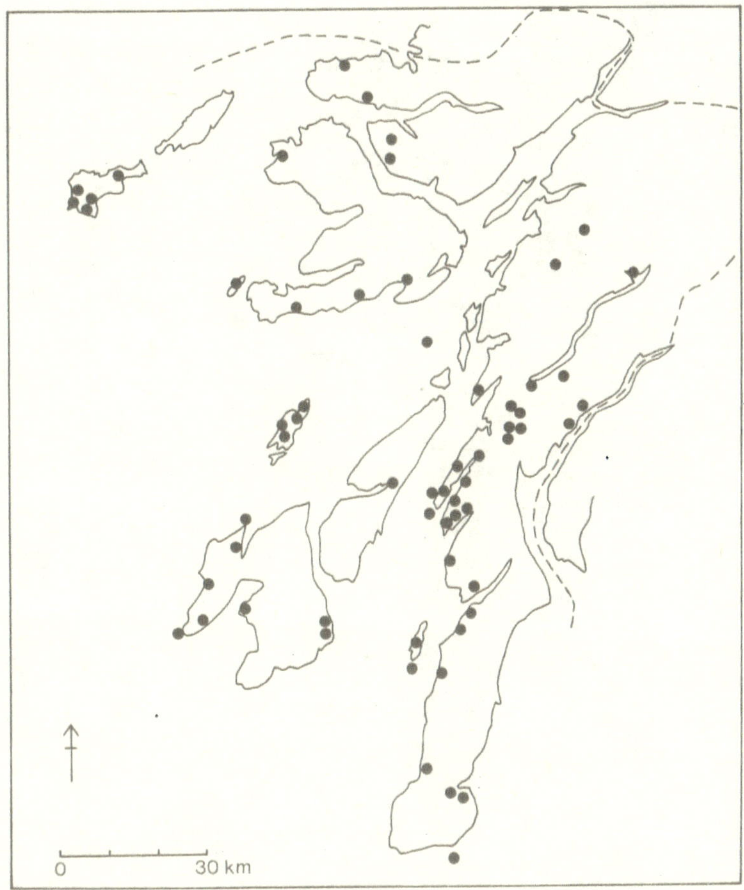

Figure 7.5 Distribution of early Christian sites with cross sculpture in the portion of Argyll bounded by the dotted line. Taken from Campbell's study of cross sculpture (1987: 108). I am grateful to the Society of Antiquaries of Scotland for permission to reproduce this illustration.

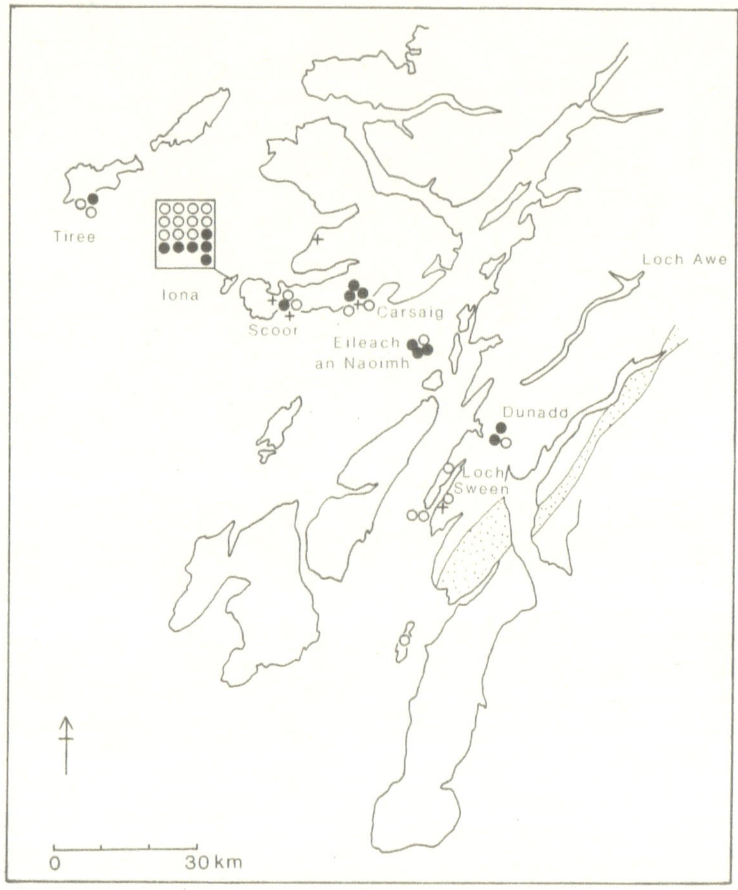

Figure 7.6 Distribution of incised crosses with expanded terminals, marked by black points (other variant terminals marked by open points and crosses). Taken from Campbell's study of cross sculpture (1987: 109). I am grateful to the Society of Antiquaries of Scotland for permission to reproduce this illustration.

aside from locations along the sea route to Ireland and those associated with Columba's travels in Pictland or Skye, all identified places lie in Tiree, Mull, Morven, Ardnamurchan, and Lorne. This is the same portion of northern Argyll in which the expanded-terminal crosses were found (Campbell 1987: 110).

The dating evidence for each carving elaborates the discussion. Individually, the seventeen expanded-terminal crosses of Argyll offer dates between the late-sixth and early-ninth centuries; Thomas dated the Barnakill stone to the seventh century by inscription, the Dunadd quern falls in the main occupation period from the late-sixth to early-ninth centuries, and from Iona the vast majority of crosses probably pre-date the Viking Age[25] (Thomas 1971: 112; Campbell 1987: 112; Fisher 2001: 10–11). Noting the restricted range of the cross form, mentioned above, Campbell suggests that the expanded-terminal cross finds its home at the earlier end of the period. This dating is consistent with Thomas's general simple cross-form dates for northern Britain and with Henderson's class IV monument dates for Pictland, both mentioned above. On geographic and temporal grounds, then, the Argyll occurrences of this cross form may be linked with the Columban familia of monastic houses of the seventh and eighth centuries.

As for the general distribution of the form, it appears largely exclusive to Ireland (probably the coastal west),[26] western Scotland, and both the Western and Northern Isles (Hamlin 1982: 289–93; Campbell 1987: 111; Fisher 2001: 29–32). This dating is consistent with a barred terminal cross found on St Ninian's Isle, Shetland, and tentatively dated to ca. 700, as well as an expanded-terminal cross from Papil, Shetland, which Thomas ascribed to the mid-eighth century (Thomas 1973: 28–9).

Campbell's typological analyses of Argyll material illustrate the potential of sophisticated comparative work on simple cross forms. Furthermore, Fisher's work on the Stavanger, Shetland, eastern Icelandic, and Faroese sculpture (mentioned earlier) demonstrates that useful interpretations may be drawn from careful consideration of typological parallels across the north Atlantic area.

Hypotheses

This chapter seeks to identify parallels for the Seljaland rock-cut crosses in order to contextualize southern Iceland's cross sculpture from artificial caves and alcoves. Three alternative hypotheses are proposed: (1) the cross sculpture is contemporary with seventeenth- and eighteenth-century inscriptions; (2) the crosses are similar to the Norse and Hiberno-Norse Christian sculpture of

Britain, Ireland, and Scandinavia; or (3) the crosses are similar to the sculpture of early Christian Britain and Ireland.

On a number of cave walls Matthías Þórðarson identified ownership marks (*búmörk*) and inscriptions from the seventeenth to twentieth centuries (Þórðarson 1931: 58; Friðriksson 1994: 25). Þórðarson proposed that cross marks cut into cave walls (which he largely omitted from his catalogue of cave sites) were of similar antiquity. He writes:

> Einar Benediktsson virðist hafa lagt mikið upp úr því, að krossmörk væru í fjóshellinum á Ægissíðu, sem sönnunargagni fyrir aldri hans og að hann væri gerður af írskum múnkum löngu fyrir landnámstíð. Nú er það svo, að krossmörk hafa menn krotað og gert með ýmsu móti fyrr og siðarr; virðist ekkert það við krossmarkið á hellisgaflinum og því siður við hin, sem bendir til að þau séu gerð löngu fyrir landnámstíð. Þau virðast eins vel geta verið frá síðustu öldum, enda eru þau það að líkindum, og ósannanlegt, að þau séu eldri. (Þórðarson 1931: 62)

> Einar Benediktsson seemed to have made much of the fact that cross marks were in the cowshed cave at Ægissíðu, as a piece of evidence for the age of the cave, and that the cave was made by Irish monks long before the time of [Norse] settlement. It is in fact the case that people have scrawled cross marks, in various fashions, through time; nothing about the cross marks on the cave wall, and even less about the others, seems to suggest that they were made long before the time of settlement. They seem just as well to be from the last centuries, and that is what they probably are, and unprovable that they are older.

Þórðarson interprets the cross sculpture from caves as an innovative and late Icelandic practice. The first hypothesis to consider then is this: the Icelandic tradition of rock-cut simple crosses (represented by the examples from Skollhólahellir cave and the Seljaland caves) is *contemporary with* seventeenth- and eighteenth-century inscriptions on cave walls.

The first hypothesis is tested in a simple way: by considering whether seventeenth- and eighteenth-century inscriptions in these caves respect or are respected by the cross sculpture – thus suggesting whether the inscriptions are pre-dated by or pre-date the crosses.

Christianity was practised extensively (and intensively in places) in Viking Age Britain and Ireland; this was also true, to some extent, of the areas of Scandinavian settlement there. As noted earlier, Frisia and Saxony were incorporated into the Christian Frankish kingdom in the early Viking Age, and Christian missions to Scandinavia were established.

Later sources such as the Icelandic *Landnámabók* assign insular and sometimes Christian origins to many early Norse settlers, with a special prominence given to the cult of Kolumkille (*Landnámabók*: ch. 15; Benediktsson 1968: 53–5; Smyth 1984: 163, 171–2; Anderson 1922: 340n1, 343n1). A Christian-influenced Hebridean or Innse Gall origin for some Norse Landnámsmenn would be consistent with Viking Age archaeological material from Iceland, such as the Foss cross mentioned earlier (Ahronson 2001). Thus, the second hypothesis to consider is this: the Icelandic tradition of rock-cut simple crosses (represented by the examples from the Seljaland caves) is *similar to* the earliest stratum of Norse and Hiberno-Norse Christianity in Britain, Ireland, and Scandinavia.

A legacy of sculpted stones and carvings survives in the caves and rock faces of Atlantic Europe's isolated coasts and islands, identifying sixth- to ninth-century monastic communities across Argyll, the Hebridean islands, Orkney, and Shetland. How far into the Atlantic Ocean did these groups venture? As we have seen in previous chapters, the first settlement of Iceland by Viking Age Scandinavians is thought to have begun ca. 870, and it may have been preceded by monastic settlement from the Scottish islands. The early Christian sculpture of western Scotland has been studied in great detail, and Fisher has brought this work together in his 2001 inventory. Thus, the crosses from western Scotland present a strong corpus with which to contrast the Icelandic sculpture. The third hypothesis to consider then is this: the Icelandic tradition of rock-cut simple crosses (represented by the examples from the Seljaland caves) is *similar to* the cross sculpture of early Christian Britain and Ireland (represented by the corpus from Scotland's western highlands and islands).

The second and third hypotheses are tested by initially classifying the Seljaland sculpture into the RCAHMS's broad cross-form categories (*incised linear*, *sunken linear*), followed by further categorization by the presence of characteristics recognized in art-historical literature (for example, *Latin*, *rounded terminals*) (Fisher 2001: 11–12). Once this categorization has been completed, consideration is given to the similarities between the Seljaland sculpture and the sculpture from Britain, Ireland, and Scandinavia.

The art-historical terminology used for classification articulates variables privileged by scholars of simple cross sculpture. For instance, if a cross is cut into rock in such a way as to create a sunken (or incised or outline) cross shape, this has been interpreted as a "meaningful" characteristic for classification (Fisher 2001; 2002; 2005). That sunken (or incised or outline) cross forms should be privileged over other variables (such as *shaft width*) is supported by its continuing survival in academic discourse. The presumption is that the exercise of scholarly discourse has discarded "unmeaningful" variables and identified potentially "meaningful" (or significant) ones. These privileged variables are likely to be eventually superseded by more refined terminology, but for the purposes of this chapter they satisfy the questions being asked of the data.

Some ambiguities are inherent in this terminology; for instance, when does a Latin cross become a Greek cross? Where there is such uncertainty in classification I mention this. Fisher's catalogue for the west highlands and islands is a model for cross sculpture study in the Atlantic area, and his categorizations, with some modification, are applied to the Seljaland data. A benefit of using Fisher's categorizations is that they are recognized divisions introduced by the RCAHMS in its inventory work for Iona. Using these categories has the additional benefit of allowing easy assessment of similarities between the Seljaland sculpture and the crosses in Fisher's catalogue. Comparisons are made along typological and contextual lines – in other words, of size and style as well as the location where a cross is found, along with any relevant material.

Method

Numerous caves in southern Iceland are artificial and have cross markings. Hjartarson et al. have done much for southern Iceland's cross sculpture, yet their preliminary illustrations of the Seljaland material (figure 7.7) are insufficient for detailed analysis. In order to test the multiple hypotheses outlined above, the following method was adopted. Investigations at Seljaland in August 2002 undertook detailed recording of nineteen large and four mid-sized crosses cut into the walls of the Seljalandshellar cave group. A further cross, from the entrance to Kverkarhellir cave, was similarly recorded. At this stage of research, simple graffito crosses in the Seljalandshellar caves (counted in September 2001 at eighty-three) were not recorded in this way, as the simplest of cross marks are the least amenable to typological analysis. The format of illustration outlined for the Seljaland corpus was then applied to a further four crosses in order to demonstrate the strength of recording the rock-cut crosses according to this method: three from alcoves in the Heimaklettur cliff face (on the Westman Islands) and one from Skollhólahellir cave at Ás farm in Rangárvallasýsla. The largest Heimaklettur cross, mentioned earlier in this chapter, is known locally as the Papakross and identified with early Irish settlers in the islands' oral traditions. The two other alcove crosses were previously unrecorded and may not be known locally.

In the recording of the Seljaland crosses, emphasis was placed upon producing a drawing. In the field, high-quality black-and-white photographs,[27] scale

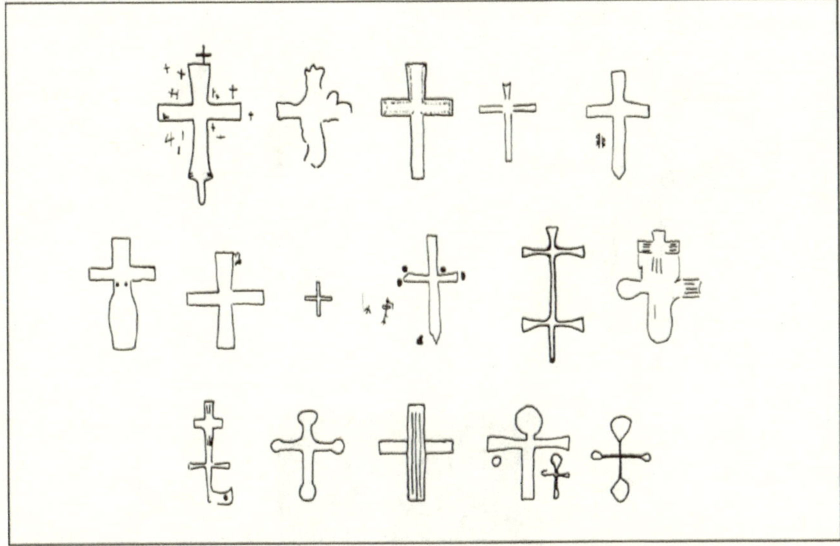

Figure 7.7 Preliminary illustrations of cross sculpture from the Seljalandshellar caves. Taken from Hjartarson et al.'s catalogue (1991: 248), with author's permission.

drawings, and wax rubbings recorded the sculpture. Publication illustrations were prepared by Ian G. Scott (formerly chief illustrator of the RCAHMS) and examined by Ian Fisher.

The Seljaland inventory of cross sculpture provides a model for recording and illustrating the southern Iceland corpus of rock-cut cross sculpture. This method is illustrated for Seljalandshellar cross B13 (see figure 7.8 for scaled rubbing, photographs, field illustration, and final drawing) and is modelled upon that practised by the RCAHMS. Rubbings and photographs of the Seljaland cross sculpture were taken, with the ultimate aim of producing a final ink drawing. In the production of these drawings, the rubbing was used for outline and size, and details were drawn from photographs; field drawings were used to overcome ambiguities in the rubbings and photographs. The final illustrations were then rigorously examined (by Ian G. Scott and me) in order to resolve potential difficulties and highlight *real* (rather than imagined) problem areas inherent in the sculpture.

As mentioned, the emphasis was placed upon producing a drawing. An alternate approach would give prominence to creating a photographic record. Photography, however, can be deceptive, casting detail into shadow and obscuring depth of features. Leslie Alcock, for instance, does not accept the

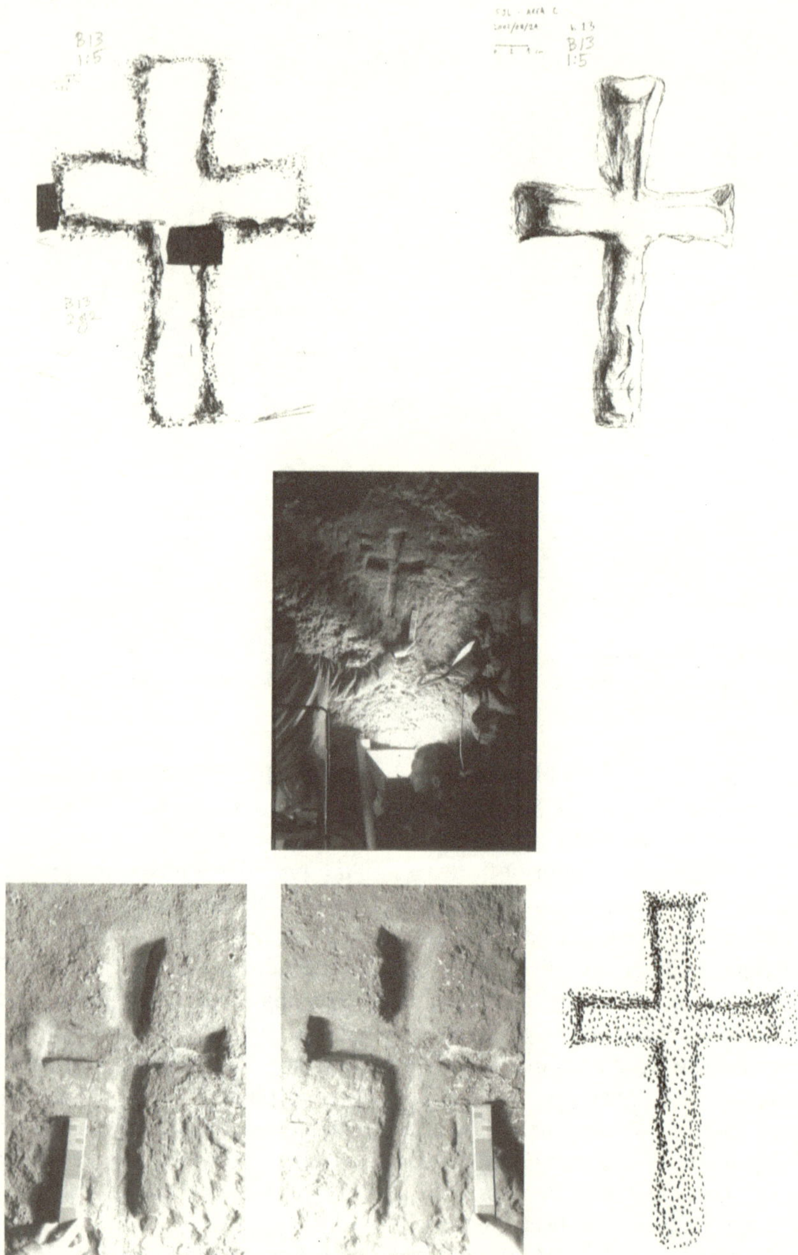

Figure 7.8 *Above.* Rubbing and field illustration of Seljalandshellar cross B13. Original scale 1:5; reproduced here at 1:10. Drawn by Kerry-Anne Mairs. *Middle.* "Action" shot. *Below.* Photographs of Seljalandshellar cross B13 and stipple illustration of cross B13. Scale 1:10. Drawing by Ian G. Scott.

"common belief that a photograph is … totally objective" (Alcock 1998: 533). Instead, he notes that "looking at stones in the field and in museums reveals the large part which lighting plays in determining what may (or may not) be seen and therefore photographed" (Alcock 1998: 533).

Scott, however, challenges the excessive detail inherent in the technique, leading him to question "the value of presenting a photograph in demonstration of an argument" (Scott 1997: 129). To elaborate the point, a drawing *is* an argument, and a good drawing conveys both confidence and uncertainty in the aspects of the sculpture that it illustrates. Scott writes that "objectivity and accuracy are admirable goals but only subjective, selective interpretation will clear away from this basic record some of the intrusive and confusing elements, and allow reconstructions to be suggested" (Scott 1996: 4). Such a subjective and selective interpretation may also convey difficulties. Scott stresses this: "A considered, studied drawing will present ambiguities, but these can be assumed to be intentional … Drawings can, and should, stimulate … questioning and not simply be an inert record of the bits and pieces: they should provide the means for a paper reconstruction and analysis" (Scott 1997: 129–32).

In the illustration of cross sculpture, then, the aim is not to produce an objective record (if this is even achievable) but rather to selectively and convincingly convey an argument for what is observed.

Taking up Scott's mandate to illustrate, an immediate concern is which method to adopt. Graham Ritchie provides a history of illustration for Meigle 10, a now-lost Perthshire carved stone slab. In his survey of drawings from 1726 to 1903, the range of technique and ability become clear, and the modern RCAHMS policy of having both a stipple drawing and a photograph demonstrates clear advantages (Ritchie 1997). Stipple drawing is not the only method used today, however, for two techniques dominate: line and stipple.

Line drawings are often presented by default in simple illustration,[28] perhaps because the technique is used for archaeological field plans and thus applied without reflection rather than as a deliberate choice. Intelligent use of line drawing has its advocates. Alcock, for instance, favours the use of line drawings, suggesting that line is less subjective than stipple (Alcock 1998: 533–4). Scott challenges the point with the counter that "line is surely the uncompromising statement of belief, ignoring the third dimension and sharpening the perception" (Scott 2005).

Scott is a proponent of the stipple technique. He cites the technique's "comparative lack of an individual 'handwriting' character (usually detectable in other styles of drawing)" (Scott 1997: 131) and that stipple allows a uniform repetition of style by others. He also notes that the technique conveys "the third dimension without giving it an affected texture when you are obliged to use only black ink for the sake of clarity in reproduction and longevity in the archive" (Scott 1997: 131). Furthermore, Scott adds that stipple, unlike other techniques, is amenable to additions and corrections, and drawings may always be improved (Scott 1996: 10; 1997: 131).

The stipple drawing technique was adopted in the illustration of the Seljaland cross sculpture. The results presented in this chapter encourage the use of stipple to illustrate Iceland's corpus of cross sculpture.

Illustrations of in situ sculpture, however, need to be physically located in order to clearly identify *which* sculpture is under discussion and to study spatial relationships (for example, to floor level or levels). Each Seljaland cross was identified on cave plans for Kverkarhellir cave and the Seljalandshellar cave group,[29] and the height above ground level of the cross's base was tabulated.

Practical limitations at times became manifest. Seljalandshellar crosses B10 and B11 were photographed only once; their height above ground level (2.70+ m) meant that ground-level lighting could not be varied effectively. Cross B11 was problematic; it was clearly perceived upon the cave wall but ambiguous in detail. Thus, light stipple outlines the cross form, conveying the difficulties inherent in this sculpture.

Two crosses were illustrated a second time, using an alternate methodology. Additional drawings of Seljalandshellar crosses B9 and B10 (figure 7.30) were made from photograph (therefore are not to scale) in order to contextualize the sculpture in relation to the surrounding wall surface.

As mentioned earlier, the methods advocated for the Seljaland cross sculpture may be applied to other rock-cut crosses. Preliminary illustrations were presented elsewhere for crosses from Heimaklettur in the Westman Islands and Skollhólahellir on Ás farm in Rangárvallasýsla (Ahronson 2000; Hjartarson and Gísladóttir 1983). The figure 7.31 drawings were made from photograph only and demonstrate how the Seljaland methodology may be applied retrospectively (see also figure 7.32). These illustrations are acceptable as work in progress, but, before their full incorporation into the corpus alongside the Seljaland sculpture, their details will have to be re-examined and a similar standard set for accompanying photographs.

The detailed recording and illustration of Seljaland cross sculpture is central to all three hypotheses proposed. The next section presents these illustrations and explores parallels for the sculpture.

Results and Discussion

Cross sculpture in the Seljaland caves is found at two sites: the Seljalandshellar cave group and Kverkarhellir cave. This section illustrates twenty-three rock-cut crosses (nineteen large and four mid-sized) from the Seljalandshellar cave group as well as a single cross from Kverkarhellir cave. Two photographs were taken of each illustrated cross (except AX2), although only one photograph is reproduced here, and includes a 0.20 m scale (figures 7.9 to 7.30). A further four crosses are illustrated: three from Hetta, on Heimaklettur in the Westman Islands; and one from Skollhólahellir cave, on Ás farm in Rangárvallasýsla (figures 7.31 and 7.32). As noted earlier, three hypotheses are considered when interpreting the data:

- The Icelandic tradition of rock-cut simple crosses (represented by examples from the Seljaland caves) is *contemporary with* seventeenth- and eighteenth-century inscriptions on cave walls.
- The Icelandic tradition of rock-cut simple crosses (represented by the examples from the Seljaland caves) is *similar to* the earliest stratum of Norse and Hiberno-Norse Christian sculpture in Britain, Ireland, and Scandinavia.
- The Icelandic tradition of rock-cut simple crosses (represented by the examples from the Seljaland caves) is *similar to* the cross sculpture of early Christian Britain and Ireland (represented by the corpus from Scotland's western highlands and islands).

The RCAHMS introduced a composite system of classification in their *Inventory of Iona*, and Fisher classifies his material according to their system. For simple cross sculpture, the carving technique (for example, incised, sunken, relief) and the cross form (for example, linear, outline) are combined (Fisher 2001: 11–12). The Seljaland and additional southern Iceland material (illustrated above) has been similarly classified into *incised linear* and *sunken linear*, with brackets indicating uncertainty, and square brackets separating out the additional Vestmannaeyjar (VE) and Skollhólahellir (SK) sculpture:

- *Incised linear*: AX2, A/B3, (B4), B5, B7, B9, B12, B15, B16, C17, C18, C19, KV, [VE3], [SK1]
- *Sunken linear*: A1, A2, B6, B8, B10, B11, B13, (B14), [VE1], [VE2]

For further development of the interpretation, the Seljaland corpus (with the additional contextual detail of the Hetta and Skollhólahellir crosses) may be additionally classified into overlapping categories as follows:

- *Latin cross*: AX2, A/B3, B4, B5, B6, B7, (B8), B9, B10, B11, B12, B13, (B14), B15, B16, (C17), C18, C19, KV, [VE1], [VE2], [VE3], [SK1]

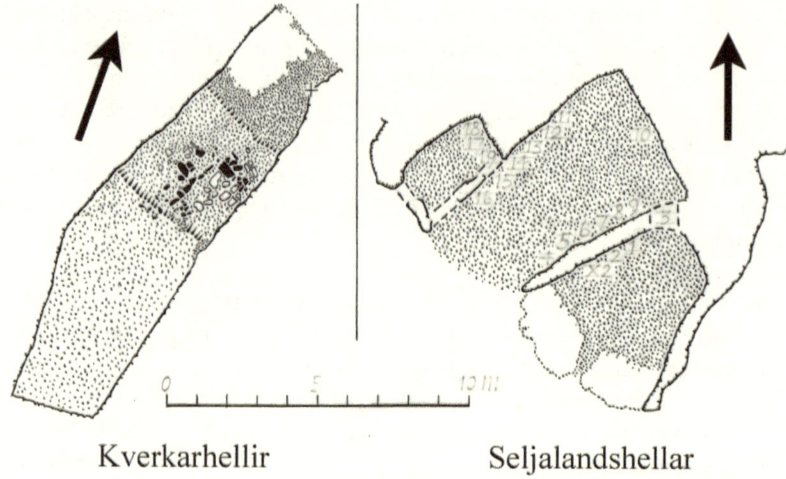

Figure 7.9 Kverkarhellir and Seljalandshellar plans. The crosshair at the eastern wall of the Kverkarhellir cave mouth indicates the site of cross KV, at a height of 1.59 m above floor level. The numbers on the Seljalandshellar plan indicate crosses SLJ A1–C19 as well as the four mid-sized crosses represented by (A)X2. The initial letter A, B, or C indicates the chamber within which the cross is located; the southeastern cave chamber (the gapi) is indicated by *A*, the middle chamber *B*, and the northwestern chamber (the stúka) *C*. The height of each Seljalandshellar cross is given in table 7.1. Drawn by Ian G. Scott.

- *Double armed*: A1, A2
- *Bold V-cut*: (B4), B9, B12, B15, [SK1]
- *Expanded terminal (incised)*: AX2(cross 4), (A/B3), B4, B7, [VE3], [SK1]
- *Expanded terminal (sunken)*: B6, B10, B13, [VE1], ([VE2])
- *Pitted terminals*: AX2(cross 1), AX2(cross 2), (A/B3), B5
- *Sinkings associated with cross*: A/B3
- *Pointed base*: AX2(cross 3), B7, B9, B12, B15, KV
- *Socket base*: B10, C18, C19
- *Foot base*: A1, A2
- *Oval head*: KV

Parallels for the Seljaland, Westman Island, and Skollhólahellir sculpture may be identified in other Icelandic rock-cut crosses. The simple Latin cross form dominates. The unusual pairing of opposite "footed" crosses at Seljalandshellar

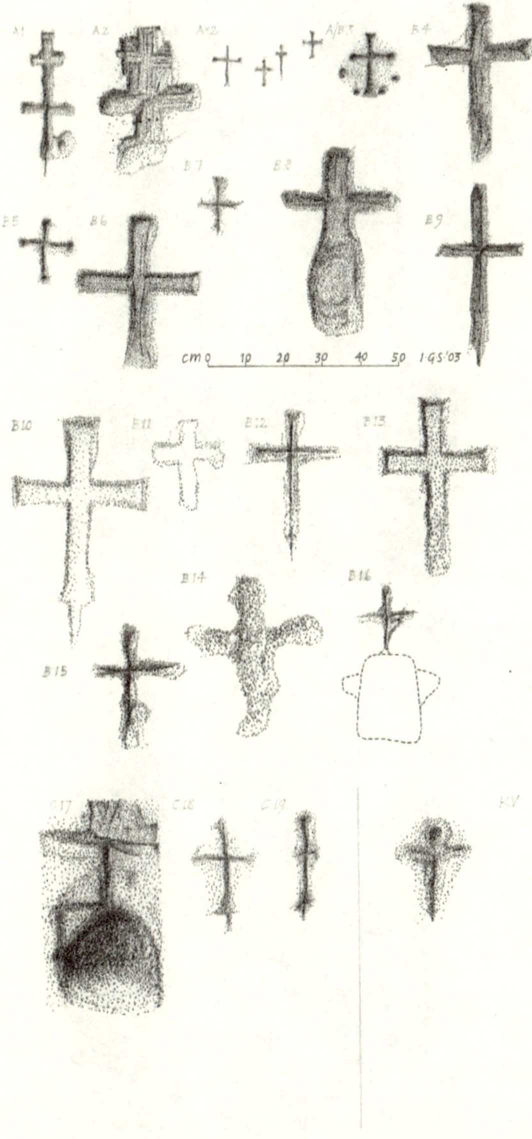

Figure 7.10 Illustrations of crosses A1–C19 and KV. Scale 1:20. Drawn by Ian G. Scott.

Figure 7.11 Cross A1.

Figure 7.12 Cross A2.

Figure 7.13 Cross A/B3 (on horizontal ledge between chambers A and B).

Figure 7.14 Cross B4.

Figure 7.15 Cross B5.

Figure 7.16 Cross B6.

Figure 7.17 Cross B7.

Figure 7.18 Cross B8.

Figure 7.19 Cross B9.

Figure 7.20 Cross B10.

Figure 7.21 Cross B11.

Figure 7.22 Cross B12.

Figure 7.23 Cross B13.

Figure 7.24 Cross B14.

Figure 7.25 Cross B15.

Figure 7.26 Cross B16.

Figure 7.27 Cross C17.

Figure 7.28 Cross C18.

Figure 7.29 Cross C19.

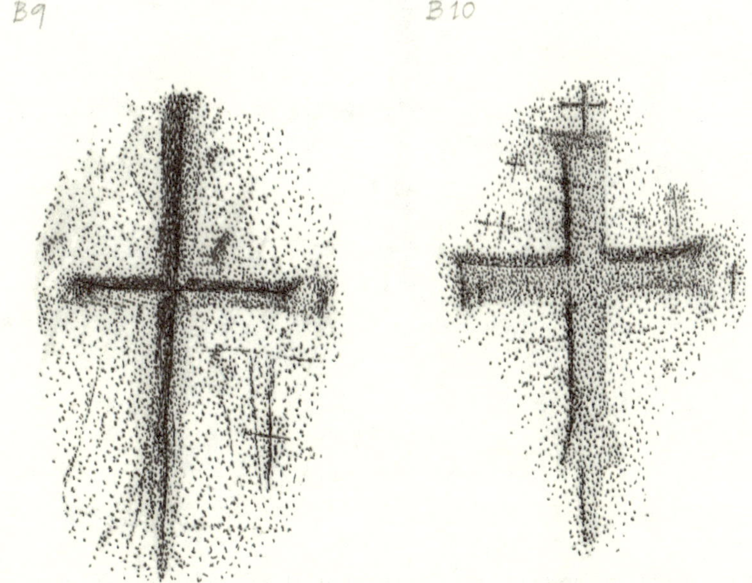

Figure 7.30 Crosses B9 (*left*) and B10 (*right*), with surrounding wall surfaces. Not to scale. Drawn by Ian G. Scott.

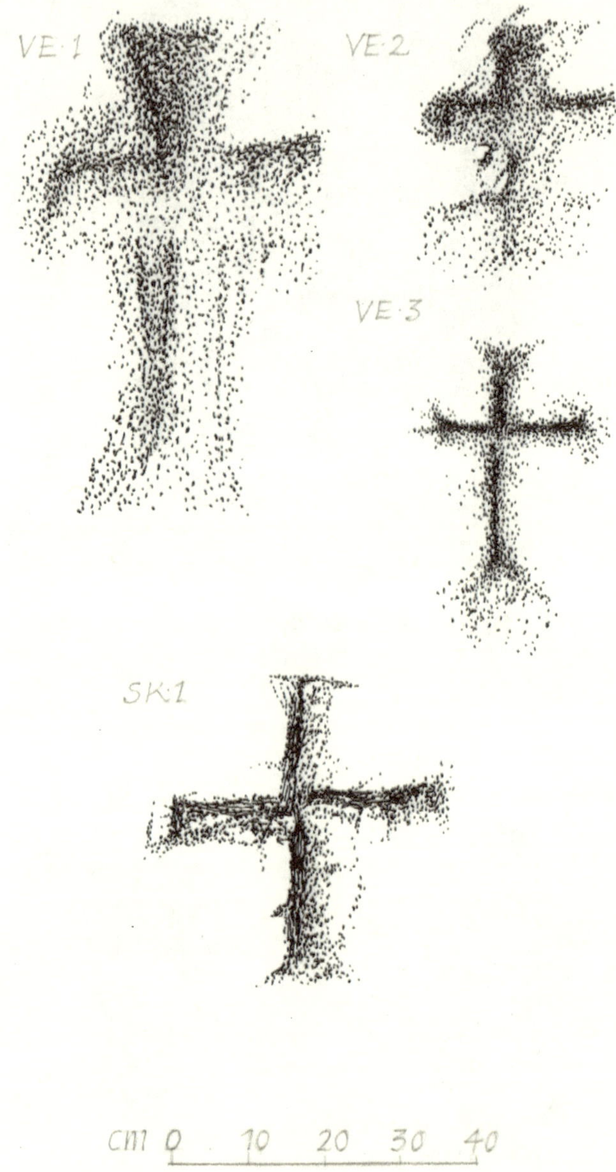

Figure 7.31 Illustrations of crosses VE1 (*Papakross*), VE2, VE3, and SK1. Scale 1:10. Drawn by Ian G. Scott.

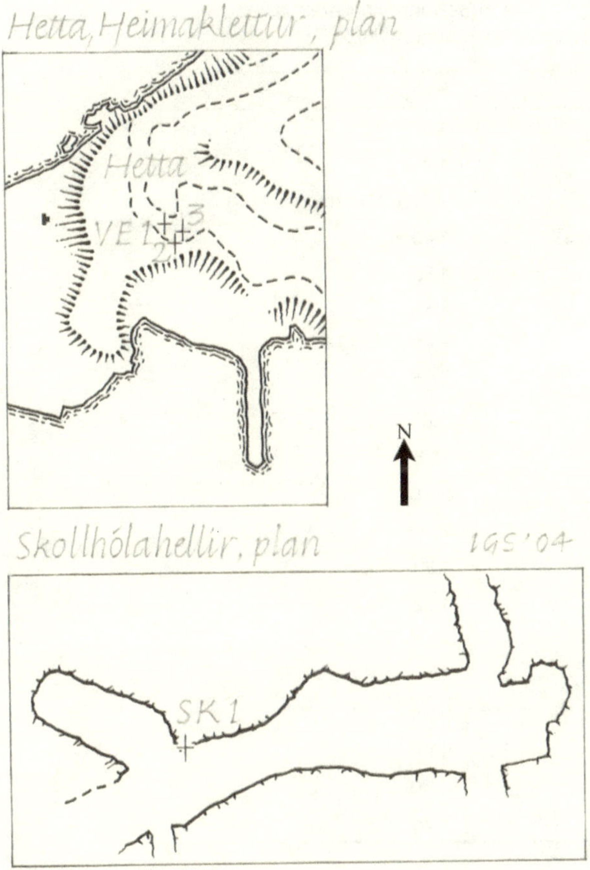

Figure 7.32 The Hetta plan (*above*) locates the three Westman Island crosses: VE1 (*Papakross*), VE2, and VE3. Scale 1:10000. The Skollhólahellir plan locates the largest cross found there, SK1. Scale 1:400. Both plans drawn by Ian G. Scott.

(A1 and A2) may be compared to what appears to be two similarly paired "footed" cross forms from Berustaðahellir, Rangárvallasýsla (Hjartarson et al. 1991: 120). Furthermore, the sunken cross form (so common at Seljaland) may also be identified in two Hetta crosses (VE1 and VE2), as well as two *krossaþrenningar* from Efri-Gegnishólar and Árbæjarhelli (Hjartarson et al. 1991: 30, 87, 195; Holt and Guðmundsson 1980: 9). Lastly, the bold V-cut of several Seljalandshellar crosses may be identified in other Icelandic cave sculpture,

Table 7.1 Height of each Seljalandshellar cross above ground level (measured in August 2002)

Cross	Height (m)
A1	1.40
A2	1.25
A/B3	2.18 (on horizontal ledge)
AX2 (4 crosses)	1.40
B4	1.35
B5	1.43
B6	1.15
B7	1.07
B8	0.87
B9	1.18
B10	2.70
B11	2.90
B12	1.33
B13	1.52
B14	1.02
B15	1.30
B16	0.84
C17	0.94
C18	0.70
C19	0.79

such as that illustrated from Skollhólahellir (SK1). The Seljaland material, then, is comparable with sculpture from other sites in southern Iceland.

Seventeenth- and eighteenth-century sculpture?

Whether seventeenth- and eighteenth-century inscriptions respect or are respected by cross sculpture may suggest that these inscriptions are pre-dated by or pre-date the crosses. This first hypothesis draws upon Matthías Þórðarson's bold argument that southern Iceland's cave crosses are contemporary with the modern inscriptions.

A close relationship between inscriptions and cross sculpture is difficult to establish, however. In order to illustrate his ideas, Þórðarson described inscriptions in Skollhólahellir cave and then used these examples in formulating his arguments. Thus, consideration of Skollhólahellir cross sculpture and inscriptions is a most appropriate test of the hypothesis. Þórðarson writes: "Í suðvesturhlutanum er á norðurveggnum, rétt fyrir innan afhellinn, ýmislegt krot, upphafsstafir og ártöl: A 1780, 1794, 1801, 1802 o.fl" (Þórðarson 1931: 36; In the southwestern part, on the north wall, right next to the entrance, are various scrawls, capital letters and dates: A 1780, 1794, 1801, 1802, et cetera.).

These markings are located on a smoothed area beneath two incised, expanded-terminal crosses.[30] Only with difficulty can the two crosses be seen to respect the inscriptions. More probable is the suggestion that the inscriptions respect the sculpture, with the cross bases effectively limiting the smoothed area of inscription. These crosses and inscriptions are illustrated in figure 7.33.

Whatever the case may be, it must be said that the first hypothesis, of seventeenth- and eighteenth-century cross sculpture in caves, does not have particularly strong data to support it. Certainly, this scenario may be imagined, but unless a convincing data set is brought to bear, special pleading must be adopted to explain the sculptural coherency among supposedly modern crosses from a number of sites in southern Iceland (for example, Seljaland, Skollhólahellir, and the Westman Islands). Furthermore, in formulating the ideas behind the hypothesis tested here, Þórðarson (the professional archaeologist) appears particularly hostile to Einar Benediktsson (the poet and businessman) and to his suggestions that early Irish hands were responsible for the cross sculpture in caves. Þórðarson's language is dismissive of Benediktsson's ideas, both in vocabulary (*fjóshellinum*, cowshed cave) and in tone (Þórðarson 1931: 62). Thus Þórðarson's own support for an otherwise weak argument may be characterized as a reaction against Benediktsson's interpretive excesses – and Benediktsson did go too far. For instance, he writes of "'krossmarki allstóru' á hellisgaflinum innst, sem hann [Benediktsson] nefnir í því sambandi kórþil" (Þórðarson 1931: 57; 'a rather large cross mark' in the innermost corner, which he [Benediktsson] refers to as choir panelling[!]). In short then, this simple test of the first hypothesis demonstrates a lack of support for the idea of cross sculpture being contemporary with seventeenth- and eighteenth-century inscriptions.

Norse and Hiberno-Norse similarities?

A comparative methodology is used to assess whether the Seljaland corpus of cross sculpture is similar to the earliest stratum of Norse and Hiberno-Norse Christian sculpture in Britain, Ireland, and Scandinavia; in other

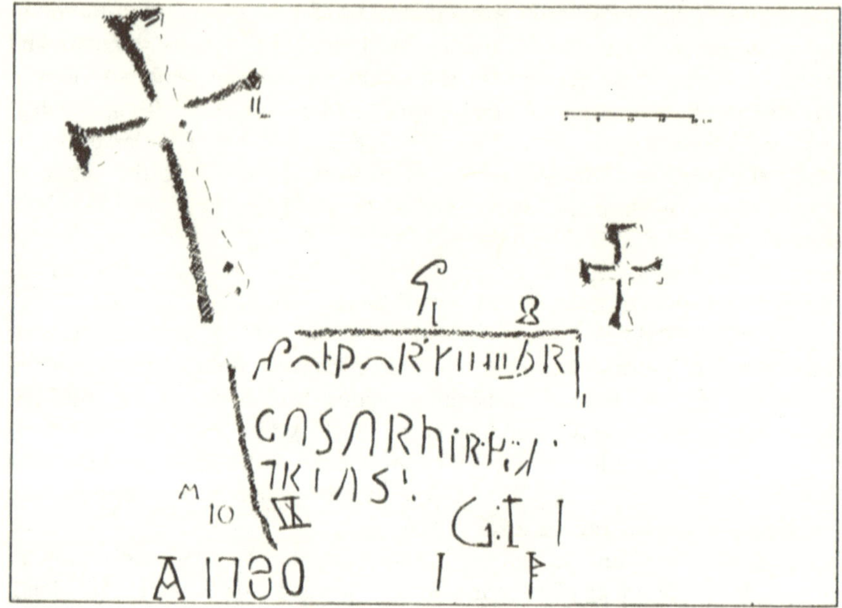

Figure 7.33 Wall markings in Skollhólahellir. Drawn by Árni Hjartarson in 1982. Taken from a study of Skollhólahellir cave (Hjartarson and Gísladóttir 1983: 130), with author's permission.

words, typological features and context are compared between the Seljaland crosses and other sculpture from the Norse and Hiberno-Norse worlds.

ICELAND

The Seljaland corpus exhibits a number of similarities with rock-cut cross sculpture from other cave and alcove contexts in Iceland. The similarities between footed, sunken, and bold V-cut types suggest that the cave and alcove rock-cut crosses form a coherent (yet undated) tradition.

As mentioned earlier, recent investigations have unearthed three standing stones from Þórarinnstaður (eastern Iceland) with an eleventh-century association. These crosses may be paralleled with a late-tenth-century cross arm from Stöng (southern Iceland) and an undated fragment from Viðey (southwest Iceland) (Kristjánsdóttir 2003: 123–4). Furthermore, Fisher identifies near-perfect parallels to this type in the Shetland islands of Yell and Unst as well as the Stavanger area of Norway (Fisher 2005; 2002: 55–6). The cross form is characterized by "a wedge-shaped top arm and short straight side-arms" (Fisher 2005), and in some cases "their top arms are asymmetrical. This feature, which at first seems accidental, is repeated in other stones along with expanded shafts, and two have central crosslets" (Fisher 2005). The rock-cut Seljaland corpus does not share features with this standing stone type from Þórarinnstaður / Unst and Yell / Stavanger, though the simple incised, pitted terminal cross form of some Seljaland Latin crosses (for example, B5 and A/B3) may have similarities with the central Greek crosslets just mentioned (Birkeli 1973: 151–6; Fisher 2001: figs. 30A and 30B; 2002: 57). Care must be taken, however, when comparing these simplest of incised crosses, especially when the contexts are not similar (that is, in cave walls rather than as decoration to standing crosses).

FAROE ISLANDS

Fisher has studied the Faroese corpus of cross-marked stones and has suggested that the Seljaland sunken cross form seen in B10 and B13 may be compared to the Skúvøy group of shallow sunken crosses (with slight curving out at the ends of the arms). However, he also notes that this comparison is far from satisfactory, as the Skúvøy examples are very shallow indeed and an unusual variant of the sunken form (Fisher, personal communication). Fisher describes the Skúvøy shallow sunken type: "This group comprises three basalt slabs or boulders bearing very shallow sunken Latin crosses … The technique [by which they were sculpted], adapted to a coarse material full of gas-bubbles, began with an incised outline whose centre was then channelled with a rounded object, perhaps a pebble. The carving was defined by differences of colour and texture due to the polishing of the resultant round-bottomed grooves, rather than by light and shade" (Fisher 2005). This Faroese type, then, makes an unconvincing comparison to the Seljaland material.

SCANDINAVIA

Crosses may be identified on approximately half of the surviving corpus of Scandinavian rune stones, stones that are understood to reflect the change from pagan to Christian burial habits. The earliest of these stones are dated to ca. 975–1050 and incorporate a simple cross and restrained runic band, both elaborated in later stones (Lager 2000; Sawyer 2000). The association of runic band with cross is not paralleled in the Seljaland corpus, nor do the cross forms appear to be comparable. For instance, Swedish Småland stone Sm69 seems to illustrate an equal-armed Greek sunken or outline form (the illustration is unclear which) (Lager 2000: 121). Further study of the rune-stone corpus would be necessary to sustain the initial analysis that the rune-stone cross forms are not comparable to the Seljaland crosses. However, Norwegian cross slabs with runic bands are illustrated in Birkeli's study (Birkeli 1973). Three of these cross forms, with slight curving out of the arms (one with pointed base), show a slight but unconvincing similarity in type, and they are of outline rather than incised or sunken form.

BRITAIN AND IRELAND

Identifying Norse and Hiberno-Norse parallels from Britain and Ireland is problematic. Incised and sunken crosses are an early Christian tradition that endures into the Viking Age, though the crosses become generally more elaborate in this later period. In other words, the dating of simple rock-cut crosses is flexible; the majority of sculpture probably originates in the early Christian period, though individual crosses may date from the Viking Age.

With reference to the corpus from western Scotland, Fisher summarizes current thinking:

> The chronology of early sculpture in Britain and Ireland is still controversial, despite much recent research, and there are few fixed points. This is true even of Anglo-Saxon England, Wales and Ireland, where there are much larger groups of ornamented sculpture to facilitate art-historical comparisons, and some inscriptions naming identifiable persons …
>
> In western Scotland, the few surviving inscriptions lack the genealogical content required to identify individuals, and epigraphic dating can only be approximate. Historical context may help to date some of the more distinctive monuments, and although the Viking raids of about 800 are no longer thought to have brought an end to monastic life at Iona, the major crosses there are so exceptional that an earlier origin seems probable. The main tool for dating remains comparative study of other areas where similar monuments occur in a comparable historical setting. (Fisher 2001: 12)

The Seljaland corpus may be divided into two general categories: *incised linear crosses* and *sunken linear crosses*. Fisher provides useful summaries of each of these cross forms within an insular context, again with reference to the western Scotland sculpture:

> *Linear incised crosses.* These simple crosses are widely distributed, occurring on about a quarter of the carved stones in the area [western Scotland], sometimes in combination with other cross-types, and on the walls of caves. They are also

> numerous in western Iceland and the Isle of Man, and in Wales where Nash-Williams suggested a 7th- to 9th-century date-bracket. Epigraphic evidence is one of the main supports for the proposed dating, and they were often used in Ireland and Wales as initial crosses on inscriptions, but the Mail-Phatraic stone from Iona is one of only two Scottish examples of this practice … [This form is] found both with plain terminals, usually rounded, and with expanded or otherwise elaborated ones …
>
> Bases are rare, although in crosses with elaborated terminals the foot of the shaft is often left plain or tapered. The small cross-bar at the foot of the shaft on the Soroby slab, which may represent the foot-rest of Christ's cross, is also found on two stones in Knapdale (Achadh na Cille; Ellary). The slab on Eithne's Grave on Eileach an Naoimh has a narrow spike below the lower terminal …
>
> *Sunken crosses.* About twenty carved stones in the area [western Scotland] bear crosses defined by straight-sided grooves of rectangular section, characteristic examples being on Iona and Tiree. Both equal-armed and Latin crosses are found, and the terminals are not normally elaborated, although the arms are sometimes expanded. Most of these carvings are of modest scale, comparable with many linear crosses, but large sunken crosses are carved on pillars on Jura and at Kilfinan …
>
> This type of technique does not appear to be usual in Ireland, although an example with barred terminals is found in Donegal and has parallels in eastern Scotland. A small slab closely paralleling the Iona stones comes from the 7th-century monastic site on Coquet Island (Northumberland). (Fisher 2001: 12, 13)

The incised linear and sunken linear forms may therefore be characterized as representing an early Christian style of sculpture, productive in Britain and Ireland in the seventh and eighth centuries but continuing into the early Viking Age (ninth century). The question of Norse and Hiberno-Norse parallels from the insular world thus becomes difficult to assess, as the sculpture chronologies generally lack the resolution to separate out the ninth century. The extracts from Fisher demonstrate, however, that these two cross-form types should be understood as primarily early Christian styles, the bulk of the sculpture dates to this period, and isolated examples are thought to continue later.

For this reason the Seljaland corpus will be compared in detail with the early Christian sculpture from Britain and Ireland in the assessment of the third hypothesis, and both the second and third hypotheses will be set against each other. Should only isolated parallels be identified with the Seljaland sculpture, then this would be most similar to the Norse and Hiberno-Norse phase of early Christian sculpture, especially if features from elsewhere in the Norse world are identified.

Early Christian similarities?

As with the second hypothesis, a comparative methodology is used to assess whether the Seljaland corpus of cross sculpture is similar to the cross sculpture of early Christian Britain and Ireland (represented by the corpus from Scotland's western Highlands and islands). Fisher's inventory of sculpture from the western highlands and islands is used in testing this hypothesis because it is the most detailed corpus available. Recent work in Brittany and western Ireland has produced promising early results (Davies et al. 2000; Herity et al. 1997), though the kind of comprehensive discussion that Fisher provides has yet to be realized. The formulation of our test, then, is indeed influenced by the strength of previous research in the field.

Generalized similarities may be noted between the expanded-terminal type (both incised and sunken) from southern Iceland and Campbell's expanded-terminal type from Argyll. Previous study has highlighted three such crosses (VE1, VE2, and VE3) from sheltered alcoves of the exposed cliff Heimaklettur on the Westman Islands. The largest cross, carved into its own alcove, is found alongside hand- and foot-holds cut into soft tuff, or palagonite. The Westman Islands lie off the southern Iceland coast, opposite the region in which the artificial caves are found. A further two crosses are cut into a soft sandstone wall of Skollhólahellir cave in mainland southern Iceland (one of these is illustrated as SK1). Simple incised crosses also decorate the walls of Skollhólahellir, and two are illustrated elsewhere (Ahronson 2000: 121).

On typological and contextual grounds, specific comparisons have been drawn between the Icelandic expanded-terminal crosses and the Argyll expanded-terminal type (Ahronson 2000), a style linked to the Columban familia of monastic houses of the seventh and eighth centuries (Campbell 1987: 112; Ahronson 2000: 119). Several of Scotland's rock-cut early Christian crosses, including a number of the Agyll expanded-terminal crosses, are found in caves, sites that Campbell suggests as "retreats or deserta for anchorites or penitents" (Campbell 1987: 108–9). A monastic association for Scotland's cross-marked cave sites is not new. In 1859 James Young Simpson commented on the "habit" of early Christian ascetics, such as the late-ninth-century "Caenchombrac of the Caves of Inis-bo-fine (AFM c. AD 898)," to "[betake] themselves to caves, natural or artificial, using them for their houses and oratories" (Simpson 1859: 522). Simpson continued: "In Scotland, we have various alleged instances of caves being thus employed as anchorite or devotional cells, and some of them still show rudely-cut altars, crosses, &c., – as the so-called Cave of St Columba on the shores of Loch Killesfort in North Knapdale, with an altar, a font or piscine, and a cross cut in the rock (Origines Prochiales, vol. ii, p. 40); the Cave of St Kieran on Loch Kilkerran in Kantyre (ibid., vol. ii, p. 12); the Cave of St Ninian on the coast of Wigtownshire (Old Statistical Account of Scotland, vol. xvii, p. 594); [and] the Cave of St Moloe in Holy Island in the Clyde" (Simpson 1859: 522).

However, though the comparable cave locations and expanded-terminal similarities just discussed may be intriguing, interpretations must be preliminary when discussion is based upon only five crosses from two sites (Ahronson 2000). The Seljaland corpus, in contrast to these isolated examples, is robust and illustrated here in sufficient detail to permit sustained assessment of similarities to the western Scotland crosses. Twenty-four crosses from Seljaland are illustrated, and they are contextualized with other Icelandic sites. Furthermore, Ian Fisher has examined the Seljaland sculpture and pointed to a number of similarities with the western Scotland crosses (Fisher, personal communication). The following paragraphs discuss these similarities, largely with reference to comparative illustrations from Fisher's *Early Medieval Sculpture* (2001: 30–3).

First, the expanded-terminal style identified at the Hetta and Skollhólahellir sites is also seen at Seljaland, in both incised and sunken variants. More significant, however, is the host of additional features that the Seljaland crosses share with the western Scotland corpus. For instance, the bold V-cut and the pointed base of a number of Seljaland examples are similar to a cross cut into the King's Cave on Arran (Fisher 2001: fig. 31MM); the bold V-cut is also seen in other carvings, such as the rock-cut Aird a'Mhòrain cross from North Uist, marking a well and a landing place (Fisher 2001: fig. 31N).[31] Furthermore, the pointed-base form is repeated on a stone from Cladh a'Bhile, Ellary, though this comparison is problematic as the Cladh a'Bhile carving is an outline cross (Fisher 2001: fig. 33U[17]).[32] A more convincing comparison is with the pointed base on one face of another stone from Cladh a'Bhile (Fisher 2001: fig. 31E[13]b).

Pitted terminals, seen on a handful of Seljaland crosses, may also be identified on "Eithne's Grave" from Eileach an Naoimh (Fisher 2001: fig. 30A) as well as on two crosses from St Columba's Cave (Ellary) (Fisher 2001: fig. 30B, 30C; Tolan-Smith 2001: 28). Furthermore, the armpit sinkings associated with one of the St Columba's Cave crosses may be compared to the Seljaland cross with pitted terminals and associated sinkings.

The spiked socket base of three Seljaland crosses is an unusual feature, conceivably inspired by a metalwork exemplar or processional crosses such as the Rupertus Cross (Webster and Backhouse 1991: 170–3; Fisher 2001: 172). Alternatively, Fisher has noted a small cross bar at the foot of the cross shaft at Cladh a'Bhile (Fisher 2001: fig. 31Ec) and at Achadh na Cille (Fisher 2001:

fig. 31JJ) as potentially representing the foot rest of Christ's cross (Fisher 2001: 12). The Seljaland spiked socket bases may be related to either of these suggestions.

Another unusual feature is the oval-headed Kverkarhellir cross. The cross head has some similarity to a small, outline, oval-head cross from St Molaise's Table on Holy Island (Arran) (Fisher 2001: fig. 63B), though this should not be overly stressed.

Turning to the sunken cross form, a number of similar examples may be identified for this predominantly western Scotland type. For instance, a cross from the isolated monastic site on North Rona (Fisher 2001: fig. 32R[2])[33] is of sunken form and convincingly similar to B6. Furthermore, the Seljaland examples of this type see generalized comparison to the sunken crosses from St Molaise's Cave on Holy Island (Arran) (Fisher 2001: fig. 32AA). In addition, the high central position of the sunken B10 cross in Seljalandshellar cave B is paralleled by the high central position of a sunken cross in St Molaise's Cave (Fisher 2001: fig. 61B). Further afield, sunken forms with socket (or metalwork-type) bases from the Breton collection of early Christian sculpture share some affinities with the Seljaland cross B10. Specifically, the seventh- to tenth-century Rimoette cross may be a good comparison (though fuller illustration of the cross is necessary to establish its sunken character) (Davies et al. 2000: 244), and the similarly dated croux Prostlon's sunken form also features a socket base (Davies et al. 2000: 224).

The two double-armed and footed-base crosses from Seljaland appear to be unique,[34] though some comparison may be made with what appear to be similarly paired footed cross forms from Berustaðahellir cave. Limited comparison of double-armed examples may be made to two incised crosses from Cladh a'Bhile and Lochead (Fisher 2001: fig. 30GG[12]b, HH[1]), though this is far from convincing. Comparison may also be made to the Breton Langombrac'h cross, with its sunken form and double arms (Davies et al. 2000: 202). This Breton cross, however, is defined by arcs whereas the Seljaland examples are not – thus limiting the value of this comparison. Another Breton sunken cross, that which fronts the Crac'h stone, is a stronger comparison with its multiple arms and footed base (Davies et al. 2000: 174). In the western Scotland corpus, the sunken, footed form – but not the double arms – may also be identified at St Molaise's Cave (Fisher 2001: fig. 61C).

In the assessment of the two final hypotheses, then, a host of parallels for the Seljaland sculpture is identifiable from across the insular world (if Brittany may be included as such). Of the insular sculpture, that from western Scotland has been the focus for comparison, and the analysis points to particular similarities between the Seljaland and western Scotland material. For instance, insular crosses of sunken form are concentrated in Scotland, with roughly twenty examples illustrated in Fisher's corpus, and seven clear examples of the type survive at Seljaland. Prominence of the sunken form in both western Scotland and the Seljaland corpus suggests particular connections between the cross sculpture of southern Iceland and western Scotland, as do the numerous shared features discussed above (for example, expanded terminals, bold V-cuts, and sinkings). Investigating whether the western Scotland corpus (rather than the Irish, Anglo-Saxon, et cetera) is indeed the best match to the Seljaland sculpture would be a useful future study.

Are the Seljaland crosses most similar to the Norse and Hiberno-Norse crosses of Britain and Ireland or to the early Christian sculpture? At present, chronological resolution makes this question difficult to resolve, though the lack of clear Scandinavian[35] or Faroese[36] features in the Seljaland corpus favours the early Christian hypothesis; the bulk of early Christian sculpture from western Scotland is understood to pre-date the Viking Age, and the Seljaland corpus finds numerous convincing similarities throughout this Scottish material. Correspondingly, the third hypothesis of early Christian insular similarities for the Seljaland corpus is favoured, though the second hypothesis of insular Norse and Hiberno-Norse affinities may also be supported to a lesser degree. Thus the simplest and most convincing hypothesis is that the cross sculpture from Seljaland is similar to the early Christian sculpture of western Scotland.

Conclusions and Further Problems

This chapter has identified Iceland's cave and alcove crosses as forming a coherent art-historical tradition. The writings of some of Iceland's prominent archaeological workers were reviewed in order to contextualize this tradition, and the spread of Christian sculptural forms to northern and insular Europe was charted in order to allow assessment of historically plausible routes for the appearance of these forms in Iceland. The study of Seljaland sculpture offered the opportunity to outline a methodology for recording and illustrating this largely overlooked body of monuments, based upon the methods developed by the Royal Commission on the Ancient and Historical Monuments of Scotland. It is hoped that this methodology, or one like it, will be applied to record the other in situ sculpture collections of southern Iceland.

Three hypotheses were assessed in order to explore the parallels with Seljaland rock-cut crosses. A seventeenth- or eighteenth-century origin for the sculpture (suggested by Þórðarson) must remain a case unproven; where it could be tested, it appeared unlikely. Comparison of the Seljaland material to the earliest Christian sculpture of Viking Age Scandinavia also did not identify convincing examples of shared features, though the hypothesis of similarities to Norse and Hiberno-Norse period crosses from Britain and Ireland finds some support. The favoured hypothesis, however, points to parallels for the Seljaland sculpture in the early Christian crosses of Britain and Ireland; a host of convincing similarities were identified in the recently published corpus from western Scotland.

The limitations of these conclusions lie in the comparative methodology used. Date brackets were obtained for the Scottish sculpture in many cases through comparison to cross forms from Ireland and Wales, which have been dated in those places by epigraphic arguments. For instance, the incised linear cross form has in this way been given a seventh- to ninth-century date bracket. Some support is therefore given to the hypothesis of Viking Age insular similarities, as studies of crosses from western Scotland inherently lack the resolution to separate out the early Christian sculpture of the seventh and eighth centuries from that which continued into the Viking Age, though most (but not all) early Christian sculpture from Scotland probably pre-dates the Viking Age. The Ionan example illustrates this last point, where monastic life and sculptural traditions continued in some form into the Viking Age – but certainly not on the scale of previous centuries. Thus, in consideration of the different hypotheses, isolated similarities in the Seljaland corpus would have strengthened the Viking Age hypothesis (especially if Scandinavian features were also identified), whereas numerous sustained similarities between the Seljaland corpus and the crosses of western Scotland would have favoured the hypothesis that pre-dates the Viking Age. In this study of the Seljaland crosses, such numerous sustained typological and contextual similarities were identified, thus supporting the idea of seventh- and eighth-century affinities.

Having established these early Christian similarities, how should they be explained (that is, by which mechanism could they have been brought about)? One way to understand these sculptural affinities is to propose a direct connection between the early Christian sculpture of western Scotland and the Seljaland corpus. Chapter 5 presented the arguments for a ca. 800 construction phase at Kverkarhellir cave, and chapter 6 described a contemporary environmental impact preserved in the sedimentary deposits at Seljaland. This ca. 800 date is earlier than current thinking would place the Scandinavian-led settlement of Iceland, but early medieval monastic settlements are known to have been established on isolated Atlantic islands, such as North Rona. These early dates from Seljaland could be integrated with contemporary textual accounts from the Gaelic world of journeys north into the Atlantic Ocean,[37] and it is possible to imagine that the ca. 800 dates from Seljaland relate to an early Christian settlement of Atlantic Gaels. Similarly, it is possible to propose that the Seljaland sculpture was produced as part of this early Christian continuum of desert places in the Ocean. Indeed, if one desired to see the Seljaland crosses as the work of early Christian communities of the Gaelic tradition, then the conclusions of this chapter's comparative study certainly suggest that the scenario is plausible.

However, though the idea of Seljaland as a desert place may be the simplest proposal, an alternate possibility may also be imagined. For instance, late medieval Icelandic texts describe a significant proportion of that island's settlers as having an origin in what W.F.H. Nicolaisen calls "Scandinavian Scotland"[38] (Nicolaisen 1980: 219–20; Gammeltoft 2001: 21n9; Crawford 1987). According to *Landnámabók*, a Bishop Patrick of the Hebridean Church (after whom Patreksfjörður in the Westfjords is said to have been named) gave the late ninth-century Norse settler Örlygur directions to Esja, near Reykjavík. We are told that upon arrival, Örlygur kept a promise to Bishop Patrick and erected a church to Kolumkilli (Columba) (*Landnámabók*: ch. 15; Benediktsson 1968: 53–5; Smyth 1984: 163, 171–2; Anderson 1922: 340n1, 343–4n1). Another more complex scenario, then, is that Scandinavian-led settlement by individuals such as Örlygur provided an opportunity for conservative sculptural forms, drawn from the insular tradition, to flourish at artificial cave sites, such as the Seljaland caves. An absence of Scandinavian-style detail on these crosses makes this idea less likely.

In conclusion, though further work on the sculpture may help resolve some ambiguities, the simplest and most robust case is for the Seljaland corpus to be of insular early Christian type, with particularly convincing similarities to the pre–Viking Age sculpture of western Scotland. An important caution, however, is that the present chapter is the first comprehensive inventory and discussion of cross sculpture from *one group* of Iceland's artificial cave sites. The next step is to assess how sculpture from other sites relates to the Seljaland collection, and to the western Scotland corpus. This chapter provides the start, and it is hoped that further work will develop the typological analyses advanced here.

Conclusion

We should no more think of Iceland as Scandinavian than we should think of Ireland as Celtic.

Rory McTurk, *Emeritus Professor of Icelandic Studies*[1]

I may be wrong and you may be right, and by an effort, we may get nearer to the truth.

Karl R. Popper (fl. 1930–94)[2]

"I believe that the advantage is always on the side of true culture," observed Karenin, raising his eyebrows slightly.

"But what are the signs of this true culture?" Pestsov asked.

"I should have thought such signs were generally well known," said Karenin. "But are they fully known?" put in Koznyshev with a subtle smile. "It is the accepted view at the present time that real culture depends on a purely classical education; but we hear violent arguments on both sides, and there is no denying that the opposite camp has some strong points in its favour."

"You are a classical scholar, Sergei Ivanich! Will you take red wine?" said Oblonsky.

"I am not speaking of my personal opinions," replied Koznyshev with a condescending smile, as though to a child, and holding out his glass. "All I say is that there are strong arguments on both sides," he went on, addressing himself to Karenin. "I had a classical education, but personally can find no place in the controversy. I see no clear reason why the classics should be preferred to a modern education."

"The natural sciences have just as great an educational value," Pestsov joined in. "Take astronomy, take botany, or zoology with its system of general principles…"

"I cannot quite agree with you there," answered Karenin. "It seems to me that one must admit that the very process of studying the forms of a language has a peculiarly beneficial effect on intellectual development. Moreover, it cannot be denied that the influence of the classical authors is in the highest degree a moral one, whereas, unfortunately, with the study of the natural sciences are associated the false and noxious doctrines which are the curse of our times."

Koznyshev was about to say something when Pestsov's deep bass interrupted him. He began warmly contesting the justice of such a view. Koznyshev quietly waited to put in a word, evidently ready with some crushing retort.

"But," said Koznyshev with his subtle smile, addressing Karenin, "one cannot help allowing that to weigh all the pros and cons of classical and scientific studies is a difficult task, and the question, which form of education is to be preferred, would not have been so quickly and conclusively decided had not classical education had on its side the advantage, as you expressed it just now, of its moral – *disons le mot* – anti-nihilist influence."

"Exactly."

"Were it not for the advantage of this anti-nihilist influence on the side of classical education, we should have given longer consideration to the question, and weighed the arguments on both sides," said Koznyshev, subtly smiling. "We should have given elbow-room to both systems. But as it is we know that these little pills of classical learning possess the medicinal property of anti-nihilism, and we boldly prescribe them to our patients … But what if they had no such medicinal property?" he concluded, adding the grain of Attic salt.

At Koznyshev's little pills, everyone laughed, and Turovtsyn in particular roared loudly and jovially, having at last heard something funny, all he ever looked for in listening to conversation.

Leo Nikolayevich Tolstoy, written 1874–6[3]

Study of the early medieval past, across a zone stretching from the Scottish coasts to Iceland, may be defined by complex interplay between established "certainties" and fundamental ambiguities. For instance, the existence of early Christian settlements within the Gaelic-speaking world is assured, while their nature and extent beyond that is unclear. Similarly, the Norse are known to have come to dominate this region by the late Viking Age, but the exact chronology and character of their earliest colonization of this zone is difficult to perceive. Iceland's artificial caves (and cross sculpture) have also provoked speculation. Thus, as we have seen in chapters 1 and 4, the desire to resolve some of these unknowns has encouraged the proposal of bold ideas. For a variety of reasons, the nineteenth century was a particularly fruitful period for bold proposals, such as those of Eugène Beauvois regarding early Christian communities of Gaels across the Scottish islands and beyond. Like many others, Beauvois was fascinated by early medieval journeys into the Ocean, and a sensitive reading of his work demonstrates how we may appreciate his continuing contribution to scholarship. At the same time, however, we may also be reminded of the dangers of theory-led conclusions that are overly reliant upon isolated material and unsupported by coherent bodies of data, and also of the mortality of our own ideas.

In focusing on relationships between the early medieval parts of this coastal and insular zone, this book has produced multidisciplinary results that are concrete and gain strength from the avowedly interdisciplinary methodology outlined in chapter 2. In other words, the philosophical discussion of that chapter articulated a method for bringing together and developing the work of the archaeologist, Celticist, Norse scholar, environmental scientist, place-name scholar, and historian, thus enabling a synthesis of research that fosters critical rigour. Therefore, we appealed to Karl Popper's inclusive concept of anti-positivist science as *a critical process with a unity of method*, and, having arrived at our explicitly interdisciplinary approach, we looked to the *Pap-* names often associated with communities of early Christian Gaels throughout our zone. An important conclusion of chapter 3 was to stress how *Pap-* names are *Old Norse* (not Old Irish) names and that they may be among the earliest Scandinavian-origin names in the north Atlantic area. Furthermore, Hebridean *Pab(b)ay* islands and *Paible* places occur in a regular distribution; most populated areas of the "Long Island," Skye, and Rum each have a *Pap-* name, and this distribution suggests a consistent role for these places within the Norse-speaking Viking Age regional structure or administration. The chapter's place-name explorations therefore underscore the ill-defined – but real – relationship between the area's Norse speakers and early Christian communities, though we may also wonder why *Pap-* names are regularly distributed in the Scottish islands but are rare and clustered in the Faroe Islands and Iceland.

Notable for both its excellent tephrochronological sequence and literary inheritance, Iceland – a true "wilderness" at the outset of the medieval period – has proven critical to exploring the uncertainties that characterize our field of study. Consequently, a suite of methodologies was deployed in order to investigate the enigmatic artificial caves whose distinctive rock-cut sculpture has encouraged long-mooted claims of early Christian "Irish" use. Awareness of these ideas and the fundamental uncertainties surrounding these sites spurred the Seljaland section (chapters 4 to 7). Given Seljaland's prominence in the landscape, its soils, access to various habitats, and attestation in Iceland's earliest literature, one would expect the region to have been exploited by human populations from an early period. Indeed, in chapter 5, tephrochronology was applied to identify cave construction at Seljaland ca. 800, a date significantly earlier than the traditional chronology for Iceland's Norse settlement. To elaborate, a number of key historical tephrae were used to date a debris-type deposit thought to have resulted from the early digging out of Kverkarhellir, one of Seljaland's artificial caves. Care should be taken with these results, however, as they suggest what may be the earliest human presence on the island. Nonetheless, Seljaland presents the clearest indicator of people in Iceland at this time, and, as a result, chapter 6 presented a discussion of palaeoenvironmental studies, which also point to a localized and early-ninth-century human impact upon the Seljaland landscape – and therefore contextualizes both the early date obtained for cave construction and indicates that affinities between cross sculpture in the Seljaland caves and the early Christian sculpture of western Scotland are possible. In exploring these early environmental changes at Seljaland, we developed and applied a new technique, tephra contouring, to assess questions of ninth-century and tenth-century deforestation, and identified evidence of the earlier than expected introduction of domesticated mammals to the area. By exposing discrete past land surfaces and vegetation cover, this new technique provided "photographs" of Iceland's first human centuries. Chapter 7 focussed upon the largely unrecorded sculptural tradition represented by Iceland's rock-cut crosses. In this final study we recorded and analysed the Seljaland corpus in order to contextualize those cross forms through comparison with other Atlantic places. After detailed consideration, the simplest and most robust interpretation was found to be that the Seljaland cross sculpture is of insular early Christian type, with notable parallels in pre–Viking Age western Scotland. It is worthwhile to stress this last point: cross sculpture in the Seljaland caves suggests a connection with Gaelic monasticism in the Scottish littoral.

From these conclusions then, two main ideas emerge: first, the Norse did not enter an "empty" landscape in Iceland; and, second, early in the period of Norse domination there was an ill-defined, but real, relationship between early Christian communities and the Norse, which is most clearly seen in the Scottish islands. In future work we may test our ideas and further refine them (and there is inevitably much that was not touched upon here). For the moment, however, we can say that we have arrived at a more complex and rounded picture of a phase of the past in a zone stretching from Scotland to Iceland.

Notes

Introduction

1 This story is taken from Annandale's 1905 study of the Faroe Islands and Iceland, published while he was Deputy Superintendent of the Indian Museum in Calcutta (Annandale 1905: 10–11).

2 Popper 1994: 145.

3 For instance, see descriptive passages in *Íslendingabók*, *Landnámabók*, and *Historia Norvegiae* (*Íslendingabók*: ch. 1; *Landnámabók*: ch. 1; Benediktsson 1968: 4–5, 31–2; Pálsson and Edwards 1972: 14; *Historia*: ch. 6; Phelpstead and Kunin 2001: ch. 6; Ekrem and Mortensen 2003: 64–7).

4 Dicuil describes an early Christian community of Gaels in what appear to be the Faroe Islands (which he claims were settled ca. AD 725) and a journey to Iceland by clerics in AD 795 (Tierney 1967: 72–7).

5 Although the migratory routes of birds are subject to rapid evolutionary change (Weidensaul 1999: 48–50), modern-day examples that travel the airways between Iceland and Scotland include the Barnacle Goose (*Branta leucopsis*) and Pink-footed Goose (*Anser brachyrhynchus*) (L. Jonsson 1999: 78, 84).

1. Nineteenth-Century Legacies

1 Trigger 1989: 150–1; Trigger 1998: 86–7, 97–8.

2 Beauvois 1883b: 75.

3 Beauvois 1875: 86–7.

4 For instance, see the contributed articles in *The Papar in the North Atlantic* (Crawford 2002).

5 Anthony D. Smith has observed that before the Second World War there was a "popular equation of 'race' with 'nation,' where the term 'race' often signified the

separate culture of a descent group" (Smith 2001: 49). Furthermore, he adds that "[we should not] overlook the great advances made in national historiography and archaeology, disciplines that, if they were fed by nationalist conceptions, also encouraged and bolstered those conceptions with apparently 'hard data' and the tangible remains of distant material cultures" (Smith 2001: 49). Expressions of the recent burgeoning of interest in the connections between nationalism and archaeology, and the political context of archaeology, include Kohl and Fawcett, Diaz-Andreu and Champion, and Diaz-Andreu and A.D. Smith (Smith 2001: 151n8; Kohl and Fawcett 1995; Diaz-Andreu and Champion 1996; Diaz-Andreu and Smith 2001).

6 *Hvítramannaland* is normally translated as "White Men's Land," but I prefer "men of white"–land because this expresses the uncertainty inherent in the *Hvítramanna-* (men of white) phrase and also has the benefit of avoiding potentially inappropriate conceptualizations of race. In parallel with *Sviþjód it mikla* (Greater Sweden) (Storm 1888[1887]: 65; Nansen 1911: 48), *Írland et mikla* is usually translated as "Greater Ireland," though the phrase literally translates into English as "Ireland the Great."

7 "*þat liggr vestr í haf nær Vínlandi enu góða*" (*Landnámabók*: M35; Benediktsson 1968: 162; it lies west in the Ocean near Vínland the good).

8 Beauvois cites, among these "savants, passablement nombreux," Caroli C. Rafn, Finn Magnusen, P.A. Munch, Torfæus, Finnus Johannæus, P.E. Müller, Karl Vilhelmi (or Wilhelmi), and Wormskjold (Rafn 1837; Rafn and Magnusen 1838; Munch 1852–3; Torfæus 1705; Johannæus 1772; Munch 1852; 1857; Müller 1817–20; Wilhelmi 1839; Wormskjold 1814).

9 This field has remained productive (though now largely the work of popular writers). For instance, Hrafn E. Jónsson published his ideas that the Saguenay and Lac Saint-Jean areas of Québec were home to "landi hvítra manna" at the time of Jacques Cartier's sixteenth-century journeys. However, Jónsson does not discuss the medieval descriptions of Írland et mikla or Hvítramannaland; thus his arguments are tangential to the topic at hand (Jónsson 1999).

10 Fridtjof Nansen adds that "[in 1910–11] Professor Moltke Moe has found a 'Tír na Fer Finn,' or White Men's Land, mentioned in Irish sagas of the thirteenth and fourteenth centuries" (Nansen 1911: 44n1).

11 In contrast, Oskamp believed that an other world "in the Ocean is undoubtedly pre-Christian in origin as it is inherent in the religious system of an island society" (Oskamp 1970: 85).

12 Gísli Sigurðsson cites T.J. Westropp in making a similar point comparing the Vínland sagas to *immrama*-type tales (Sigurðsson 1988: 61–2; Westropp 1913: 235–6). Furthermore, this concept of perceived reality is articulated in a recent study by Michael Livingston, though his goal is to suggest the survival of a

Vínland concept in late medieval English literature and cartography: "Along the outer rim of the map – the location for those places thought to be at the very borders of the world – we find the now-expected sequence of northwestern European locations including Denmark, Thule, Vínland, Iceland and Norway … The places on these maps were places that one would have little trouble – if one had the time, the money, and the inclination – getting to via land or sea; all that was needed was a good set of directions. There is no Avalon, Atlantis, or other legendary location on the maps" (Livingston 2004: 41).

13 I am also guilty of missing Beauvois's contribution (e.g., Ahronson 2002a); I had previously been unaware of his explorations of the topic.

14 In the second edition of their *Kinder- und Hausmärchen* (Grimm 1856; 1884; Thompson 1946: 368).

15 In her Master of Philosophy research, Laura Taylor undertook a recent study of *Landnámabók* (Taylor 2003). See also Benediktsson 1968; 1969; and Rafnsson 1974.

16 Beauvois gives his own translation, working from the editions of his day: "… leurs fils était Aré, qui fut poussé par une tempête dans le Hvítramannaland que quelques-uns appellent Írland it mikla (Grande-Irlande). Ce pays est situé à l'ouest, dans la mer, près du Vínland it gódha (le bon pays du vin) et, dit-on, à six jours de navigation de l'Irlande. Ce récit a été fait d'abord par Hrafn *Hlymreksfaré* (le voyageur à Limerick), qui avait longtemps habité Hlymrek, en Irlande. Thorkel Gellisson rapporta aussi que des Islandais disaient avoir appris de Thorfinn *jarl* (duc) des Orkneys (Orcades), que Aré avait été reconnu dans le Hvítramannaland et qu'il ne pouvait en sortir, mais qu'il y était traité avec honneur" (Beauvois 1875: 43–4).

17 Beauvois translates: "Poussés par un vent du sud, ils arrivèrent dans le Markland, où ils trouvèrent cinq Skrælíngs. L'un d'eux était barbu et il y avait deux femmes et deux enfants. Les gens de Karlsefné s'emparèrent de ces derniers, tandis que les autres s'échappèrent et disparurent sous terre (probablement dans une des caverns qui leur servaient de demeure). Les enfants emmenés par eux, apprirent leur langue et furent baptises. Ils appelaient leur mère Vetthilde (variants: Weihilldé, Veinhildé, Vætilldé, etc) et leur père Uvæge (variants: Vægé, Ægé, Ovægé, Ovæe). Ils rapportèrent que deux rois gouvernaient les Skrælíngs, l'un nommé Avalldania (var.: Avalldaina, Avaldamon, Avalldumon); l'autre, Valldidida (var. Avaldidida); qu'il n'y avait pas de maisons dans le pays; que les habitants couchaient dans des caverns ou des trous; qu'une autre grande contrée située en face de leur pays était habitée par des gens qui marchaient vêtus de blancs, portant devant eux des perches où étaient fixes des drapeaux et criant fort. On pense que c'était le Hvítramannaland ou Írland it mikla" (Beauvois 1875: 60–1).

18 In his 1875 article Beauvois gives a translation of the entire chapter, as well as a related section from chapter 47: "Il partit avec un vent du nord-est, qui souffla

presque continuellement cet automne et de longtemps on n'entendit parler de ce navire" (ch. 47).

Gudhleif, fils de Gudhlaug-le-Riche, du Straumfjœrdh, et frère de Thorfinn, l'ancêtre des Sturlúngs, était un grand armateur. Il possédait un grand navire et Thórólf, fils d'Eyralopt, en avait un autre; de concert, ils livrèrent bataille au fils de Sigvaldé jarl, à Gyrdh, qui perdit un œil. Vers la fin du règne de Saint-Ólaf, Gudhleif, ayant fait un voyage à Dublin, naviguait vers l'ouest pour retourner en Islande, et il se trouvait à l'ouest de l'Irlande, lorsqu'un grand vent du nord-est le poussa si loin en mer, vers l'ouest et le sud-ouest, qu'il ne savait plus où se trouvait la terre. Comme l'été était avancé, ils firent de nombreux vœux pour être preserves d'un naufrage, et il arriva qu'ils aperçurent la terre. C'était une grande contrée qu'ils ne connaissaient pas. Gudhleif et les siens prirent la resolution d'y débarquer, parce qu'ils étaient fatigues d'avoir été longtemps ballottés sur mer. Ils trouvèrent un bon port et ils étaient à terre depuis peu de temps, lorqu'il arriva des gens dont pas un ne leur était connu, mais il leur semblait fort que ceux-ci parlaient l'irlandais. Bientôt cette multitude s'étant accrue au nombre de plusieurs centaines, assaillit les navigateurs, s'empara d'eux tous, les chargea de liens et les emmena vers le haut pays. Conduits à une assemblée pour y être jugés, ils comprirent que les uns voulaient les massacrer de suite; les autres, les partager entr'eux et les réduire à l'esclavage. Pendant les délibérations ils virent approcher une troupe de cavaliers avec un étendard, d'où ils conclurent qu'il devait y avoir un chef dans cette troupe. Lorsque celle-ci fut arrivée, ils virent chevaucher sous l'étendard un homme grand et vigoureux, déjà très-âgé et à cheveux blancs. Tous les assistants s'inclinèrent devant ce personnage et l'accueillirent de leur mieux, c'est à lui que fut laissée la decision de l'affaire. Le vieillard envoya chercher Gudhleif et ses gens, leur addressa la parole en langue norraine et leur demanda de quel pays ils étaient. Ils répondirent qu'ils étaient Islandais pour la plupart. "Et quels sont les Islandais parmi vous?" Gudhleif dit qu'il en était un et salua le vieillard qui lui fit bon accueil et lui demanda de quel contrée de l'Islande il était. Gudhleif dit qu'il était du canton de Borgarfjœrdh. "Et de quel endroit?" Renseigné sur ce point par Gudhleif, il l'interrogea sur presque tous les personnages considérables du Borgarfjœrdh. Et dans ces entretiens, il s'informa exactement à tous égards, d'abord de Snorré Godhé et de sa sœur Thuride de Fródhá, et surtout de Kjartan, fils de cette dernière, lequel était alors maître de Fródhá. Les indigènes de leur côté criaient qu'il fallait prendre une résolution quelconque relativement à l'équipage du navire. Alors le chef se mit à l'écart et choisit douze de ses hommes, avec lesquels il délibéra longtemps. Ensuite ils revinrent vers la foule et le chef dit à Gudhleif et aux siens: "Nous avons délibéré à votre égard avec les gens du pays, et ils s'en sont remis à ma décision: je vous laisse libres d'aller où il vous plaira, mais alors même que l'été vous semblerait bien avancé, je vous conseille de vous éloigner promptement, car il ne faut pas se fier aux indigènes, et il ne fait pas bon avoir affaire à eux; ils croient d'ailleurs que la loi a été violée à leur préjudice." "Mais," dit Gudhleif, "s'il nous est donné de revoir notre patrie, comment nommerons-nous celui qui nous a sauvés?" "Je ne puis vous le dire," répondit-il, "car je ne veux pas que mes parents ou mes frères d'armes fassent un voyage comme celui que vous auriez fait si je n'eusse été présent pour vous protéger. Maintenant je suis arrivé à un âge où je puis m'attendre, à chaque instant, à succomber de vieillesse. Mais quand même je vivrais encore quelque temps, il y a dans le pays des chefs plus puissants que moi; ils ne sont pas actuellement dans la contrée où vous avez abordé; mais s'ils viennent, ils auront peu de ménagement pour les étrangers." Ensuite il fit appareiller leur navire et resta là jusqu'à ce qu'il s'élevât un vent favorable pour partir. Mais avant de les quitter, il tira de son doigt un anneau et le confia à Gudhleif, ainsi qu'une bonne épée, en lui disant: "Sil t'est donné de retourner en Islande, tu remettras cette épée à Kjartan, le maître de Fródhá, et cet anneau à Thurídhe, sa mère." "Mais," demanda Gudhleif, "de qui dirai-je que viennent ces présents?" "Dis comme c'est la vérité, qu'ils sont envoyés par une personne qui était en meilleurs termes avec la dame de Fródhá qu'avec son frère le Godhé de Helgafell. Mais si quelqu'un croit savoir à qui ont appartenu ces objects, dis-leur de ma part que je défends à qui que ce soit de venir me trouver; car c'est une entreprise périlleuse, à moins que l'on n'ait, comme vous, la chance de trouver un lieu d'abordage favorable. Ce pays est étendu et mal pourvu de ports, et partout un mauvais accueil attend les étrangers, à moins qu'ils ne soient dans les mêmes circonstances que vous." Après quoi Gudhleif et les siens se mirent en mer et arrivèrent en Irlande à une époque avancée de l'automne. Ils passèrent l'hiver à Dýflinn (Dublin) et, l'été suivant, ils firent voile pour l'Islande, où ils remirent les présents aux destinataires. Des personnes tiennent pour certain que le chef indigène était Bjœrn Breidhvíkíngakappé, mais il n'y a pas d'autres notions certaines à cet égard que celles que l'on a rapportées. (ch. 64)

19 It is true that the *Eiríks saga rauða* passage includes description of how the two Skæling children "*sukku í jorð niðr*" (sink deep into the earth); however, this may be understood in a mundane way. For instance, Beauvois glosses the phrase by suggesting the children fled "probablement dans une des cavernes qui leur servaient de demeure."

20 Here Beauvois refers to the following passage from the *Historia Norvegiæ*, which Munch discovered in 1849 and published the following year: "*Papæ vero propter albas vestes, quibus ut clerici induebantur vocati sunt, unde in teutonicâ linguâ omnes clerici: papæ dicuntur; adhuc quædam insula Papey ab illis denominatur/*

Les Papas sont ainsi nommés à cause des habits blancs dont ils se vêtaient comme les clercs; car, en langue teutonique, tous les clercs sont appelés papas; aujourd'hui encore une île de Papey rappelle leur nom" (Beauvois 1875: 70, 70n4). It is of note that the portion of the passage is omitted that identifies the *papæ* in the following way: "*Sed ut per habitum et apices librorum eorum ibidem derelictorum notatur, Africanus fuerent judaismo adhærentes* / But as is observed from their habit and the writings of their books abandoned there, they were Africans, adhering to Judaism" (Storm 1880: 90; Anderson 1922: 331).

This passage still troubles scholars (see, for instance, commentary in Phelpstead as well as Ekrem and Mortensen [Phelpstead and Kunin 2001: 85; Ekrem and Mortensen 2003: 126]). As I hope to show in detail elsewhere, it may be that the *Historia Norvegiæ* author is making a politically motivated reinterpretation of the early Christian past of the "Orchades" (a region that the *Historia* seems to define as Shetland, Orkney, and the Hebrides (*Historia*: ch. 5; Phelpstead and Kunin 2001: 83; Ekrem and Mortensen 2003: 125). The *Historia Norvegiæ* text is clear in denying Orchades links to the Scottish mainland. Orchades is described with two ancient races, both now disappeared, without connection to contemporary Scottish populations: the *peti* (picts) are "*paruo superantes pigmeos statura in structuris orbium uespere et mane mira operantes, meredie uero cunctis uiribus prosus destituti in subterraneis domunculis pre timore latuerunt* / only a little taller than pygmies, [and] accomplished miraculous achievements by building towns, morning and evening, but at midday every ounce of strength deserted them and they hid for fear in underground chambers" (*Historia*: ch. 5); while the *papæ* are Africans practising Judaism. Thus I suggest the *Historia* author is deliberately making claims for Norway's sovereignty over the Orchades in such a way as to counter potentially competing claims from Scotland. For instance, the *peti* in Orchades are not related to Scottish populations, but instead the claim is made that "*Qui populus unde illuc aduentasset penitus ignoramus* / We do not know at all where these people came from" (*Historia*: ch. 6). Futhermore, remembering that the Orchades in the *Historia* included the Hebrides, then it is remarkable that the *papæ* (a "race" presumably inspired by the region's early Christian past) be identified not with Gaels but instead with "Affricani fuerent iudaismo adherentes" (*Historia*: ch. 6). In making this last identification, the *Historia* author may be engaging with a floating "lost people" legend potentially current in the Norman and Scandinavian worlds.

I will briefly elaborate. First, it appears that eleventh- and twelfth-century authors used *African* in the sense of "North African" (i.e., from the old Roman province) rather than our modern definition (Metcalfe 2003: 56). Second, large communities of Jews existed in medieval North Africa (Goitein 1967–93), and there was also an apparently baseless belief that the Berbers were Jews

(Hirschberg 1963). Significant Arabic-speaking Jewish communities were also to be found in Norman Sicily (Metcalfe 2003: 68). Third, there was a Judaeo-Christian legend that the Girgashites (one of the peoples whom the Iraelites dispossessed from Canaan) migrated en masse to North Africa: "The Girgashites evacuated, believed in the Holy One, praised be He, and went to Africa (the Roman province of Africa on the southern shore of the Meditarranean)" (*Talmud*: Tractate Kilaim, Shevi'it ch. 6; Guggenheimer 2001: 501). This legend appears not only in the Palestinian Talmud but also in the *Midrashim* (*Midrashim*: Leviticus xvii:6, Deuteronomy v.14; Iraelstam and Slotki 1939: 220–1; Rabbinowitz 1939: 116) and in early Christian texts (Hirschberg 1974: 23, 45–7; Monceaux 1902: 2–3). Fourth, contacts existed between Britain and Sicily in the Norman period (Johns 2002: 4; Haskins 1911). This was true also of Scandinavian Britain and thus "the presence in southern Italy and Sicily of more than a handful of Normans who still bore Norse personal names" (Johns 2002: 4). Furthermore, direct connections between Scandinavia and Sicily are testified to by medieval Icelandic reports of Norwegian crusaders spending a "comfortable and lengthy stay in Sicily in the splendour of Count Roger II's court" (Doxey 1996: 149).

The idea of a "lost people" of North African Jews was current among Jewish populations in tenth-century Sicily, but its spread to Latin-speaking peoples on the island after the Norman conquest is uncertain (Jeremy Johns, personal communication). However, if one were to imagine the legend's currency in Norman Sicily, then the connections between that island and northwest Europe outlined above allow us to propose that this "lost people" legend may have been one of the *Historia* author's materials.

21 As mentioned earlier, ideas of "Welsh-speaking Indians" were attacked by Thomas Stephens in 1858.

22 Trigger discusses Lafitau (Trigger 1989: 65; Washburn and Trigger 1996: 72; Trigger 1998: 50–1).

23 Beauvois's "restes de murs en pierre" may be related to nineteenth-century discoveries of structural features and manipulated landscapes associated with early modern fishing rooms, such as those currently being investigated by Peter Pope in Newfoundland's Petit Nord (http://niche-canada.org/member-projects/petit-nord/pnhome.html).

24 Titled "*Kitāb Nuzhat al-mushtāq fī-khtirāq al-afāq* / L'Agrément de celui qui est passioné pour la pérégrination à travers le monde" or "*Kitāb Rujār* / Livre de Roger" (Bresc and Nef 1999: 13).

25 Dunlop reproduces maps that accompany this text and appear in *Book of Roger* manuscripts (Dunlop 1947). The most recent edition of the passage (which builds upon Jaubert's translation) reads:

Entre l'extrémité de l'Écosse, île déserte, et l'extrémité de l'île d'Irlande, on compte deux jours de navigation vers l'occident.

L'Irlande est une île très considerable. Entre son extrémité supérieure et la Bretagne, on compte troisjours et demi de navigation. Et l'auteur du *Livre des merveilles* affirme que l'on y trouve trois villes. Il affirme aussi qu'un people y vit et que les bateaux avaient l'habitude d'y passer, de s'y arrêter et d'y acheter de l'ambre et des pierres colorées, mais que des affrontements éclatèrent entre les habitants. Certains cherchèrent alors à prendre le pouvoir sur les autres et les combatirrent avec leur famille. L'animosité s'installa entre les habitants pour cette raison. Ils s'anéantirent réciproquement, certains d'entre eux allèrent s'installer sur la côte du continent, leurs villes furent détruites, et aucun d'eux ne demeura en Irlande.

De l'extrémité de l'Angleterre à l'île du Danemark, un jour de navigation. De l'extrémité septentrionale de l'Écosse à l'île de l'Islande (*R.s.lânda*), trois jours. De l'extrémité de l'Islande à celle de la Grande Irlande, un. De l'extrémité de l'Islande à l'île de Norvège (*N.r.bâgha*), douze milles vers l'est. L'Islande mesure quatre cents milles de long sur cent cinquante de large. (*Idrîsî*: VII, 2; Bresc and Nef 1999: 461)

26 Thus Wittek's reinterpretation cautions against using *b.rlanda* as evidence for this section of the *Book of Roger* being drawn ultimately from a French-speaking informant.

2. A Fruitful Conversation between Disciplines

1 Popper 1994: 34. Italics in original.
2 Ibid., 36–7.
3 In this way, future work might profitably set the ideas explored in this chapter against John Hines's reflections on archaeology and literature (Hines 2004).
4 Crumley outlines her reasoning in selecting only anthropologists to formulate historical ecology: "Although the topic could prompt lively discussion among geographers, historians, natural scientists, and philosophers (to name a few), all the seminar participants are anthropologists. This choice was made so a common vocabulary would undergird the discussion of a difficult topic" (Crumley 1994: xiii).
5 See especially his last treatment of these ideas (Popper 1994).
6 The *realist* assumption may also be contrasted with *non-cognitivism* or *error theory*, for instance (Darwall et al. 1997; Craig 1998).
7 Strictly speaking, Trigger was here referring to American society in the 1980s; however, I suspect that his comments have some relevance for global society today.
8 Popper sees Bacon as a "logically and rationally quite unimportant philosopher" (Popper 1994: 195). Nonetheless, his importance for science is unassailable and is itself a topic that Popper explores (Popper 1994: 195–201).

9 Popper describes the process, in the 1960s, by which he came to be unfairly labelled a positivist:

It was in this paper [by Jürgen Habermas], I think, that the term "positivism" first turned up in this particular discussion: I was criticized as a *positivist*. This is an old misunderstanding created and perpetuated by people who know of my work only at second-hand. Owing to the tolerant attitude adopted by some members of the Vienna Circle, my book, *Logik der Forschung*, in which I criticized this positivist Circle from a realist and anti-positivist point of view, was published in a series edited by Moritz Schlick and Philipp Frank, two leading members of the Circle. And those who judge books by their covers (or by their editors) created the myth that I had been a member of the Vienna Circle and a positivist. Nobody who has read that book (or any other book of mine) would agree – unless indeed he believed in the myth to start with, in which case he may of course find evidence to support his belief. (Popper 1994: 67)

10 The following two quotations from Popper illustrate his "continually revolutionary science":

As I have suggested before, scientific progress is revolutionary. Indeed, its motto could be that of Karl Marx: "Revolution in permanence." However, scientific revolutions are rational in the sense that, in principle, it is rationally decidable whether or not a new theory is better than its predecessor. Of course, this does not mean that we cannot blunder. There are many ways in which we can make mistakes …

New ideas should be regarded as precious, and should be carefully nursed – especially if they seem to be a bit wild. I do not suggest that one should be eager to accept new ideas *just* for the sake of their newness. But we should be anxious not to suppress a new idea even if it does not appear to us to be very good. (Popper 1994: 12, 14)

11 Elaborating this point, Popper writes: "Kuhn has discovered something which I had failed to see, and I have derived considerable enlightenment from his discovery… Kuhn discovered what he has called 'normal science' and the 'normal scientist.' This name refers to a phenomenon which in his opinion, as the name indicates, is 'normal.' I admit to the existence of the phenomenon (which I had before overlooked or not seen in its full significance); but I do not admit the evaluation hinted at by the term 'normal': I do not only dislike the phenomenon, but I think that it has only recently become very important and, in my opinion, a danger to science" (Popper 1974: 1145; see also Bird 1975: 160, 163n37).

12 For instance, Popper points to Windelband, Rickert, Dilthey, Collingwood, Trevor-Roper, and Berlin (Popper 1994: 139).

3. Pabbays and Paibles

1 Wilson 1851: 486.

2 See also Ian Simpson and Barbara Crawford's Scottish *Papar Project* (www.paparproject.org.uk).
3 In its modern form, *Papies Holm* has a Scots English plural morpheme. The Scots English ending of *Papies* should not be seen as a difficulty for identifying *Papies Holm* as a North Atlantic *Pap-* name, however, as morphological morphemes are rather unstable and often "updated" to new linguistic conditions, such as internal language-structural changes as well as language change (Sandnes 2003: 291–2).
4 This is not to say that "breast, teat" names need refer to paired paps; consider *Pap of Glencoe* (one peak) or *Paps of Jura* (three peaks).
5 In the twelfth-century *Historia Norvegiae*, Scotland's Atlantic islands are described thus: "Que quidem diuersis incolis acculte nunc in duo regna sunt diuise: sunt enim Meridiane insule [Suðreyjar or Hebrides] regulus sublimate, Brumales uero comitum presidio decorate, qui utrique regibus Norwegie non modica persoluunt tributa." (They are populated by different peoples and now split into two domains; the southern isles [Suðreyjar or Hebrides] have been elevated by petty kings, the northern graced by the protection of earls, both of whom pay no mean tribute to the kings of Norway.) *Historia*: ch. 5; Ekrem and Mortensen 2003: 64–5; Phelpstead and Kunin 2001)
6 Taken from Beauvois, though he himself extracts this folktale from Schrœter.
7 In chapter 1 we proposed that the claim of Orkney's papae being "Africanus … judaismo adhærentes" was politically driven rather than historically legitimate. In 1995 Raymond Lamb proposed an identification for Orkney's papar as "Roman Churchmen" comparable to those of Frankish Gaul and Anglo-Saxon England (Lamb 1995: 26). However, the North Atlantic distribution of *Pap-* names, incorporating Scotland's Western Isles, instead suggests an association with the northwards-looking Church of the Scottish west.
8 That is not to say that *all* earlier scholarship shared these ideas. Indeed, in Iceland especially, there has been criticism of the idea that *Pap-* names remember early Christian papar; see for instance Sveinbjarnardóttir's criticisms (Sveinbjarnardóttir 1972; 2002: 101). Furthermore, other novel approaches to *Pap-* names have been proposed by Icelandic scholars. For example, Sturla Friðriksson suggested *Pap-* island names were given because of puffin colonies at these places and that puffin colouring is reminiscent of priest's robes – thus the proposed original meaning for *Papey* of "priest or puffin island" (Friðriksson 1982). However, the necessary antiquity of *papi* as an alternate name for a puffin is not established, nor does this meaning account for *Pap-* farm names or the proximity of these names to early Christian sculpture sites (Fisher 2002).
9 One of the more recent writers to work with this idea was Gillian Fellows-Jensen, when she suggested that *Pap-* names may have been applied, during Scandinavian colonization, to sites recently abandoned by early churchmen (Fellows-Jensen 1996: 116; Gammeltoft 2003: 44).

10 This syncope (or vowel resolution/vowel simplification) was also active in Old Icelandic, though to a lesser degree than in Old Norwegian. Gammeltoft discusses many of these linguistic points in relation to *Pap-* names (Gammeltoft 2004b: 41–2). This syncope may be chronologically constrained, and we will return to the implications of this in a detailed assessment of the hypotheses.
11 Beauvois provides an example of this late medieval Germanic usage of the word: "C'est en effet dans le sens que le mot *papa* est employé dans la *Poëme Frison* (Thet Freske Riim, vers 1476), chronique rimée en vieux frison, publié par la Société provinciale Frisonne (Van Leeuwen 1835: 49, 81)" (Beauvois 1875: 70n3).
12 "*I got. kalenderfragment fines vid 29.10. bi Werekan papan*" (Thors 1957: 37–8; In the Gothic calendar fragment the word is used for 29.10.: bi Werekan papan).
13 "*Jak troer then mann vil illa rapa; Some y wil elska prest eller papa*" (Thors 1957: 37–8).
14 Note, however, that the South Uist *Pabbay* is the name given to two islands.
15 The spirit of this argument should also apply to the Western Isles, regardless of whether they were largely Pictish speaking or, as Cox believes, Gaelic speaking before Norse colonization in that area (Cox 2002: 107, 114–18).
16 Admittedly, *Pap-* names do appear in proximity to some cross sculpture sites, but this sculpture is mostly earlier (that is, of early Christian date).

4. Seljaland, Vestur-Eyjafjallahreppur, Iceland

1 Jónsson 1902: 29; Friðriksson 1994: 24.
2 Þórðarson 1931: 57.
3 Tómasson í Skógum 1997: 148–9.
4 We shall return to the scholarship of Jónsson, Benediktsson, Þórðarson, and later writers in greater depth in chapter 7 (Jónsson 1900; 1902; 1906; Benediktsson 1905a; 1905b; Þórðarson 1931).
5 For instance, consider Sveinbjarnardóttir's 1972 observation that "lítið hefur verið gert til að varpa ljósi á þá. Síðustu rannsóknir á þeim voru gerðar í kringum 1930" (Sveinbjarnardóttir 1972: 17; little has been done to cast light upon them [the caves]. The latest research on them was carried out around 1930). Holt and Guðmundsson as well as Hjartarson, Guðmundsson, and Gísladóttir have since reinitiated study of these caves (Holt and Guðmundsson 1980; Hjartarson et al. 1991).
6 The eleventh-century author Adam of Bremen outlined that Icelanders live in caves (though his account is fantastic in parts): "in subterraneis habitant speluncis, communi tecto et strato gaudentes cum pecoribus suis" (*Adam*: bk. 4, ch. 36, skol 153; Schmeidler 1917: 272). They live in underground caves, glad to have roof and food and bed in common with their cattle (Tschan 1959: 217).

7 Although this point appears clearly established for the Hebrides, Iceland's clustered distribution of these names (in contrast to Atlantic Scotland's more regular distribution) hints at further complexities.

8 This material is discussed in Macniven, Sveinbjarnardóttir, and Eldjárn and Friðriksson (Macniven 2003: 96; Sveinbjarnardóttir 1982; Eldjárn and Friðriksson 2000: 48, 393–5).

9 These three include Holt (Holtsós), Þrasastaðir (near Eystriskógar), and Steinfinnstaðir (which has been equated with Kápa in Almenning). Macniven gives an overview of this discussion (Macniven 2003: 99–101).

10 *Landnámabók* tells how the region "*á millim Hornafjarðar ok Reykjaness varð seinst albyggt*" (*Landnámabók*: H294; Benediktsson 1968: 337; between Hornafjörður and Reykjanes was last to be completely settled).

11 *Landnámabók*: S339, S341, M4, M6, H297, H299; Benediktsson 1968: 340–1, 343.

12 Cleasby, Vigfusson, and Craigie define Icelandic *sel* as "a shed on a mountain pasture, but within the landmarks of each farm" (Cleasby et al. 1957: 521).

13 It is described as a church site in Páll Jónsson's *Kirknatal* (Macniven 2003: 101; DI12 1923–32: 6).

14 In my work I use the singular *tephra* and plural *tephrae*. Among tephrochronologists the English conjugation of the Greek feminine noun *tephra* is a point of contention and has yet to be standardized, with variant forms of the plural including *tephras* and *tephra*. Following the normal "Latinizing" rules for borrowing a Greek word into English, I advocate the use of *tephrae* as the plural form and I have found that this usage enables me to express my meaning more clearly.

15 An earlier survey of Eyjafjallasveit, published in 2000 and of a different scale, provides a good introduction to the impressive survival of visible archaeological features in the area (Sveinbjarnardóttir and Gunnarsdóttir 2000: 187–97).

16 A memorial inscription at Kverkin describes the planting of woodland in 1981.

17 Intriguingly, *Papahellir* (Papar cave) is an alternate place name for *Seljalandshellar* (Seljaland caves) (Hálfdan Ómar Hálfdanarson, personal communication).

18 As mentioned earlier, the rock-cut cross sculpture at a number of these sites has attracted comparisons to the early Christian sculpture of Britain and Ireland and shall be explored at length in chapter 7.

19 Vésteinsson refers to models of settlement, with particular emphasis upon medieval farms (Vésteinsson 1998).

5. Dating the Cave

1 Ager 1993: 53.

2 Schiffer 1987: 58.

3 *Biskupa sögur I–II* (1858–1878), Híð Íslenzka Bókmenntafélag, Copenhagen, I:320, 346–7. Cited in Friðriksson 1994: 25.

4 In contrast with Atlantic Scotland, those Icelandic *Pap-* names not demonstrating archaic linguistic features – such as the syncope in *Papey* names discussed in chapter 3 – may formally have been coined at any point since the island's Norse settlement. The coincidence of papar folklore with potentially modern *Pap-* names thus highlights the complex interactions between the folkloric and place-name material related to these caves.

5 One tradition regards the healing properties ascribed to the water from a basin that is cut into the westernmost of the Seljalandshellar chambers. This basin has three holes drilled down into the wall fabric, and water springs from them to collect in the basin. The wall fabric exposed by the basin is in similar condition to that of the surrounding wall; thus construction is unlikely to be recent. The date of the drilling is uncertain but is conceivably contemporary with the basin's construction.

6 *Early historic* is used here to refer to the first centuries of medieval settlement in Iceland.

7 Folk tradition describes the use of Kverkarhellir for human habitation in the 1500s (Árnarson 1856 [1993]: 200–2).

8 Size range terminology is drawn from Jones, Tucker, and Hart's guidelines for Quaternary researchers (Jones et al. 1999: 43).

9 The stratigraphy of the younger sediments contains apparent complexities that neither add nor detract from the matter at hand; correspondingly, discussion of this is left for detailed treatment elsewhere.

10 A comparable sample column was excavated in trench D1; however, considering the uncertainties regarding the tephra identifications for that trench, this data was deemed immaterial to the present argument. Similarly, the trench D4 sample column produced data clearly of much value, though the bulk of this lacks relevance to the current question and will be pursued in another context.

11 The tephra layers discussed are referred to using a two-element system. The first element abbreviates the source volcanic system to one letter (H for Hekla, K for Katla, V for Vatnaöldur), while the second element expresses the AD date (H1947 for Hekla AD 1947).

12 The black Katla R (Reykjavík) tephra of c. 920 is thus named because ash from the eruption was blown towards Reykjavik (Hafliðarson et al. 1992).

13 This interpretation is based upon Dugmore and Erskine's estimates for sediment accumulation rates at Seljaland (Dugmore and Erskine 1994).

14 "*Non sunt multiplicanda entia praetor necessitatem*/entities are not to be multiplied beyond necessity" (Juhl and Markestad 1991).

15 Unresolved controversy surrounds suggestions made for the Westman Islands (Hermanns-Auðardóttir 1989; 1991; 1992; Vilhjálmsson 1992: 167–81), while

more recent fieldwork in Reykjavík identified a field boundary sealed by an ash layer that was suggested to be in situ landnám tephra, and thus dated this feature to, perhaps, c. 850 (Roberts et al. 2002: 35–9).

6. Three Dimensions of Environmental Change

1 Jones et al. 1999: 17.
2 Buckland 1981: 383.
3 Ian A. Simpson et al. discuss in detail the method and data sets used in formulating this palaeoecological reconstruction (Simpson et al. 2001: 182–4).
4 Heavily sedimented lowland coastal plain.
5 This estimate of 300 hectares of woodland was prepared by Amanda Thomson through application of her model for surface vegetation in Eyjafjallasveit to an area bounded by the Seljalandsá (to the north), the 10 m contour line (to the west and south), the 300 m contour line (to the east), and Seljalandskóli (to the southeast).
6 That is, the *form* of an ash layer.
7 Statistically quantifying the confidence of conclusions drawn from tephra contours is a goal for future work at Seljaland (and elsewhere).
8 The 9cm hole in the K920 tephra layer was discovered in 2001 during the preliminary development of this technique in a section of area A1 that bordered area A2 and is therefore included in the discussion (but not the illustration) of the results of the A2 trench (Ahronson 2003b: 63–7).

7. The Crosses of a Desert Place?

1 Gerard Murphy edits and translates the poem, citing Mugrón, abbot of Iona and Kells, as author of this Middle Irish *lorica*, though one manuscript attributes this *crosradhach* to Columba (Murphy 1998 [1956]: 32–5; Fisher 2001: 1, 156n1.
2 These particular inscriptions and graffito crosses are associated with Vigleikr prestsson and other members of Hákon Hákonarson's fleet during their 1263 visit to Melasey (Molaise's Island or Eilean Molaise) (Fisher 2001: 61–5).
3 Matthías Þórðarson exemplifies this approach in his seventy-six-page study of artificial caves in Rangárvallasýsla and Árnessýsla. His study explored the caves' inscriptions and *búmörk* (ownership marks) rather than cross sculpture (Þórðarson 1931; Friðriksson 1994: 24–5). For discussion of the inscriptions, Þórður Tómasson (í Skógum) has published on *búmörk* (Tómasson [í Skógum] 1976), while Þórgunnur Snædal collects much of the work on runic inscriptions in her register of 96 carvings with "55 on (grave)stones or in caves" (Snædal 2003: 67).

4 Árni Hjartarson and Hallgerður Gísladóttir credit Einar Benediktsson with the first effort at cataloguing artificial cave sites including rock-cut crosses (Hjartarson and Gísladóttir 1993).

5 Taken from an unpublished Þjóðminjasafn Íslands internal report on artificial cave sites after two earthquakes on 17 and 21 June 2000 (Þjóðminjasafn Íslands 2000). Guðmundur Ólafsson also authored a formal report, *Hellir að Seli, Ásahreppi. Rannsóknarskýrslur Fornleifadeildar 1991*.

6 Þórðarson very briefly refers to and discounts the cross sculpture (Þórðarson 1931: 28, 50, 57, 62).

7 These articles appeared in *Morgunblaðið* on 1 and 12 December 1929 as well as in the Christmas supplement of *Lesbók Morgunblaðsins* (1929: 397–8).

8 A similar text appeared later (Sveinsson 1948).

9 Illustrated in Collingwood's *Northumbrian Crosses of the Pre-Norman Age* (1927: 3, 13), *Proceedings of the Royal Irish Academy* (1961: 101–5), and in Lethbridge (1950: 84).

10 Þórður Tómasson later published on another cave site. This cave, Hrútshellir, has been the subject of much antiquarian and later interest (Tómasson [í Skógum] 1986).

11 Cave sites are recognized, for instance, in a recent survey of Icelandic archaeology (Friðriksson 1994: 24–6).

12 The expression *sem var í marki* incorporates the archaic term *marki*, which I tentatively translate as "that were in position."

13 Torfason uses the variant form *Keltakross*, though it is possible he coins the name.

14 Hjartarson et al. undertook a mammoth task in *Manngerðir Hellar á Íslandi*. Their work is excellent and of broad remit; cross sculpture is included, but illustrations are not the focus of their catalogue and are necessarily simple.

15 *Northwest Europe* is used in its loosest sense for the region encompassing the peninsulas of Brittany and Normandy, the British and Irish islands, the north Atlantic archipelagos, and the Scandinavian peninsulas and islands.

16 Mystery cults allowed more personal and intimate interaction with the deity. The most successful of the oriental mystery cults was the religion of Christ. A branch of Judaism, the earliest Christianity was characterized by belief in an afterlife and in congregational worship at a ritual building. A font was often located outside to allow ritual baptism before entry to a temple. The cult was secretive but of open membership and excluded, in theory but not early practice, joint belief in other gods. The secrecy, owing to intermittent persecution, made early evidence for the cult ambiguous and uncertain, and the true extent of Christian practice within the early empire is problematic. For two views of the extent of Christianity in Roman Britain, see Salway and Arnold (Salway 1993: 519–29; Arnold 1984: 142–56).

The finding of lead fonts with inscribed Christian symbols has allowed the identification of some ritual buildings. However, assemblies in cities often gathered not in temple or church but in a "series of rooms set aside for the various liturgical purposes within the bishop's house ... it is hardly distinguishable from the private house, except by some lucky find of furnishings or decoration" (Salway 1993: 519). Such appears to be the case at Lullingstone, for instance, where Christian wall painting is found in a domestic context (Meates 1979; Mawer 1995; Thomas 1981: 181). Even then, however, Christian symbolism may be problematic.

To illustrate the difficulties, consider the Christian symbols found in Roman Britain's mosaic tiles. Were they displayed as an act of faith? A complication for interpretation arises if "the owner of the building commissioned the particular designs because of the stock-in-trade of the mosaicist" (Arnold 1984: 145). The answer changes the nature and meaning of the symbols for, as Salway notes, "the iconography of one religion was often adapted and given a new meaning by another" (Salway 1993: 496).

17 Ann Hamlin outlines ideas that Laing and Laing follow here (Hamlin 1972: 24).

18 Although the term insular has sometimes been used to describe only Ireland and the Celtic areas of Britain, I use it in its most inclusive sense: as an adjective signifying Britain and Ireland and their islands.

19 If the hammer rings are accepted as a *reaction* to Christian cross amulets, care must be taken not to overstress the point. For instance, Gabriel Turville-Petre saw objects such as the pewter cross from Foss (Arnarssýsla, Iceland) as "a compound of a hammer and a cross, even the work of a man of mixed religion" (Turville-Petre 1964: 83). My own work, however, challenges the hammer-like character of the Foss object. Elsewhere, I interpret the Foss object as a *cross* – produced in a Norse Christian milieu and betraying insular influence (Ahronson 2001; Eldjárn 1981; 1983).

20 Mentioned in *Vita Anskarii*, chapters 13 and 14 (Waitz 1884), and identified as near Itzehoe in Holsten (Nyberg 2000: 24; Freytag 1977: 147).

21 Lager uses Anne-Sofia Gräslund's chronological system (Gräslund 1994).

22 The Selja cave is also mentioned in the ca. 1380 manuscript *Flateyjarbók*.

23 A late-tenth-century cross arm was discovered at Stöng in southern Iceland's Þjórsárdalur, and an undated fragment was recovered from the monastic ruins on Viðey, near Reykjavík (Kristjánsdóttir 2003: 124; Vilhjálmsson 1996: 133).

24 Simon Taylor surveys the substantial number of Columban dedications in eastern Scotland and suggests that these names reflect similarly early Columban activity (Taylor 2000).

25 However, Iona remained occupied until the twelfth century, with the "continuing use of the monastery and burial-ground after the disruptive attacks of the

ninth-century, … marked by St Matthew's Cross, and other fragmentary crosses" (Fisher 2001: 11).

26 Hamlin characterizes the Irish distribution of simple cross forms thus:

It seems at present, in the absence of a full corpus, that the distribution of these stones is very heavily western and coastal, concentrated in the seaboard counties and islands from Cork and Kerry to Donegal. This western area is poorly covered by written sources and the stones often occur at sites whose history is shadowy or quite unknown. These stones thus assume a historical importance beyond their undoubted aesthetic value …

Carved stones of the kind under review are not common in the east, at known early episcopal centres. Could these pillar stones with their western distribution, their early, exotic, borrowed elements, be pointers to a very early *stratum* of monasticism in western Ireland, introduced in the sixth and seventh centuries when the diocesan church elsewhere was still strong? The regional variety already touched on, together with the markedly western and coastal distribution, would suggest varied maritime contacts, still to be worked out in detail. This leads to another speculation. The quite extraordinary concentrations of ecclesiastical sites in some western areas, like the Dingle and Iveragh peninsulas, have never been fully explained. These are areas of great natural beauty, rugged and inhospitable, not obviously attractive for settlement, but if these coastal regions were indeed the earliest centres of Irish monasticism they could have attracted ecclesiastical settlers over many centuries, producing the wealth of material remains which impress but puzzle us today. (Hamlin 1982: 289–93)

27 Two photographs (with different lighting) for each cross.

28 I have used the technique myself in a preliminary discussion of southern Iceland cross sculpture (Ahronson 2000).

29 The Kverkarhellir plan was drawn from a 2001 survey, whereas the Seljalandshellar plan was drawn from a simple scaled drawing in *Manngerðir Hellar* (Hjartarson et al. 1991: 246).

30 The larger one is illustrated here as SK1, and the smaller has been illustrated elsewhere (Hjartarson and Gísladóttir 1983: 130; Ahronson 2000: 119).

31 A deep cut may also be seen in carvings from Kilmun (Fisher 2001: fig. 31M), Kirkapoll (Tiree) (Fisher 2001: fig. 31N), and Kilfinan (Cowal) (Fisher 2001: fig. 32V[1]), though this last is more sunken.

32 This carving may pre-date the eighth century (Fisher, personal communication).

33 Fisher provides a good commentary on the island: "'Rona of the ocean,' as it was designated in the 16th century, lies 72 km NNE of the Butt of Lewis and about the same distance NW of Cape Wrath, and 17 km E of the rock of Sula Sgeir. The main part measures 1.6 km from E to W by 0.8 km, with a low promontory

extending almost 1 km to the N … Monro noted the existence of 'St Ronan's chapell,' which in 1549 was being used for burials, and later writers recounted the legend, current in Lewis tradition, of Ronan's departure from that island to live as a hermit on Rona. Although the island probably takes its name from the Norse Hraun-ey ('rough island') rather than from the saint, there are important remains of Early Christian occupation" (Fisher 2001: 114).

34 Conceivably influenced by the patriarchal crosses of Byzantine art?

35 For instance, there is no significant correspondence between the Seljaland sculpture and the outline crosses included in Birkeli's Norwegian corpus.

36 The Faroese technique of shallow pecking, for instance, is absent in the Seljaland examples.

37 As mentioned previously, a tradition of such journeys is evident in Dicuil's *Liber de mensura orbis terrae* (Tierney 1967) and Adomnán's *Life of Columba* (Anderson and Anderson 1991; Sharpe 1995), as well as in Irish voyage literature generally.

38 Nicolaisen's term was coined in Latin as *Scotia Scandinavica*.

Conclusion

1 Quoted out of context, with permission.

2 Popper 1994: xii.

3 Tolstoy 1954: pt. 4 ch. 10, 411–12.

References

Adam. Edited and translated by Schmeidler (1917) and Tschan (1959).

Ager, D.V. 1993. *The Nature of the Stratigraphical Record*. 3rd ed. Chichester, UK: John Wiley & Sons.

Ahronson, K. 2000. "Further evidence for a Columban Iceland: Preliminary results of recent work." *Norwegian Archaeological Review* 33 (2): 117–24. http://dx.doi.org/10.1080/002936500423484.

Ahronson, K. 2001. "Hamarinn frá Fossi." *Árbók hins Íslenzka Fornleifafélags* 1999: 185–9.

Ahronson, K. 2002a. "Testing the evidence for northern North Atlantic *papar*: A cave site in southern Iceland." In *The Papar in the North Atlantic: Environment and History. The Proceedings of a day conference held on 24th February 2001. The 'Papar' Project. Volume 1*, edited by B. Crawford, 107–20. St Andrews, Scotland: The Committee for Dark Age Studies, University of St Andrews.

Ahronson, K. 2002b. "Pabbay Place-name Inventory: Including the Pab(b)ay Islands of Harris, Skye/Strath, South Uist, and Barra in the Western Isles of Scotland." Unpublished report.

Ahronson, K., ed. 2003a. "Atlantic Peoples between Fire, Ice, River and Sea: Past Environments in Southern Iceland." Special issue, *Northern Studies* 37: 49–111.

Ahronson, K. 2003b. "One North Atlantic cave settlement: Preliminary archaeological and environmental investigations at Seljaland, southern Iceland." In "Atlantic Peoples between Fire, Ice, River and Sea: Past Environments in Southern Iceland," edited by K. Ahronson, Special issue, *Northern Studies* 37: 53–70.

Ahronson, K. 2004. "The crosses of Columban Iceland: A survey of preliminary research." In *Vínland Revisited: The Norse World at the Turn of the First Millenium. Selected Papers from the Viking Millenium International Symposium, 15–24 September 2000, Newfoundland and Labrador*, edited by S. Lewis-Simpson, 75–82. St John's, NL: Historic Sites Association of Newfoundland and Labrador, Inc.

Ahronson, K. 2007. *Viking-Age Communities: Pap-Names and Papar in the Hebridean Islands*. Oxford: BAR British Series 450.

Ahronson, K., and T.M. Charles-Edwards. 2010. "Prehistoric Annals and early medieval monasticism: Daniel Wilson, James Young Simpson and their cave sites." *Antiquaries Journal* 90: 455–66. http://dx.doi.org/10.1017/S0003581510000028.

Ahronson, K., W. Gillies, and F. Hunter. 2006. "Early Christian activity at Scottish cave sites." *Church Archaeology* 7/8/9: 123–5.

Alcock, L. 1998. "From realism to caricature: Reflections on Insular depictions of animals and people." *Proceedings of the Society of Antiquaries of Scotland* 128: 515–36.

Annandale, N. 1905. *The Faroes and Iceland: Studies in Island Life*. Oxford: Clarendon Press. http://dx.doi.org/10.2307/198214.

Anderson, A.O., ed. and trans. 1922. *Early Sources of Scottish History, AD 500 to 1286: Volume I*. Edinburgh: Oliver and Boyd.

Anderson, A.O., and M.O. Anderson, eds. and trans. 1991. *Adomnan's Life of Columba*. Oxford: Oxford University Press.

Árnarson, J. [1856] 1993. *Íslenzkar þjóðsögur og Ævintðri IV.* New edition, edited by Á. Böðvarsson and B. Vilhjálmsson. Reykjavík: Bókaútgáfan þjóðsaga Prentsmiðjan Hólar H.F.

Arnold, C.J. 1984. *Roman Britain to Saxon England: An Archaeological Study*. London: Croon Helm.

Arnold, M. (1867) 1962. "On the study of Celtic literature." In *Lectures and Essays in Criticism*, edited by R.H. Super, 291–386. Ann Arbor: University of Michigan Press.

Ashburn, D., M.P. Kirkbride, and A.J. Dugmore. 2003. "Post-settlement land disturbance indicated by magnetic susceptibility of aeolian soils at Seljaland." In *Atlantic Peoples between Fire, Ice, River and Sea: Past Environments in Southern Iceland*, edited by K. Ahronson, Special issue, *Northern Studies* 37: 81–94.

Ashe, G. 1962. *Land to the West: St Brendan's Voyage to America*. St James's Place, London: Collins.

Babcock, W.H. 1915. "Indications of visits of White Men to America before Columbus." *Congrès international des américanistes* 19: 469–78.

Barnes, G. 2001. *Viking America: The First Millenium*. Cambridge: D.S. Brewer.

Bately, J., ed. 1980. *The Old English Orosius*. London: Oxford University Press.

Beauvois, E. 1859. "Découvertes des Scandinaves en Amérique du dixième au treizième siècle, fragments de sagas islandaises, traduits pour la première fois en français." *Revue orientale et américaine*, 1859, 9–32, 48–65.

Beauvois, E. 1875. "La découverte du Nouveau Monde par les Irlandais et les premières traces du Christianisme en Amérique avant l'an 1000." *Congrès international des américanistes* 1: 41–93.

Beauvois, E. 1877a. "Les colonies européennes du Markland et de l'Escociland (domination canadienne) au XIVe siècle et les vestiges qui en subsistèrent jusqu'aux XVIe et XVIIe siècles." *Congrès international des américanistes* 2: 25–84, 174–227.

Beauvois, E. 1877b. "Les derniers vestiges du christianisme prêché du 10e au 14e siècles dans le Markland et la Grande Irlande: Les Porte-Croix de la Gaspésie et de l'Acadie (domination canadienne)." *Annales de philosophie chrétienne*, 1877, 284ff.

Beauvois, E. 1879a. "La Norambègue: Découverte d'une quatrième colonie précolombienne dans le Nouveau Monde avec des preuves de son origine scandinave." *Congrès international des américanistes* 3.

Beauvois, E. 1879b. "Les Skrælings, ancêtres des Esquimaux dans les temps précolombiens." *Revue orientale et américaine*, 1879, 48 pages.

Beauvois, E. 1881. "La grande terre de l'Ouest dans les documents celtiques du moyen âge." *Congrès international des américanistes* 4: 45–74.

Beauvois, E. 1883a. "L'autre vie dans la mythologie scandinave." *Le Muséon: Revue internationale. Études de linguistiques, d'histoire et de philosophie* 2: 189–209.

Beauvois, E. 1883b. "Les relations précolombiennes des Gaëls avec le Mexique." *Congrès international des américanistes* 5: 74–97.

Beauvois, E. 1883–4. "L'élysée transatlantique et l'Eden occidental." *Revue de l'histoire des religions* 6: 273–318; 7: 265–331.

Beauvois, E. 1884a. "L'élysée des Mexicains comparé à celui des Celtes." *Revue de l'histoire des religions* 10:1–42, 265–331.

Beauvois, E. 1884b. "La fontaine de Jouvence et le Jourdain dans les traditions des Antilles et de la Floride." *Le Muséon: Revue internationale. Études de linguistiques, d'histoire et de philosophie* 3: 404–29.

Beauvois, E. 1885. "L'histoire de l'ancien Mexique: Les antiquités mexicains du P. Duran comparées auz régés des P.P.J. Tobar et J. d'Acosta." *Revue des quéstions historiques*, 1885, 109–65.

Beauvois, E. 1886. "Deux sources de l'histoire des Quetzalcoatl: Les anciennes interprétations italienne et espagne du codex vaticanus no 3738 et du codex tellerianus." *Le Muséon: Revue internationale. Études de linguistiques, d'histoire et de philosophie* 5: 427–44, 597–604.

Beauvois, E. 1887. "La légende de Saint Columba chez les Mexicains du Moyen Age." *Le Muséon: Revue internationale. Études de linguistiques, d'histoire et de philosophie* 6: 156–72, 298–310.

Beauvois, E. 1888. "Premiers chrétiens des îles nordatlantiques." *Le Muséon: Revue internationale. Études de linguistiques, d'histoire et de philosophie* 7: 315–30, 408–33.

Beauvois, E. 1889a. "Les chrétiens d'Islande au temps de l'Odinisme. IXe et Xe siècles." *Le Muséon: Revue internationale. Études de linguistiques, d'histoire et de philosophie* 8: 340–54, 430–43.

Beauvois, E. 1889b. "Echos de croyances chrétiennes chez les Mexicains du moyen-age et chez d'autres peuples voisins." *Revue de l'Histoire des Religions* 18.

Beauvois, E. 1891. "La Tula primitive berceau des Papas du Nouveau Monde." *Le Muséon: Revue internationale. Études de linguistiques, d'histoire et de philosophie* 10: 206–31.

Beauvois, E. 1892. "Migration des Gaëls en Amérique au moyen-âge." *Congrès international des américanistes* 8: 200–1.

Beauvois, E. 1893. "Les papas du Nouveau-Monde: Rattachés à ceux des îles britanniques et nordatlantiques." *Le Muséon: Revue internationale. Études de linguistiques, d'histoire et de philosophie* 12: 171–88, 213–34.

Beauvois, E. 1895. "Les Gaulois en Amérique au XIIieme siècle." *Le Muséon: Revue internationale. Études de linguistiques, d'histoire et de philosophie* 15.

Beauvois, E. 1896. "Pratiques et institutions religieuses d'origine chrétienne chez les Mexicains du moyen âge." *Revue des questions scientifiques* 2: 10.

Beauvois, E. 1898. "Le contrefaçon du Christianisme chez les Mexicains du moyen age." *Le Muséon: Revue internationale. Études de linguistiques, d'histoire et de philosophie* 17: 122–94, 223–42.

Beauvois, E. 1902. "Les croix précolombiennes chez les Mayas du Yucatan et des contrées voisines." *Revue des questions scientifiques* 3 (2): 93–126.

Beauvois, E. 1903. "La Grande-Irlande ou pays des blancs précolombiens du Nouveau-Monde." *Journal de la société des américanistes de Paris* 1: 189–229.

Beauvois, E. 1904. "La fable des Amazones chez les indigènes de l'Amérique précolombienne." *Le Muséon: Revue internationale. Études de linguistiques, d'histoire et de philosophie*, 1904, 287–326.

Beauvois, E. 1907. "Le Paradis de l'Atlantique d'après les traditions concordantes de l'Ancien et du Nouveau Monde." *Le Muséon: Revue internationale. Études de linguistiques, d'histoire et de philosophie*, 1907, 41–99.

Beeston, A.F.L. 1950. "Idrisi's account of the British Isles." *Bulletin of the School of Oriental and African Studies. University of London. School of Oriental and African Studies* 13 (02): 265–80. http://dx.doi.org/10.1017/S0041977X00083464.

Benediktsson, E. 1905a. "Íra-býlin I." In *Fjallkonan*. Reykjavík.

Benediktsson, E. 1905b. "Íra-býlin II." In *Fjallkonan*. Reykjavík.

Benediktsson, E. 1918. *Thules beboere: Brudstykker til belysning af Islands forhistorie*. Kristiania, Norway: Raadhustrykkeriet A/S.

Benediktsson, J., ed. 1968. *Íslendingabók Landnámabók*. Reykjavík: Hið Íslenzka Fornritafélag.

Benediktsson, J. 1969. "Landnámabók: Some remarks on its value as a historical source." *Saga-Book* 17:275–92.

Benfey, T. 1859. *Pantschatantra: Fünf Bücher indischer Fablen, Märchen, und Erzählungen*. 2 vols. Leipzig: F.W. Brockhaus.

Bird, J.H. 1975. "Methodological implications for geography from the philosophy of K.R. Popper." *Royal Scottish Geographical Society* 91 (3): 153–63. http://dx.doi.org/10.1080/00369227508736316.

Birkeli, F. 1973. *Norske Steinkors i Tidlig Middelalder: Et bidrag til belysning av overgangen fra norrøn religion til kristendom.* Oslo: Universitets forlaget.

Bosworth, J. 1855. *A Literal English Translation of King Alfred's Anglo-Saxon Version of Orosius.* London: Longman.

Bowler, P.J. 1989. *The Invention of Progress: The Victorians and the Past.* Oxford: Basil Blackwell.

Branigan, K., and M.J. Dearne, eds. 1992. *Romano-British Cavemen: Cave Use in Roman Britain.* Oxbow Monograph 19. Oxford: Oxbow Books.

Bresc, H., and A. Nef. 1999. *Idrîsî, La Première Géographie de l'Occident.* Translated by P.A. Jaubert and A. Nef. Paris: GF Flammarion.

Buckland, P.C. 1981. "Tephrochronology and palaeoecology: The value of isochrones." In *Tephra Studies: Proceedings of the NATO Advanced Study Institute 'Tephra Studies as a Tool in Quaternary Research,' held in Laugarvatn and Reykjavík, Iceland, June 18–29, 1980*, edited by S. Self and R.S.J. Sparks, 381–7. Dordrecht, Netherlands: Reidel Publishing.

Campbell, E. 1987. "A cross-marked quern from Dunadd and other evidence for relations between Dunadd and Iona." *Proceedings of the Society of Antiquaries of Scotland* 117: 105–17.

Campbell, E. 2007. *Continental and Mediterranean Imports to Atlantic Britain and Ireland, AD 400–800.* York: Council for British Archaeology.

Campbell, J.F. 1893. *Popular Tales of the West Highlands: Orally Collected.* New ed., vol. 4. Paisley, Scotland: Alexander Gardner.

Carey, J. 1983. "The location of the Otherworld in Irish traditions." *Eigse* 19 (1982/3): 36–43.

Carney, J. 1963. "Review of Navigatio Sancti Brendani abbatis edited by Carl Semper." *Medium Ævum* 32: 37–44.

Charles-Edwards, T. 1976. "The social background to Irish *peregrinatio*." *Celtica* XI: 43–59.

Cleasby, R., G. Vigfusson, and W.A. Craigie, eds. 1957. *An Icelandic-English Dictionary.* Oxford: Clarendon Press.

Clunies Ross, M. 1997. "Textual territory: The regional and genealogical dynamics of medieval Icelandic literary production." In *New Medieval Literatures.* vol. 1, edited by W. Scase, R. Copeland, and D. Lawton, 9–30. Oxford: Oxford University Press.

Collingwood, R.G. 1939. *An Autobiography.* Oxford: Oxford University Press.

Cox, R.A.V. 2002. *The Gaelic Place-names of Carloway, Isle of Lewis: Their Structure and Significance.* Dublin: School of Celtic Studies, Dublin Institute for Advanced Studies.

Craig, E., ed. 1998. *Routledge Encyclopedia of Philosophy*. London: Routledge.

Craigie, W.A. 1917. "'Iraland' in King Alfred's 'Orosius.'" *Modern Languages Review* xii.

Crawford, B.E. 1987. *Scandinavian Scotland*. Leicester, UK.

Crawford, B.E., ed. 2002. *The Papar in the North Atlantic: Environment and History. The Proceedings of a day conference held on 24th February 2001. The 'Papar' Project, volume 1.* St John's House Papers no. 10. St Andrews, Scotland: The Committee for Dark Age Studies, University of St Andrews.

Cronau, R. 1892. *Amerika: Die Geschichte seiner Entdeckung von der ältesten bis auf die neueste Zeit. Eine Festschrift zur 400 jährigen Jubelfeier der Entdeckung Amerikas durch Christoph Columbus*. 2 vols. Leipzig: Abel und Müller.

Crumley, C.L., ed. 1994. *Historical Ecology: Cultural Knowledge and Changing Landscapes*. Santa Fe, NM: School of American Research Press.

Cunliffe, B. 2001. *Facing the Ocean: The Atlantic and Its Peoples, 8000 BC–AD 1500*. Oxford: Oxford University Press.

Cunliffe, B. 2002. *The Extraordinary Voyage of Pytheas the Greek*. London: Penguin Books.

Damas, D. 1996. "The Arctic from Norse contact to modern times." In *The Cambridge History of the Native Peoples of the Americas,* vol. 1, *North America. Part 2*, edited by B.G. Trigger and W.E. Washburn, 329–99. Cambridge: Cambridge University Press. http://dx.doi.org/10.1017/CHOL9780521573931.007.

Darwall, S., A. Gibbard, and P.A. Railton, eds. 1997. *Moral Discourse and Practice: Some Philosophical Approaches*. Oxford: Oxford University Press.

Davies, W., J. Graham-Campbell, M. Handley, P. Kershaw, J.T. Koch, G. Le Duc, and K. Lockyear. 2000. *The Inscriptions of Early Medieval Brittany/Les inscriptions de la Bretagne du Haute Moyen Âge.* Celtic Studies Publications V. Aberystwyth, Wales: Celtic Studies Publications.

de Roo, P. 1900. *History of America before Colombus According to Documents and Approved Authors*. Philadelphia: Lippincott.

Deslongchamps, L. 1838. *Essai sur les fables indiennes*. Paris: Techener, Librairie.

Diaz-Andreu, M., and T. Champion, eds. 1996. *Nationalism and Archaeology in Europe*. London: UCL Press.

Diaz-Andreu, M., and A.D. Smith, eds. 2001. "Nationalism and Archaeology." Special issue: *Nations and Nationalism* 7, 4.

Diplomatorium Islandicum. 1923–32. Vol. 12, *1200–1554*. Reykjavík: Hið Íslenzka Bókmenntafélags.

Doxey, G.B. 1996. "Norwegian Crusaders and the Balearic Islands." *Scandinavian Studies* 68 (2): 139–60.

Dugmore, A.J. 1987. "Holocene glacier fluctuations around Eyjafjallajökull, South Iceland: A tephrochronological study." PhD diss., University of Aberdeen.

Dugmore, A.J., and C.C. Erskine. 1994. "Local and regional patterns of soil erosion in southern Iceland." In *Environmental Change in Iceland*, edited by J. Stötter and J.F. Wilhelm, 63–78. Munich: Münchener Geographische Abhandlungen.

Dugmore, A.J., A.J. Newton, D.E. Sugden, and G. Larsen. 1992. "Geochemical stability of fine-grained silicic Holocene tephra in Iceland and Scotland." *Journal of Quaternary Science* 7 (2): 173–83. http://dx.doi.org/10.1002/jqs.3390070208.

Dugmore, A.J., A.J. Newton, G. Larsen and G.T. Cook. 2000. "Tephrochronology, environmental change and the Norse settlement of Iceland." *Environmental Archaeology* 5 (1): 21–34. http://dx.doi.org/10.1179/146141000790523377.

Dugmore, A.J., and I.A. Simpson. Forthcoming. "1,200 years of Icelandic landscape change reconstructed using tephrochronology." *Earth Surface Processes and Landforms*.

Dumville, D. 1976. "*Echtrae* and *Immram*: Some problems of definition." *Ériu* 27: 73–94.

Duncan, A.S. 2001. "A pollen analytical study to show how human settlement can influence the vegetation of a virgin landscape, in relation to the Landnám tephra layer in southwest Iceland." BSc. Honours diss., University of Edinburgh.

Dunlop, D.M. 1947. "Scotland according to al-Idrîsî, c. A.D. 1154." *Scottish Historical Review* 26: 114–18.

Dunlop, D.M. 1957. "The British Isles according to medieval Arabic authors." *Islamic Quarterly: A Review of Islamic Culture* 4: 11–28.

Dunnell, R.C. 1984. "The Americanist literature for 1983: A year of contrast and challenges." *American Journal of Archaeology* 88 (4): 489–513. http://dx.doi.org/10.2307/504738.

Edwards, K.J., D. Borthwick, G. Cook, A.J. Dugmore, K.-A. Mairs, M.J. Church, I.A. Simpson, and W.P. Adderley. 2005. "A hypothesis-based approach to landscape change in Suðuroy, Faroe Islands." *Human Ecology* 33 (5): 621–50. http://dx.doi.org/10.1007/s10745-005-4746-0.

Eiríks. Edited by Halldórsson (1985).

Ekrem, I., and L.B. Mortensen. 2003. *Historia Norwegie*. Translated by P. Fisher. Copenhagen: Museum Tusculanum Press, University of Copenhagen.

Eldjárn, K. 1981. "The bronze image from Eyrarland." In *Speculum Norroenum: Norse Studies in Memory of Gabriel Turville-Petre*, 73–84. Odense.

Eldjárn, K. 1983. Þórslíkneski svonefnt frá Eyrarlandi. *Árbók hins Íslenzka Fornleifafélags*, 1982, 62–75.

Eldjárn, K., and A. Friðriksson. 2000. *Kuml og haugfé úr heiðinum sið á Íslandi*. Reykjavík: Mál og Menning.

Emerson, D.F. 1916. Iraland. *Modern Languages Review* xi (1916).

Eyrbyggja. Edited by Sveinsson and Þórðarson (1935).

Fell, C.E. 1984. "Some questions of language." In *Two Voyagers at the Court of King Alfred: The Ventures of Ohthere and Wulfstan Together with the Description of Northern Europe from the Old English Orosius*, edited by N. Lund, 56–63. York, England: William Sessions Limited.

Fellows-Jensen, G. 1996. "Language contact in Iceland: The evidence of names." In *Language Contact across the North Atlantic*, edited by P.S. Ureland and I. Clarkson, 115–24. Tübingen, Germany: Niemeyer. http://dx.doi.org/10.1515/9783110929652.115.

Feyerabend, P.K. 1975. *Against Method*. London: New Left Books.

Finsen, V., ed. (1852) 1974. *Grágás: Konungsbók*. Reprinted 1974. Odense, Denmark: Odense Universitetsforlag.

Fisher, I. 2001. *Early Medieval Sculpture in the West Highlands and Islands*. Monograph 1. Edinburgh: RCAHMS / SOC ANT SCOT.

Fisher, I. 2002. "Crosses in the Ocean: Some *papar* sites and their sculpture." In *The Papar in the North Atlantic: Environment and History. Proceedings of the St. Andrews Dark Age Conference, 2002*. Edited by B. Crawford, 39–58. St Andrews, Scotland.

Fisher, I. 2005. "Cross-Currents in North Atlantic Sculpture." In *Viking and Norse in the North Atlantic: Select Papers from the Proceedings of the Fourteenth Viking Congress, Tórshavn, 19–30 July 2001*, edited by A. Mortensen and S.V. Arge, 160–81. Tórshavn, Faroe Islands: Føroya Fródhskaparfelag,.

Forbes, A.R. 1923. *Place-Names of Skye and Adjacent Islands: With Lore, Mythical, Traditional and Historical*. Paisley, Scotland: Alexander Gardner Ltd.

Freytag, E. 1977. "Die Klöster als Zentren kirchlichen Lebens." In *Schleswig-Holsteinische Kirchengeschichte I: Anfänge und Ausbau*, 147–202. Neumünster, Germany: Karl Wachholtz.

Friðriksson, A. 1994. *Sagas and Popular Antiquarianism in Icelandic Archaeology*. Avebury, UK: Ashgate.

Friðriksson, S. 1982. "Papey eða lundey." *Árbók hins Íslenzka Fornleifafélags*, 1982, 176–80.

Gammeltoft, P. 2001. *The Place-Name Element in Old Norse bólstaðr in the North Atlantic Area*. Navnestudier 38. Copenhagen: Reitzels Forlag A/S.

Gammeltoft, P. 2003. "Contact or conflict? What can we learn from the island-names of the Northern Isles?" In *Scandinavia and Europe, 800–1350: Contact, Conflict, and Coexistence*, edited by J. Adams and K. Holman, 89–97. Turnhout, Belgium: Brepols.

Gammeltoft, P. 2004a. "Among *Dímons* and *Papeys*: What kind of contact do the names really point to?" *Northern Studies* 38: 31–49.

Gammeltoft, P. 2004b. "Scandinavian-Gaelic contacts: Can place-names and place-name elements be used as a source for contact-linguistic research?" *NOWELE* 44 (March): 51–90.

Gobineau, J.-A. 1853–5. *Essai sur l'inégalité des races humaines.* 4 vols. Paris: Didot.

Goitein, S.D. 1967–93. *A Mediterranean Society. The Jewish Communities of the Arab World as Portrayed in the Documents of the Cairo Geniza.* 6 vols. London: University of California Press.

Gräslund, A.-S. 1994. "Rune stones: On ornamentation and chronology." In *Developments around the Baltic and the North Sea in the Viking Age. The Twefth Viking Congress. Birka Project,* edited by B. Ambroisani and H. Clark, 117–31. Stockholm: Riksantikvarieämbetet och Statens historiska museer.

Grimm, W. 1856. *Kinder- und Hausmärchen.* Vol. 3. Leipzig: Rekham.

Grimm, W. 1884. *Grimm's Household Tales.* Vol. 2. Translated by M. Hunt. London.

Grönvold, K., N. Óskarsson, S.J. Johnsen, H.B. Clausen, C.U. Hammer, G. Bond, and E. Bard. 1995. "Ash layers from Iceland in the Greenland GRIP ice core correlated with oceanic and land sediments." *Earth and Planetary Science Letters* 135 (1–4): 149–55. http://dx.doi.org/10.1016/0012-821X(95)00145-3.

Guðmundsson, H. 1997. *Um haf innan. Vestrœnir menn og íslenzk menning á miðöldum.* Reykjavík: Háskólaútgáfan.

Guggenheimer, H.W. 2001. *The Jerusalem Talmud. First Order: Zeraïm. Tractates Kilaim and Seviït.* Berlin: Walter de Gruyter.

Hafliðarson, H., G. Larsen, and G. Ólafsson. 1992. "The recent sedimentation history of Thingvallavatn, Iceland." *Oikos* 64 (1/2): 80–95. http://dx.doi.org/10.2307/3545044.

Halldórsson, Ó. 1985. *Eiríks saga rauða. Texti Skálholtsbókar AM 557 4to.* Reykjavík: Hið Íslenska Fornritafélag.

Hamlin, A. 1972. "A Chi-rho carved stone at Drumqueran, Co. Antrim." *Ulster Journal of Archaeology* 35: 22–8.

Hamlin, A. 1982. "Early Irish stone carving: Content and context." In *The Early Church in Western Britain and Ireland,* edited by S.M. Pearce, 283–96. Oxford: BAR British Series 102.

Hannon, G.E., and R.H.W. Bradshaw. 2000. "Impacts and timing of the first human settlement on vegetation of the Faroe Islands." *Quaternary Research* 54 (3): 404–13. http://dx.doi.org/10.1006/qres.2000.2171.

Haraldsson, H. 1981. *The Markarfljót Sandur Area, Southern Iceland: Sedimentological, Petrological and Stratigraphical Studies.* Striae vol. 15. Uppsala, Sweden: Striae.

Haskins, C.H. 1911. "England and Sicily in the twelfth century." *English Historical Review* XXVI (CIII): 433–47, 641–65. http://dx.doi.org/10.1093/ehr/XXVI.CIII.433.

Hastrup, K. 1998. *A Place Apart: An Anthropological Study of the Icelandic World.* Oxford: Clarendon Press.

Henderson, I. 1987. "Early Christian monuments of Scotland displaying crosses but no other ornament." In *The Picts: A New Look at Old Problems,* edited by A. Small, 45–58. Dundee, Scotland.

Herity, M., D. Kelly, and U. Mattenberger. 1997. "List of early Christian cross slabs in seven north-western counties." *Journal of the Royal Society of Antiquaries of Ireland* 127: 80–124.

Hermanns-Auðardóttir, M. 1989. *Islands tidiga bosättning. Studier med utgångspunkt i merovingertida-vikingatida gårdslämningar i Herjólfsdalur, Vestmannaeyjar, Island.* Umeå, Sweden: Umeå Universitet Arkeologiska Institutionen.

Hermanns-Auðardóttir, M. 1991. "The early settlement of Iceland: Results based on excavations of a Merovingian and Viking farm site at Herjólfsdalur in the Westman Islands, Iceland." *Norwegian Archaeological Review* 24 (1): 1–9. http://dx.doi.org/10.1080/00293652.1991.9965524.

Hermanns-Auðardóttir, M. 1992. "The beginning of settlement in Iceland from an archaeological point of view." *Acta Borealia* 9 (2): 85–135. http://dx.doi.org/10.1080/08003839208580418.

Hermannsson, H., ed. (1944) 1966. *Islandica: An Annual Relating to Iceland and the Fiske Icelandic Collection in Cornell University Library.* Vol. 30, *The Vinland Sagas.* New York: Kraus Reprint. First published in Ithaca, NY.

Higham, M.C. 1995. "Scandinavian settlement in north-west England, with a special study of *Ireby* names." In *Scandinavian Settlement in Northern Britain: Thirteen Studies of Place-Names in Their Historical Context*, edited by B.E. Crawford, 195–205. London: Leicester University Press.

Hines, J. 2004. *Voices in the Past: English Literature and Archaeology.* Cambridge: D.S. Brewer.

Hirschberg, H.Z.J.W. 1963. "The problem of the Judaized Berbers." *Journal of African History* 4 (03): 313–39. http://dx.doi.org/10.1017/S0021853700004278.

Hirschberg, H.Z.J.W. 1974. *A History of the Jews in North Africa. Second, Revised Edition, Translated from the Hebrew.* Vol. 1, *From Antiquity to the Sixteenth Century with 4 Maps.* Leiden, Netherlands: E.J. Brill.

Historia. From editions and translations by Ekrem and Mortensen (2003) and Phelpstead and Kunin (2001).

Hjartarson, Á., and H. Gísladóttir. 1983. "Skollhólahellir." *Árbók hins Íslenzka Fornleifafélags*, 1982, 123–33.

Hjartarson, Á., and H. Gísladóttir. 1985. "Hellamyndir Johannesar S. Kjarval." *Árbók hins Íslenzka Fornleifafélags*, 1984, 167–82.

Hjartarson, Á., and H. Gísladóttir. 1993. "Hellarannsókna leiðangur Einars Benediktssonar 1915." *Árbók hins Íslenzka Fornleifafélags*, 1992, 135–44.

Hjartarson, Á., G.J. Guðmundsson, and H. Gísladóttir. 1991. *Manngerðir Hellar á Íslandi.* Reykjavík: Menningarsjóður.

Hogan, E. 1910. *Onomasticon Goedelicum Locorum et Tribuum Hiberniae et Scotiae.* Dublin.

Holt, A., and G.J. Guðmundsson. 1980. *Um manngerða hella á Suðurlandi*. Framlag til alþýðlegra fornfræða 1. Reykjavík.

Hommedal, A.T. 1996. "Fra heller til pilegrimskyrkje. Heilagstaden på Selja." In *Frå hedendom til kristendom*, edited by M. Rindal. Oslo: Ad notan Gyldendal.

Hreinsson, V., ed. 1997. *The Complete Sagas of Icelanders. Including 49 Tales*. Reykjavík: Leifur Eiríksson Publishing.

Huber, F.W. 2000. Tors Hammare: En studie över vikingatida amuletthängsmycken i Skandinavien. CD-uppsats, Sweden: Umeå University

Huber, F.W. 2002. "Thor's Hammer and the Christian Cross." Unpublished report.

Idrîsî. From editions and translations by Jaubert (1836) and Bresc and Nef (1999).

Ingram, J. 1807. *An Inaugural Lecture on the Utility of Anglo-Saxon Literature; To Which Is Added the Geography of Europe by King Alfred*. Oxford: Oxford University Press.

Iraelstam, J., and J.J. Slotki, eds. and trans. 1939. *Leviticus* (Midrash Rabbah, edited by H. Freedman and M. Simon). London: Soncino Press.

Íslendingabók. Edited by Benediktsson (1968).

Jaubert, P.A., ed. and trans. 1836. *Géographie d'Édrisi. Traduite de l'Arabe en Francais d'après deux manuscrits de la Bibliothèque du Roi et accompagnée de notes. Tome Premier*. Paris: L'Imprimerie Royale.

Jehel, G., and P. Racinet. 2000. "Diffusion des savoirs et échanges entre l'Orient musulman et l'Occident latin." In *Les relations des pays d'Islam avec le monde latin du Xe siècle au milieu du XIIe siècle*, 186–207. Paris: Éditions du temps.

Johannæus, F. 1772. *Historia ecclesiastica Islandiæ*. Copenhagen.

Jóhansen, J. 1985. *Studies in the Vegetàtional History of the Faroe and Shetland Islands*. Annales Societatis Scientarum Faeroensis Supplementum XI. Tórshavn, Faroe Islands: Føroya fróðskapparfelag.

Johns, J. 2001. "Arabic 'June' (*brutuyun*) and 'July' (*istiriyun*) in Norman Sicily." *Bulletin of the School of Oriental and African Studies. University of London. School of Oriental and African Studies* 64 (01): 98–100. http://dx.doi.org/10.1017/S0041977X01000064.

Johns, J. 2002. *Arabic Administration in Norman Sicily: The Royal Dîwân*. Cambridge: Cambridge University Press. http://dx.doi.org/10.1017/CBO9780511550386.

Jones, A.P., M.E. Tucker, and J. Hart, eds. 1999. *The Description and Analysis of Quaternary Stratigraphic Field Sections*. Technical Guide no. 7. London: Quaternary Research Association.

Jónsson, B. 1900. "Rannsókn í RangárÞingi sumarið 1899." *Árbók hins Íslenzka Fornleifafélags*, 1900, 1–8.

Jónsson, B. 1902. "Rannsókn í RangárÞingi sumarið 1901." *Árbók hins Íslenzka Fornleifafélags*, 1902, 1–32.

Jónsson, B. 1906. "Rannsókn í ÁrnesÞingi sumarið 1904." *Árbók hins Íslenzka Fornleifafélags*, 1905, 52–5.

Jónsson, H.E. 1999. "Sagney: landið dularfulla í vesturheimi." *Lésbók Morgúnblaðsins*, 27 Febrúar 1999, 8 tbl, 74 árg: 6–8.

Jonsson, L. 1999. *Birds of Europe with North Africa and the Middle East, with Illustrations by Magnus Ullman*. Translated by D. Christie. London: Christopher Helm and C. Black.

Juhl, K., and P. Markestad. 1991. "Lies, damned lies and statistics." *Norwegian Archaeological Review* 24 (2): 113–22. http://dx.doi.org/10.1080/00293652.1991.9965537.

Keillar, I. 1994. "North East Studies: Names in North-East Scotland." Project. *Place-names and Settlement Patterns in Part of the Laich of Moray*.

Knight, J.K. 1999. *The End of Antiquity: Archaeology, Society and Religion, AD 235–700*. Stroud, UK: Tempus.

Kohl, P., and C. Fawcett, eds. 1995. *Nationalism, Politics and the Practice of Archaeology*. Cambridge: Cambridge University Press.

Koht, H. 1909. "Sons of Harald." *Norsk Historisk Tidsskrift* 4: 6.

Kristjánsdóttir, S. 2003. "Timburkirkja og grafreitur úr frumskristni: Af fornleifa-fauppgreftri á Þórarinsstöðum í Seyðísfirði." *Árbók hins Íslenzka Fornleifafélags*, 2000–1, 113–42.

Kruse, A. 2005. "Explorers, raiders and settlers: The Norse impact upon Hebridean place-names." In *Cultural Contacts in the North Atlantic Region*, edited by P. Gammeltoft, C. Hough, and J. Waugh, 155–72. Lerwick, Scotland: NORNA, Scottish Place-Name Society and Society for Name Studies in Britain and Ireland.

Kuhn, T.S. [1962] 1970. *The Structure of Scientific Revolutions*. London: University of Chicago Press.

Lafitau, J.-F. 1723. *Mœurs des sauvages Américains, comparées aux mœurs des premiers temps*. Paris.

Lager, L. 2000. "Art as a reflection of religious change." *Archaeological Review from Cambridge* 17:117–32.

Laing, L., and J. Laing. 1990. *Celtic Britain and Ireland, AD 200–800: The Myth of the Dark Ages*. Dublin: Irish Academic Press.

Laliberté, M. 1999. "Le sylvicole moyen dans la vallée de la rivière des Outaouais/ The Middle Woodland in the Ottawa Valley." In *La préhistoire de l'Outaouais/ Ottawa Valley Prehistory*, edited by J.-L. Pilon, 69–81. Hull, QC: Société d'histoire de l'Outaouais.

Lamb, R. 1995. "Papil, Picts and Papar." In *Northern Isles Connections: Essays from Orkney and Shetland Presented to Per Sveaas Andersen*, edited by B. Crawford, 9–27. Kirkwall, Scotland: Orkney Press.

Landnámabók. Edited by Benediktsson (1968).

Lang, A. 1893. Introduction to *Cinderella*, edited by M.R. Cox. Publications of the Folk-Tale Society no. 31. London.

Larsen, G. 1979. "Um aldur Eldgjárhrauna." *Náttúrufræþingurinn* 49: 1–26.

Larsen, G. 1984. "Recent volcanic history of the Veiðvötn fissure swarm in Southern Iceland: An approach to volcanic risk assessment." *Journal of Volcanology and Geothermal Research* 22 (1-2): 33–58. http://dx.doi.org/10.1016/0377-0273(84)90034-9.

Larsen, G. 2000. "Holocene eruptions within the Katla volcanic system, south Iceland: Characteristics and environmental impact." *Jökull* 49: 1–28.

Larsen, G., A.J. Dugmore, and A.J. Newton. 1999. "Geochemistry of historical-age silicic tephras in Iceland." *Holocene* 9 (4): 463–71. http://dx.doi.org/10.1191/095968399669624108.

Larsen, G., A.J. Newton, A.J. Dugmore, and E.G. Vilmundardóttir. 2001. "Geochemistry, dispersal, volumes and chronology of Holocene silicic tephras from the Katla volcanic system, Iceland." *Journal of Quaternary Science* 16: 119–32. http://dx.doi.org/10.1002/jqs.587.

Le Clerq, C. 1691. *Nouvelle relation de la Gaspésie, qui contient les mœurs et la religion des sauvages Gaspésiens, Porte-Croix, adorateurs du soleil, et d'autres peuples de l'Amérique septentrionale, dite Canada*. Paris.

Lethbridge, T.C. 1950. *Herdsmen and Hermits: Celtic Seafarers in the Northern Seas*. Cambridge: Bowes and Bowes.

Livingston, M. 2004. "More Vinland maps and texts: Discovering the New World in Higden's *Polychronicum*." *Journal of Medieval History* 30 (1): 25–44. http://dx.doi.org/10.1016/j.jmedhist.2003.12.001.

Lowe, C. 2002. "The *papar* and Papa Stronsay: 8th-century reality of 12th-century myth?" In *The Papar in the North Atlantic: Environment and History. The proceedings of a day conference held on 24th February 2001. The 'Papar' Project*, vol. 1, edited by B. Crawford, 83–95. St Andrews, Scotland: The Committee for Dark Age Studies, University of St Andrews.

Lund, N., C.E. Fell, O. Crumlin-Pedersen, and P.H. Sawyer, eds. and trans. 1984. *Two Voyagers at the Court of King Alfred: The Ventures of Ohthere and Wulfstan together with the Description of Northern Europe from the Old English Orosius*. York, UK: William Sessions Limited.

MacDonald, A. 1977. "Old Norse *Papar* names in N and W Scotland: A summary." In *Studies in Celtic Survival*, edited by L. Laing, 107–11. Oxford: BAR British Series 37.

MacDonald, A. 2002. "The *papar* and some problems: A brief review." In *The Papar in the North Atlantic: Environment and History. The proceedings of a day conference held on 24th February 2001. The 'Papar' Project. Volume 1*, edited by B. Crawford, 13–30. St Andrews, Scotland: The Committee for Dark Age Studies, University of St Andrews.

Mackeprang, M. 1938. "Thors Hammer." *Tilskueren*, 1938, 170–81.

Mackintosh, H.B. 1928. *The Lossie and the Loch of Spynie*.

Mac Mathúna, S. 1999. "*Hvítramannaland* revisited." In *Islanders and Water-Dwellers. Proceedings of the Celtic-Nordic-Baltic Folklore Symposium held at University College Dublin. 16–19 June 1996*, edited by P. Lysaght, S. Ó Catháin, and D. Ó hÓgáin, 177–87. Blackrock, Co. Dublin: DBA Publications.

Macniven, A. 2003. "Where are Eyjafjallasveit's earliest settlement sites? A review of the documentary evidence." In "Atlantic Peoples between Fire, Ice, River and Sea: Past Environments in Southern Iceland," edited by K. Ahronson, Special issue, *Northern Studies* 37: 95–103.

Magnússon, M., and H. Pálsson. 1965. *The Vinland Sagas: The Norse Discovery of America; Grænlendinga Saga and Eirik's Saga*. Harmondsworth, UK: Penguin.

Mairs, K.-A. 2003. "Using volcanic ash to establish past environments at Langanes in the Markarfljót valley." Unpublished report.

Malone, K. 1930. "King Alfred's North: A study in mediaeval geography." *Speculum* 5 (2): 139–67. http://dx.doi.org/10.2307/2847864.

Malone, K. 1933. "On King Alfred's geographical treatise." *Speculum* 8 (1): 67–78. http://dx.doi.org/10.2307/2846850.

Matras, C. 1934. "Papýli í Føroyum." *Varðin* 14: 185–7.

Mawer, C.F. 1995. *Evidence for Christianity in Roman Britain: The Small Finds*. BAR British Series 243. Oxford: Tempus Reparatum.

McAleese, K. 2004. "*Skrælingar* abroad – *Skrælingar* at home?" In *Vínland Revisited: The Norse World at the Turn of the First Millenium. Selected Papers from the Viking International Symposium, 15–24 September 2000, Newfoundland and Labrador*, edited by S. Lewis-Simpson, 353–64. St John's, NL: Historic Sites Association of Newfoundland and Labrador, Inc.

McMahon, A., and R. McMahon. 2003. "Finding families: Quantitative methods in language classification." *Transactions of the Philological Society* 101 (1): 7–55. http://dx.doi.org/10.1111/1467-968X.00108.

Meates, G.W. 1979. *The Roman Villa at Lullingstone, Kent*. Vol. 1, *The Site*. Monograph Series of the Kent Archaeological Society. Maidstone, UK: Kent Archaeological Society.

Metcalfe, A. 2003. *Muslims and Christians in Norman Sicily*. London: Routledge Curzon.

Midrashim. Leviticus edited and translated by Iraelstam and Slotki (1939). Deuteuronomy edited and translated by Rabbinowitz (1939).

Miller, D., ed. 1983. *A Pocket Popper*. Oxford: Fontana Paperbacks.

Monceaux, P. 1902. "Les colonies juives dans l'Afrique romaine." *Revue des études juives* 44:1–28.

Müller, P.E. 1817–20. *Saga Bibliothek*. Copenhagen.

Munch, P.A. 1852. "Geographiske Oplysinger om Orknœerne." *Annaler for nordisk Oldkyndighed og Historie*, 1852.

Munch, P.A. 1852–3. *Det Norske Follks Historie*. Christiania, Denmark.

Munch, P.A. 1857. "Geographiske Oplysinger om Hjaltland." *Annaler for nordisk Oldkyndighed og Historie*, 1857.

Murphy, G. [1956] 1998. *Early Irish Lyrics: Eighth to Twelfth Century*. Dublin: Four Courts Press.

Nansen, F. 1911. *In Northern Mists: Arctic Exploration in Early Times*. Vol. 2. Translated by A.G. Chater. London: William Heineman. http://dx.doi.org/10.5962/bhl.title.6529.

Newnham, R.M., D.J. Lowe, M.S. McGlone, J.M. Wilmhurst, and T.F.G. Higham. 1998. "The Karahoa tephra as a critical datum for earliest human impact in northern New Zealand." *Journal of Archaeological Science* 25 (6): 533–44. http://dx.doi.org/10.1006/jasc.1997.0217.

Nicolaisen, W.F.H. 1980. "Place-names as evidence for linguistic stratification in Scotland." In *NORNA-Rapporter 18. Sprogvidenskabelig udnyttelse af stednavnematerialet*, edited by V. Dalberg, B. Holmberg, J. Sørensen Kousgård. Uppsala, Sweden.

Nyberg, T. 2000. *Monasticism in North-Western Europe, 800–1200*. Aldershot, UK: Ashgate.

Ó Corráin, D. 1998. "Viking Ireland: Afterthoughts." In *Ireland and Scandinavia in the Early Viking Age*, edited by H.B. Clarke, N.M. Máire, and Ó.F. Raghnall, 421–52. Bodmin, UK: Four Courts Press.

Odess, D., S. Loring, and W.W. Fitzhugh. 2000. "*Skraeling*: First Peoples of Helluland, Markland, and Vinland." In *Vikings: The North Atlantic Saga*, edited by W.W. Fitzhugh and E.I. Ward, 193–205. Washington, DC: Smithsonian Institution Press/National Museum of Natural History.

Ogilvie, A.E.J., L.K. Barlow, and A.E. Jennings. 2000. "North Atlantic climate c. AD 1000: Millennial reflections on the Viking discoveries of Iceland, Greenland, and North America." *Weather* 55 (2): 34–45. http://dx.doi.org/10.1002/j.1477-8696.2000.tb04028.x.

Oleson, T. 1963. *Early Voyages and Northern Approaches, 1000–1632*. The Canadian Centenary Series. Toronto: McClelland & Stewart.

O'Loughlin, T. 1999. "Distant islands: The topography of holiness in the *Nauigatio sancti Brendani*." In *The Medieval Mystical Tradition: England, Ireland and Wales. Exeter Symposium VI. Papers read at Charney Manor, July 1999*, edited by M. Glasscoe, 1–20. Woodbridge, UK: Brewer.

Olsen, O. 1966. *Horg*. Copenhagen: Hov og Kirke.

Oman, G. 1971. "al-Idrîsî." In *The Encyclopedia of Islam*. New Edition, vol. 3, *H-IRAM*, edited by B. Lewis, V.L. Ménage, C. Pellat, and J. Schacht, 1032–5. Leiden, Netherlands: Brill.

Orosius. Edited and translated by Bately (1980) and Lund (1984).

Oskamp, H.P.A. 1970. *The Voyage of Máel Dúin: A Study in Early Irish Voyage Literature Followed by an Edition of Immram curaig Máele Dúin from the Yellow Book of Lecan in Trinity College, Dublin*. Groningen, Netherlands: Wolters-Noordhoff Publishing.

Page, R.I. 1995. *Chronicles of the Vikings: Records, Memorials, and Myths*. Avon, UK: British Museum Press.

Pálsson, H. 1955. "Minnisgreinar um Papa." *Saga: Tímarit Sögufélags* 5: 112–22.

Pálsson, H. 1960. "Hvítramannaland." *Tímarit Máls og Menningar* 21:48–54.

Pálsson, H. 1996. *Keltar á Íslandi*. Reykjavík: Háskólaútgáfan.

Pálsson, H. 2000. "Vínland revisited." *Northern Studies* 35: 11–38.

Pálsson, H., and P. Edwards, eds. and trans. 1972. *The Book of Settlements Landnámabók*. Winnipeg: University of Manitoba Press.

Pálsson, H., and P. Edwards, eds. and trans. 1973. *Eyrbyggja Saga*. Edinburgh: Southside.

Pálsson, H., and P. Edwards, eds. and trans. 1989. *Eyrbyggja Saga*. London: Penguin.

Peacock, J.D. 1968. *Geology of the Elgin District*. Edinburgh.

Perkins, R. 1993. "Arabic sources for Scandinavia(ns)." In *Medieval Scandinavia: An Encyclopedia*, edited by P. Pulsiano, K. Wolf, P. Acker, and D.K. Fry. New York: Garland Publishing.

Perkins, R. 2004. "Medieval Norse visits to America: Millenial stocktaking." *Saga-Book* 28: 29–69.

Phelpstead, C., ed., and D. Kunin, trans. 2001. *A History of Norway and the Passion and Miracles of the Blessed Óláfr.* Text Series 13. London: Viking Society for Northern Research.

Pope, P. 2004. "Did the Vikings reach North America without discovering it? The Greenland Norse and Zuan Caboto in the Strait of Belle Isle." In *Vínland Revisited: The Norse World at the Turn of the First Millenium. Selected Papers from the Viking International Symposium, 15–24 September 2000, Newfoundland and Labrador*, edited by S. Lewis-Simpson, 341–52. St John's, NL: Historic Sites Association of Newfoundland and Labrador, Inc.

Popper, K.R. 1972. *Objective Knowledge*. Oxford: Oxford University Press.

Popper, K.R. 1974. "Replies to my critics." In *The Philosophy of Karl Popper*, edited by P.A. Schlipp, 961–1197. La Salle, IL: Open Court.

Popper, K.R. 1992. *In Search of a Better World: Lectures and Essays from Thirty Years*. Translated by L.J. Bennett and M. Mew. London: Routledge.

Popper, K.R. 1994. *The Myth of the Framework: In Defence of Science and Rationality*. London: Routledge.

Rabbinowitz, J. 1939. *Deutoronomy.* Midrash Rabbah, edited by H. Freedman and M. Simon. London: Soncino Press.

Rafn, C.C. 1837. *Antiquitates Americanæ, sive scriptores septentrionales rerum ante Colombianarum in Americâ.* Copenhagen: Schultz.

Rafn, C.C., and F. Magnusen. 1838. *Grœnlands historiske Mindesmærker.* Copenhagen: Brünnichske Bogtrykkeri.

Rafnsson, Sveinbjörn. 1974. *Studier i Landnámabók: Kritiska bidrag till den Isländska fristatstidens historia.* Lund: CWK Gleerup.

Renfrew, C. 1999. "Reflections on the archaeology of human diversity." In *The Human Inheritance: Genes, Language and Evolution*, edited by B. Sykes, 1–32. Oxford: Oxford University Press.

Ritchie, J.N.G. 1997. "Recording early Christian monuments in Scotland." In *The Worm, the Germ and the Thorn: Pictish and Related Studies Presented to Isabel Henderson*, edited by D. Henry, 119–28. Balgavies, Scotland: Pinkfoot Press.

Roberts, H.M., M. Snæsdóttir, and O. Vésteinnsson, eds. 2002. *Fornleifarannsóknir við Aðalstræti 2001. Áfanfaskýrsla./Archaeological Investigations in Aðalstræti 2001.* Interim report. Reykjavík: Fornleifastofnun Íslands.

Ross, S. 1987. "The submerged forest in Burghead Bay." In *MFC*, ed. Bull.

Russell, A.J., and P.M. Marren. 1999. "Proglacial fluvial sedimentary sequences in Greenland and Iceland: A case study from active proglacial environments subject to jokulhlaups." In *The Description and Analysis of Quaternary Stratigraphic Field Sections, Technical Guide no. 7*, edited by A.P. Jones, M.E. Tucker, and J. Hart, 171–208. London: Quaternary Research Association.

Ryan, A. 1985. "Popper and liberalism." In *Popper and the Human Sciences*, edited by G. Currie and A. Musgrave, 89–104. Dordrecht, Netherlands: Martinus Nijhoff Publishers. http://dx.doi.org/10.1007/978-94-009-5093-1_6.

Said, E.W. [1978] 2003. *Orientalism.* London: Penguin.

Salway, P. 1993. *The Oxford Illustrated History of Roman Britain.* Oxford: Oxford University Press.

Sandnes, B. 2003. *Fra Starafell til Starling Hill. Dannelse og utvikling av norrøne stedsnavn på Orknøyene.* Trondheim, Norway.

Sawyer, B. 2000. *The Viking-Age Rune-Stones: Custom and Commemoration in Early Medieval Scandinavia.* Oxford: Oxford University Press.

Schiffer, M.B. 1976. *Behavioral Archaeology.* New York: Academic Press.

Schiffer, M.B. 1987. *Formation Processes of the Archaeological Record.* Albuquerque: University of New Mexico Press.

Schledermann, P. 2000. "Ellesmere: Vikings in the Far North." In *Vikings: The North Atlantic Saga*, edited by W.W. Fitzhugh and E.I. Ward, 248–56. Washington, DC: Smithsonian Institution Press/National Museum of Natural History.

Schmeidler, B., ed. 1917. *Adam von Bremen, Hamburgische Kirchengeschichte. Dritte Auflage.* Scriptores rerum Germanicarum in usum scholarum. Hanover, Germany: Hahnsche Buchhandlung.

Schmidt, E. 1879. "Vestiges du Christianisme et de l'homme blanc en Amérique avant sa découverte par Christophe Colomb." *Congrès international des américanistes* 3 (1): 493–507.

Schrœter, J.H. 1849–51. "Færœiske Folkesagn." *Antikvarisk Tiddsskrift.*

Schwarz-Mackensen, G. 1978. "Thorshämmer aus Haithabu: Zur Deutung wikingerzeitlicher Symbole." *Berichte über die Ausgrabung in Haithabu* 12: 85–93.

Scisco, L.D. 1908. *American Historical Magazine* III.

Scott, I. 1996. "Archaeological illustration: Personal experience and the drawing of carved stones for publication." *Graphic Archaeology: The Journal of the Association of Archaeological Illustrators and Surveyors* 1996, 1–13.

Scott, I. 1997. "Illustrating early medieval carved stones." In *The Worm, the Germ and the Thorn: Pictish and Related Studies Presented to Isabel Henderson*, edited by D. Henry, 129–32. Balgavies, Scotland: Pinkfoot Press.

Scott, I. 2005. "The bulls of Burghead and Allen's technique of illustration." In *Able Minds and Practiced Hands: Scotland's Early Medieval Sculpture in the 21st Century*, edited by S.M. Foster and M. Cross, 215–20. Leeds, UK: Society for Medieval Archaeology.

Seaver, K.A. 1999. "How strange is a stranger? A survey of opportunities for Inuit-European contact in the Davis Strait before 1576." In *Meta Incognita: A Discourse of Discovery; Martin Frobisher's Arctic Expeditions, 1576–1578*, edited by T. Symons, 523–52. Hull, QC: Canadian Museum of Civilization.

Sharpe, R., ed. and trans. 1995. *Adomnan of Iona: Life of St Columba.* St Ives, UK: Penguin.

Sigurðsson, G. 1988. *Gaelic Influence in Iceland: Historical and Literary Contacts; A Survey of Research* (Bókmenntafræðistofnun Háskóla Íslands. Studia Islandica Íslensk Fræði 46 Hefti). Reykavík: Bókaútgáfa Menningarsjóðs.

Sigurðsson, M.H. 2005. "Papar og brjóst: Papaörnefni í nýju ljósi." *Lesbók Morgunblaðsins*, 22 Janúar, 6–7.

Sigurðsson, M.H. 2008. "'Perfectly mamillary': On breasts, nipples and teats in West Norse toponymy." In *Norræn nöfn-Nöfn á Norðurlöndum. Hefðir og endurnýun. Nordiska namn-Namn i Norden. Tradition och förnyelse. Handlingar från den fjortonde nordiska namnforskarkongressen i Borgarnes 11–14 augusti 2007*, edited by G. Kvaran, H.J. Ámundason, J. Hafsteinsdóttir, and S. Sigmundsson, 297–307. Uppsala, Sweden: NORNA-Rapporter 84.

Simpson, I.A., B. Crawford, and B. Ballin-Smith. 2005. "*Papar* place-names in the Northern and Western Isles of Scotland: A preliminary assessment of their association with agricultural land potential." www.paparproject.org.uk/agricultural.html.

Simpson, I.A., A.J. Dugmore, A. Thomson, and O. Vésteinsson. 2001. "Crossing the thresholds: Human ecology and historical patterns of landscape degradation." *Catena* 42 (2-4): 175–92. http://dx.doi.org/10.1016/S0341-8162(00)00137-5.

Simpson, I., and E.B. Guttman. 2002. "Transitions in early arable land management in the Northern Isles: The *papar* as agricultural innovators?" In *The Papar in the North Atlantic: Environment and History. The proceedings of a day conference held on 24th February 2001. The 'Papar' Project. Volume 1*, edited by B. Crawford, 59–67. St Andrews, Scotland: The Committee for Dark Age Studies, University of St Andrews.

Simpson, J.Y. 1859. "On an old stone-roofed cell or oratory in the island of Inchcolm." *Proceedings of the Society of Antiquaries of Scotland*, 1859, 489–528.

Smith, A. 1842. "Addition to the account of Holme and Paplay." In *The New Statistical Account of Scotland*, vol. 15, *Orkney*. Edinburgh.

Smith, A.D. 2001. *Nationalism: Theory, Ideology, and History.* Key Concepts. Cambridge: Polity.

Smith, K.T., and K. Ahronson. 2003. "Dating the cave? The preliminary tephra stratigraphy at Kverkin, Seljaland." In "Atlantic Peoples between Fire, Ice, River and Sea: Past Environments in Southern Iceland," edited by K. Ahronson, Special issue, *Northern Studies* 37: 71–80.

Smyth, A.P. 1984. *Warlords and Holy Men: Scotland, AD 80–1000*. Edinburgh.

Snædal, Þ. 2003. "Rúnarristur á Íslandi." *Árbók hins Íslenzka Fornleifafélags*, 2000–1, 5–68.

Sorenson, J.L., and M.H. Raish. 1996. *Pre-Columbian Contact with the Americas across the Oceans: An Annotated Bibliography*. Vols. 1–2. 2nd. ed., rev. Provo, UT: Research Press.

Staecker, J. 1999a. "Rex regum et dominus dominorum. Die wikingerzeitlichen Kreuz- und Kruzifixanhänger als Ausdruck der Mission in Altdänemark und Schweden." *Lund Studies in Medieval Archaeology* 23.

Staecker, J. 1999b. "Thor's Hammer: Symbol of Christianization and Political Delusion." *Lund Archaeological Review* 5.

Stevenson, W.B. 1948. "Idrisi's map of Scotland." *Scottish Historical Review* 27: 202–4.

Stokes, G. 1998. *Popper: Philosophy, Politics and Scientific Method.* Padstow, UK: Polity Press.

Stokoe, W.C. 1957. "On Ohthere's *Steorbord*." *Speculum* 32 (2): 299–306. http://dx.doi.org/10.2307/2849120.

Storm, G., ed. 1880. *Monumenta historica Norvegiæ. Latinske kildeskrifter til Norges historie i middelalderen.* Kristiania, Norway.

Storm, G. [1887] 1888. *Studier over Vinlandsreiserne.* Copenhagen: Vinlands Geografi og Ethnografi. Reprinted from *Aarbøger for nordisk Oldkyndighed*

Ström, K. 1984. "Thorshammerringe und andere Gegenstände des heidnischen Kults." In *Birka II:1. Systematische Analysen der Gräberfunde*, edited by G. Arvidsson, 127–40. Stockholm: Kgl. Vitterhets Hist. Akad.

Sutherland, P.D. 2000. "The Norse and Native North Americans." In *Vikings: The North Atlantic Saga*, edited by W.W. Fitzhugh and E.I. Ward, 238–47. Washington, DC: Smithsonian Institution Press/National Museum of Natural History.

Sveinbjarnardóttir, G. 1972. "*Papar*: Ritgerð til B.A.-prófs í sagnfræði í janúar 1972." *Mími* 19: 1–20.

Sveinbjarnardóttir, G. 1982. "Byggðaleifar á Þórsmörk." *Árbók hins Íslenzka Fornleifafélags*, 1982: 20–61.

Sveinbjarnardóttir, G. 1991. "Shielings in Iceland: An archaeological and historical survey." *Acta Archaeologica* 61: 73–93.

Sveinbjarnardóttir, G. 2002. "The question of *papar* in Iceland." In *The Papar in the North Atlantic: Environment and History. The proceedings of a day conference held on 24th February 2001. The 'Papar' Project. Volume 1*, edited by B. Crawford, 97–106. St Andrews, Scotland: The Committee for Dark Age Studies, University of St Andrews.

Sveinbjarnardóttir, G., and S. Gunnarsdóttir. 2000. *Fornleifar í Rangárvallarsýslu II: Svæðisskráning fornleifa í Eyjafjallahreppi og Landeyjum: 2. hefti - Fornleifar undir Eyjafjöllum*. Reykjavík: Fornleifastofnun Íslands.

Sveinsson, E.Ó. 1945. "Papar." *Skírnir: Tímarit hins Íslenzka Bókmenntafélags* 119, 170–203.

Sveinsson, E.Ó. 1948. *Landnám í Skaftafellsþingi*. Reykjavík: Skaftfellingafélagið.

Sveinsson, E.Ó., and M. Þórðarson. 1935. *Eyrbyggja Saga. Brands Þáttr Örva. Eiríks Saga Rauða. Grœnlendinga Saga. Grœnlendinga Þáttr*. Íslenzk Fornrit. IV Bindi. Eyrbyggja Saga. Grœnlendinga Sögur. Reykjavík: Hið Íslenzka Fornritafélag.

Talmud. Edited and translated by Guggenheimer (2001).

Taylor, L. 2003. "Your Place or Mine? The Representation of Land Ownership in Medieval Icelandic Texts." MPhil. diss., St John's College, Oxford University.

Taylor, S. 2000. "Columba east of Drumalban: Some aspects of the cult of Columba in eastern Scotland." *Innes Review* 51 (2): 109–30. http://dx.doi.org/10.3366/inr.2000.51.2.109.

Taylor, S. 2002. "Report on comparative study of settlement place-names: Papar Project." Unpublished report.

Þjóðminjasafn Íslands. 2000. "Manngerðir hellar á Suðurlandi: Skemmdir eftir Suðurlandsskjálfta sumarið 2000." Unpublished report.

Thomas, C. 1971. *The Early Christian Archaeology of North Britain: The Hunter Marshall Lectures Delivered at the University of Glasgow in January and February 1968*. London: Oxford University Press.

Thomas, C. 1973. "Sculptured stones and crosses from St. Ninian's Isle and Papil." In *St. Ninian's Isle and its Treasure*, vol. 1, edited by A. Small, C. Thomas, and D.M. Wilson, 8–44. Oxford: Oxford University Press.

Thomas, C. 1981. *Christianity in Roman Britain to AD 500*. London: Batsford Academic and Educational.

Thompson, S. 1946. *The Folktale*. New York: Dryden Press.

Thomson, A. 2003. "The agricultural potential of West Eyjafjallasveit at the time of Norse Settlement (Landnám)." Unpublished report.

Thors, C.-E. 1957. *Den kristna terminologian i fornsvenskan*. Helsinki, Finland.

Þórarinsson, S. 1954. "The tephra-fall from Hekla on March 29th 1947." In *The Eruption of Hekla, 1947–1948, II. 3*, edited by T. Einarsson, G. Kjartansson and S. Þórarinsson, 1–68. Reykjavík: Visindafélag Íslendinga. Societas Scientiarum Islandica.

Þórarinsson, S. 1967. "The eruptions of Hekla in historical times." In *The Eruption of Hekla, 1947–1948, I*, edited by T. Einarsson, G. Kjartansson and S. Þórarinsson, 1–170. Reykjavík: Visindafélag Íslendinga. Societas Scientarrum Islandica.

Þórarinsson, S. 1975. "Katla og annáll Kötlugosa" (Katla and the Annals of Katla tephras). *Árbók Ferðafélags Íslands*, 1975: 125–49.

Þórðarson, M. 1931. "Manngerðir hellar í Rangárvallasýslu og Árnessýslu." *Árbók hins Íslenzka Fornleifafélags*, 1930–1, 1–76.

Tierney, J., ed. and trans. 1967. *Dicuili: Liber de mensura orbis terrae*. Dublin: Dublin Institute of Advanced Studies.

Tolan-Smith, C. 2001. *The Caves of Mid Argyll: An Archaeology of Human Use*. Society of Antiquaries of Scotland Monograph Series no. 20. Edinburgh: Short Run Press.

Tolstoy, L.N. 1954. *Anna Karenin*. Translated by R. Edmonds. London: Penguin.

Tómasson (í Skógum), Þ. 1976. "Föng til búmarkafræði." *Árbók hins Íslenzka Fornleifafélags*, 1975.

Tómasson (í Skógum), Þ. 1986. *Hrútshellir*. Selfoss, Iceland: Goðasteinn.

Tómasson (í Skógum), Þ. 1997. *Setið við sagnabrunn*. Reykjavík: Mál og Mynd.

Torfæus, Th. 1705. *Historia Vinlandiæ antiquæ seu partis Americæ septentrionalis*. Copenhagen.

Torfason, Ó.H. 2000. *Nokkrir Íslandskrossar*. Reykjavík.

Trigger, B.G. 1985. "Writing the history of archaeology: A survey of trends." In *History of Anthropology*, vol. 3, edited by G.W. Stocking, Jr., 218–35. Madison: University of Wisconsin Press.

Trigger, B.G. 1989. *A History of Archaeological Thought*. Cambridge: Cambridge University Press.

Trigger, B.G. 1998. *Sociocultural Evolution: Calculation and Contingency*. Oxford: Blackwell.

Trillmich, W., ed. 1961. *Rimbert, Vita Anskarii in Quellen des 9. und 11. Jahrhunderts zur Geschichte der hamburgischen Kirche und des Reiches. Ausgewählte Quellen zur Deutschen Geschichte des Mittelalters 11*, 1–133. Darmstadt, Germany: Freiherr vom Stein-Gedächtnisausgabe.

Tschan, F.J. 1959. *Adam of Bremen: History of the Archbishops of Hamburg-Bremen*. New York: Columbia University Press.

Turville-Petre, E.O.G. 1953. *Origins of Icelandic Literature*. Oxford: Clarendon Press.

Turville-Petre, E.O.G. 1964. *Myth and Religion of the North: The Religion of Ancient Scandinavia*. London: Weidenfeld & Nicolson.

Van Leeuwen, J., ed. 1835. *Thet Freske Riim*. Brandenburgh: Workum.

Vésteinsson, O. 1998. "Patterns of settlement in Iceland: A study in prehistory." *Saga-Book* 25: 1–29.

Vilhelmi, K. 1839. *Heidelberger Jahrbücher des Literatur* 1839, Feb.

Vilhjálmsson, V.Ö. 1992. "The early settlement of Iceland: Wishful thinking or archaeological innovation." *Acta Archaeologica* 62: 167–81.

Vilhjálmsson, V.Ö. 1996. "Gård og kirker på Stöng i Þjórsárdalur." In *Nordsjøen: Handel, religion og politik. Karmøyseminariet 94/95*, 119–39. Karmøy, Norway.

Wainwright, F.T. 1962. *Archaeology and Place-Names and History: An Essay on Problems of Co-ordination*. London: Routledge & Kegan Paul.

Waitz, G., ed. 1884. *Vita Anskarii auctore Rimberto (Scriptores rerum Germanicarum)*. Hanover, Germany: MGH.

Washburn, W.E., and B.G. Trigger. 1996. "Native Peoples in Euro-American historiography." In *The Cambridge History of the Native Peoples of the Americas*, vol. 1, *North America: Part 1*, edited by B.G. Trigger and W.E. Washburn, 61–124. Cambridge: Cambridge University Press.

Wawn, A. 2001. "Victorian Vínland." In *Approaches to Vínland: A Conference on the Written and Archaeological Sources for the Norse Settlements in the North-Atlantic Region and Exploration of America. The Nordic House, Reykjavík 9–11 August 1999. Proceedings*, edited by A. Wawn and Þ. Sigurðardóttir. Reykjavík: Sigurður Nordal Institute.

Wawn, A. 2003. "Review of *Viking America: The First Millenium* by Geraldine Barnes." *Saga-book* 27: 150–2.

Webster, L., and J. Backhouse, eds. 1991. *The Making of England: Anglo-Saxon Art and Culture, AD 600–900*. London: British Museum Press.

Weidensaul, S. 1999. *Living on the Wind: Across the Hemisphere with Migratory Birds*. New York: North Point Press.

Westropp, T.J. 1913. "Brasil and the legendary islands of the North Atlantic: Their history and fable; A contribution to the 'Atlantic' problem." *Proceedings of the Royal Irish Academy* 30 C (1912–13): 223–63.

Wilhelmi, K. [1842] 1967. *Island, Hvitramannaland, Grönland und Vinland oder der Norrmänner Leben auf Island und Grönland und deren Fahrten nach Amerika schon über 500 Jahre vor Columbus. Borzüglich nach altscandinavischen Quellenschriften*. Amsterdam: Meridian Publishing.

Williams, G.A. 1987. *Madoc: The Making of a Myth*. Oxford: Oxford University Press.

Wilson, D. 1851. *Archæology and Prehistoric Annals of Scotland*. Edinburgh: Hugh Paton.

Winterhalder, B.P. 1994. "Concepts in Historical Ecology." In *Historical Ecology: Cultural Knowledge and Changing Landscapes*, edited by C.L. Crumley, 17–41. Santa Fe, NM: School of American Research Press.

Wittek, P. 1951. "*ad BSOAS.*, xiii, 1950, p. 275: grkh frt = Oxford." *Bulletin of the School of Oriental and African Studies, University of London* 13 (04): 1045. http://dx.doi.org/10.1017/S0041977X00124206.

Wittek, P. 1955. "Additional notes to Idrisi's account of the British Isles." *Bulletin of the School of Oriental and African Studies. University of London* 17 (02): 365–6. http://dx.doi.org/10.1017/S0041977X00111784.

Wolf, E.R. 1982. *Europe and the People without History*. Berkeley: University of California Press.

Wooding, J.M. 2000. "Monastic voyaging and the *Navigatio*." In *The Otherworld Voyage in Early Irish Literature*, edited by J.M. Wooding, 226–45. Dublin: Four Courts Press.

Wooding, J.M. 2011. "The date of *Navigatio S. Brendani abbatis*." *Studia Hibernica* 37:9–27.

Wormskjold, M. 1814. "Gammelt og nyt om Grœnlands, Viinlands og nogle flere af Forfædrene kjendte Landes formeentlige Beliggende." *Skandinaviske Literatur-Selskapbs Skrifter*, 1814, 298–403.

Wright, J.V. 1999. *A History of the Native People of Canada*. Vol. 2, *1,000 B.C.–A.D. 500*. Hull, QC: Canadian Museum of Civilization.

Young, J. 1937. "Some traditions showing traces of Irish influence." *Études Celtiques* 2: 118–26.

Young, R. 1871. *The Parish of Spynie*. Elgin, Scotland.

Zeiten, M.K. 1997. "Amulets and amulet use in Viking Age Denmark." *Acta Archaeologica* 68: 1–74.

Zielinski, G.A., M.S. Germani, G. Larsen, M.G.L. Baille, S. Whitlow, M.S. Twickler, and K. Taylor. 1995. "Evidence of the Eldgjá (Iceland) eruption in the GISP2 Greenland ice core: Relationship to eruption processes and climatic conditions in the tenth century." *Holocene* 5 (2): 129–40. http://dx.doi.org/10.1177/095968369500500201.

Zielinski, G.A., P.A. Mayewski, L.D. Meeker, K. Grönvald, M.S. Germani, S. Whitlow, M.S. Twickler, and K. Taylor. 1997. "Volcanic aerosol records and tephrochronology of the Summit, Greenland, ice cores." *Journal of Geophysical Research* 102 (C12): 26625–6. http://dx.doi.org/10.1029/96JC03547.

Toronto Old Norse and Icelandic Series

1 *Einarr Skulason's* Geisli*: A Critical Edition*, edited and translated by Martin Chase
2 *Anglo-Saxon England in Icelandic Medieval Texts*, by Magnus Fjalldal
3 *Sanctity in the North: Saints, Lives, and Cults in Medieval Scandinavia*, edited by Thomas DuBois
4 *Snorri Sturluson and the* Edda*: The Conversion of Cultural Capital in Medieval Scandinavia*, by Kevin J. Wanner
5 *Myths, Legends, and Heroes: Essays on Old Norse and Old English Literature in Honour of John McKinnell*, edited by Daniel Anlezark
6 *The Legends of the Saints in Old Norse-Icelandic Prose*, by Kirsten Wolf
7 *Essays in Eddic Poetry*, by John McKinnell
8 *Into the Ocean: Vikings, Irish, and Environmental Change in Iceland and the North*, by Kristján Ahronson

www.ingramcontent.com/pod-product-compliance
Lightning Source LLC
LaVergne TN
LVHW090156080826
844660LV00013B/826/J

* 9 7 8 1 4 4 2 6 4 6 1 7 9 *